# Questions
### from **Seventh Period**

# Questions
## from **Seventh Period**

**Doc Pennock Answers Teens' Questions
on Life,  Love, and the Catholic Faith**

Michael Francis PENNOCK, Ph.D.

ave maria press AmP notre dame, indiana

Excerpts from *The New Jerusalem Bible*, copyright © 1985 by Darton, Longman & Todd, Ltd., and Doubleday, a division of Bantam Doubleday Dell Publishing Group, Inc. Used with permission of the publisher.

---

© 1996, 2006 by Ave Maria Press, Inc.

Originally published as *What We Really Want to Know* in 1996.

Founded in 1865, Ave Maria Press is a ministry of the United States Province of Holy Cross.

www.avemariapress.com

ISBN-10 1-59471-101-1  ISBN-13  978-1-59471-101-5

Cover and text design by John Carson

Cover photo © Dynamic Graphics Group / Creatas / Alamy

Printed and bound in the United States of America.

*Library of Congress Cataloging-in-Publication Data*
Pennock, Michael.
   Questions from seventh period : Doc Pennock answers teens' questions on life, love, and the Catholic faith / Michael Francis Pennock. -- [Rev. ed.].
      p. cm.
   Rev. ed. of: What we really want to know-- . 1996.
   Includes bibliographical references and index.
   ISBN-13: 978-1-59471-101-5 (pbk.)
   ISBN-10: 1-59471-101-1 (pbk.)
   1. Catholic teenagers--Religious life--Miscellanea. 2. Catholic Church--Doctrines--Miscellanea. 3. Christian life--Catholic authors--Miscellanea. I. Pennock, Michael. What we really want to know-- . II. Title.

BX2355.P43 2006
248.8'3088282--dc22

2006008487

*I rededicate this book to the memory of Ronald Bugala, a loving Catholic husband, father, friend, and seeker of the Lord. All who knew Ron grew closer to the Lord because of him.*

# ACKNOWLEDGMENTS ➤ ➤ ➤ ➤ ➤ ➤ ➤

I want to thank Ken and Luanne Lashutka whose generosity allowed me to have a sabbatical from teaching to work on this and other writing projects. Their Christian witness has helped further the cause of Catholic education in so many places.

I also wish to thank Fr. Tim Kesicki, S.J., president of St. Ignatius High School, Cleveland, Ohio, who granted me a year of grace to write. He is an outstanding leader at my beloved alma mater, the school at which I was privileged to teach for so many years.

Further, I wish to express my gratitude to my editors, Mike Amodei and Peter Gehred, for their continuing help and inspiration. I am very blessed to have such talented, encouraging, and insightful hands guiding my efforts.

Thanks, too, to the more than 12,000 students who have been asking me questions over my teaching career and the correspondents from around the country who provided some of the questions for the first edition of this book. They have helped me to grow in the knowledge of my Catholic faith.

In the final analysis, our faith tells us that Jesus Christ is the answer to our heart's longing and our deepest questions. May he bless you, the reader of this book, and grant you his joy and peace.

# Contents

# INTRODUCTION ➤ ➤ ➤ ➤ ➤ ➤ ➤ ➤ ➤ ➤

Q uestions, questions, questions! This book is about real questions asked by real teens. The philosopher Voltaire said, "Judge a man by his questions rather than by his answers." By this measure, despite much agonizing about the state of today's youth, today's young people are by and large insightful and searching. They deeply care about the truth, God, faith, and all those people they love. They care about unborn life and those suffering from extreme privation throughout the world. They care, and they want answers to their many heartfelt questions.

I have been privileged to teach more than twelve thousand teens over a thirty-six–year teaching career. In many of my courses, I had students write questions on index cards that I would address throughout the semester. Many of these questions appear in this book, as well as ones submitted by teens, teachers, and youth ministers from around the country. Included are perennial, tough faith questions like "Why do we have to die?" and "Why do innocent people suffer?" Others come from today's headlines like "How are we supposed to respond to terrorists?" and "Why is the Church against the marriage of homosexual couples?"

These are real questions asked by real teens. They want to know the answers—the how and why of the Church's teaching on these issues of concern. *Questions from Seventh Period* addresses ninety questions in the areas of teen relationships, important Catholic teachings and practices, the mysteries of life, sexuality, and Christian living, controversial topics in the headlines, and more. My hope is that you will use the book as a springboard for further questions and lively discussion. For this purpose, the book periodically poses some critical thinking and opinion questions after some of the answers. The last chapter of this revised edition also includes some basic and interesting information on Catholic living, Jesus, the Church, saints,

Catholic symbols, famous Catholics, terms, websites, and prayers.

In Catholic high schools, teachers may wish to set aside twenty minutes a week or so to read some questions and answers to stimulate student discussion and query.

Youth ministers can use the questions as part of faith-sharing sessions or even as a stimulus for a day or weekend retreat.

Parents can use the questions to help formulate answers posed by their own teenage sons and daughters and to help begin a dialogue on these and other important issues.

Finally, I have found that my own students have enjoyed reading the book as a supplementary text in various courses. Although there are many books that address the faith questions of adults, there are too few for teens. A wise person observed that truth does not fear questions. Adults should not fear honest, down-to-earth teen questions. Young people deserve honest answers to their real questions.

No matter how you personally choose to use this book, my hope for you is that you will continue to seek all answers in the Lord Jesus. God bless you.

## Chapter ONE

# PARENTS AND OTHER MYSTERIES OF LIFE

### Some Concrete Help with Life Difficulties, Your Friends, and Mom and Dad

A highly regarded expert on parenting once gave a lecture called "Ten Commandments for Parents." Then, he fell in love, married, and became a father and changed the title of the lecture to "Ten Hints for Parents." Another child arrived, and he began speaking on "Some Suggestions for Parents."

When the third child arrived, he stopped lecturing.

Parents quickly learn that children complicate any child-raising theories. You help your parents grow in wisdom and appreciation of the difficult task of growing up as they raise you in a complex, mostly anti-family society. Please be patient with them.

Patience is a good virtue for all relationships, including those with your peers. Good communication is also necessary for your relationships to survive and grow. Think of the times you've been hurt because you were misunderstood or someone misjudged you or talked behind your back. Without your commitment to be patient and communicate honestly, you simply would not have been able to salvage those relationships.

This chapter treats some thorny questions you might have in relating to your parents and your peers. Apply some of the questions and answers to your own life.

# one ➤ ➤ ➤ ➤ ➤ ➤ ➤ ➤ ➤ ➤ ➤ ➤

*I have a tough time communicating with my parents. What can I do to improve?*

A wise person said the toughest part of communication is being able to hear what is not being said. This is true of everyone we meet, but especially tough with parents who have authority over you. Surely, the age difference—also known as the "generation gap"—adds to problems in communication. You think you are right (and you may be). Parents think they are right (and they may be).

First, some general points: *Do* make an effort to communicate. Resist the tired excuses to shut down communication:

"They don't take me seriously."

"We'll argue."

"They've made up their minds."

Believe one of these and you won't even try to talk to your parents.

Second, play fair. Don't take on any roles or moods that block honest communication. For example, have you been guilty of any of the following?

*Non-talker*: You clam up and don't let them know your true thoughts and feelings.

*Sulker*: You let your anger seethe under the surface. Moping around the house is your way to get even.

*Shouter*: You think the loudest opinions are the right ones.

*Sneaker*: You let your folks think you will go along with their wishes, but then you do what you want anyhow.

*Comparer*: You play favorites with your parents by comparing them to one another or you belittle them by criticizing their ways with those of your friends' folks who are "always better."

These mind games and many like them destroy dialogue between teens and their parents. Effective communication is a two-way exchange that involves both *speaking* and *listening*. It should result in discussion, not argument. Discussions are healthy and build relationships; arguments seek to "win" someone over to one's point of view, resulting in winners and losers. Here are some tips to use the next time you discuss (not argue) an important issue with your mom and dad.

## When you speak . . .

1. *Make sure your folks know you love them.* It's hard to get angry when you know the dialogue begins and ends in love.
2. *Always be honest and report both your ideas and feelings.* Don't tell your folks what you think they want to hear simply to end the conversation. Tell the truth.
3. *Don't blame. Suspend judgment.* Instead of saying, "You don't care" or "You're old-fashioned," say "I'm not sure where you're coming from. Help me to understand."
4. *Stick to one topic.* Dragging out past hurts won't help solve the current issue.
5. *Seek mutual understanding, not victory.* Look for areas of common ground and agreement. Remember the purpose of your conversation is to come to a peaceful resolution.
6. *Keep the noise level down.* Loud arguing sheds more heat than light. Civilized conversation requires calm exchanges.

## When you *listen* . . .

1. *Listen with your heart as well as your ears.* Pay attention to the meanings of the words your parents are using. What are they feeling? Make eye contact. Notice non-verbal communication. All of these will help you pick up "unspoken messages" that are often at the heart of disagreements.

2. *Give them a chance to respond.* Try not to anticipate what they are going to say. Be patient and hear them out. Don't interrupt.
3. *Empathize with your parents.* Above all, realize they love you and are trying to do their best. Put yourself in their shoes. What would you say to you?
4. *Promise to give serious consideration to their ideas.* Repeat what they've said to make sure you understand.

The secret ingredient for successful communication in families is love. Taking the time to discuss without anger and bitterness is itself an act of love. Love itself thrives on communication. The effort is worth it. Don't give up. Ask Jesus to bless you and your parents as you engage in dialogue. He'll be with you to help you all grow into a closer family. Be sure to ask for his help.

> *"When I was fourteen years old, I thought my father was an old ignoramus. When I became twenty-one, I was surprised at how much the old man had learned in seven years."*
>
> ~ MARK TWAIN

## Thorny Issues

You might wish to practice some of the tips for speaking and listening with your parents by discussing (not arguing) some of these "thorny" issues. Note which steps worked well for you, ways to improve, and what you learned about yourself and your folks through your discussions.

- Establishing a good curfew time and a fair punishment if a curfew is violated.
- What to do if your parents don't like one of your friends.
- Whether parents have the right to look through their teen's belongings.

- Should you go to Mass if your folks don't?
- Is there any music you should not be allowed to listen to?

# two ▻ ▻ ▻ ▻ ▻ ▻ ▻ ▻ ▻ ▻ ▻ ▻

## Why do I have to "honor my parents"?

Teens sometimes ask this question because their parents often seem unreasonable. In fact, they agree with Samuel Butler who, tongue-in-cheek, once said, "Parents are the last people on earth who ought to have children."

We must honor and obey our parents because the fourth commandment obliges us to do so. When they record this commandment, the Old Testament books of Exodus and Deuteronomy use the word honor to encompass the virtue of obedience. The New Testament shows the link between these two words:

> Children, obey your parents [in the Lord], for this is right. "Honor your father and mother." This is the first commandment with a promise "that it may go well with you and that you may have a long life on earth" (Eph 6:1–3).

Note that God rewards those who honor their parents. God has willed that parents have authority over their children and that children should obey them.

What if your folks make "unreasonable" demands? As a teen, you do have the right to express your views. You can try to change their minds. Badgering and sulking, however, are counterproductive and signs of immaturity. And if they still insist on a particular course of action, you must obey.

What if your parents are hypocritical, for example, they tell you to go to Sunday Mass, but they find excuses not to go? This shows that your parents are weak and all-too-human. They are enforcing a good rule that you should obey, even though they don't have the common sense to follow it themselves. You should listen to them, but then pray for them. Perhaps your good example will lead them to do what in their hearts they know is the right thing to do.

When we honor someone, we are showing respect and recognizing the person's authority over us. By virtue of their God-given role, parents and other authority figures, like teachers and officers of the law, deserve our obedience and respect. In a special way, parents deserve gratitude for the gift of life they have shared with us.

Like everyone else, however, parents are imperfect and do err in their judgments. Also, they sometimes act on "hunches," thus they cannot always explain their reasons for requiring something of you. You still owe them honor, respect, and obedience. A good rule of thumb: As long as you live in your parents' house, you should obey their rules and commands. It is a sin to disobey.

The one exception to obeying your parents or other authority figures is if they order you to do something you know is immoral. Obedience to God's law overrides the responsibility to obey one's parents.

The ancient philosopher Aristotle insightfully wrote, "Wicked men obey from fear, good men, from love." Obedience is an act of love. The New Testament (Heb 5:8) tells us that Jesus himself—God's own Son—learned obedience through his sufferings that have won us eternal salvation. When we obey, we imitate Jesus, our Lord of love. This is what it means to be his disciple.

One final word, the fourth commandment applies to parents and other authority figures as well. As the *Catechism of the Catholic Church* teaches, parents must respect their children, provide for them, create a loving home, raise and educate them in the faith, and give them the freedom to choose their own profession and state in life. Political and civil officials must see the purpose of their authority as one of serving others by respecting the fundamental human rights of persons and by promoting true freedom (*CCC*, 2221–2237).

> [Jesus] went down with them and came to Nazareth, and was obedient to them; and his mother kept all these things in her heart. And Jesus advanced [in] wisdom and age and favor before God and man (Lk 2:51–52).

# three ▸ ▸ ▸ ▸ ▸ ▸ ▸ ▸ ▸ ▸

*My parents give me grief over the music I listen to and the movies I go to see. Why can't they get with the times?*

Music and movies are two of the greatest of all art forms. The ancient philosopher Plato said that music "gives soul to the universe, wings to the mind, flight to the imagination, a charm to sadness, and life to everything." The popular author of *Harry Potter and the Sorcerer's Stone*, J.K. Rowling, wrote, "Ah, music. A magic beyond all we do here!" And Thomas Carlyle observed that music is the "speech of angels."

And movies! They have the ability to involve us totally, affecting our minds, our imaginations, and our intellects. They can transport us to other times and places, divert us from everyday cares, make us laugh or bring tears to our eyes. Imagine life without film!

Both the music we listen to and the films we see can be good and make us better people. But like any good gift from God, music and movies can be perverted and misused by appealing to our worst instincts. This is true with all of God's gifts. For example, the misuse of wine leads to alcoholism. Or a perversion of sex slips into harmful and debasing behavior. Similarly, some music and movies can result in "mind pollution" and emotional manipulation that is not good for you psychologically or spiritually. And this is what your parents are worried about. They know all too well the warning of computer programmers, "Garbage in, garbage out!"

How do you judge if the music you listen to is good or bad? Jesus gave us a good principle to follow when he told us to judge things by their fruits (Mt 7:16–18). If something is good, it will bear good fruit. Ask yourself if the music you listen to, or the movies you routinely view, enhance any of the "fruits of the Holy Spirit." Do they make you more

- loving?
- joyful?
- peaceful?
- patient?
- kind?
- generous?
- faithful?
- mild?
- chaste?

If so—and a lot of contemporary Christian music and many good films do—then they are morally acceptable.

Philippians tells us to think about whatever is true, honorable, just, pure, lovely, and gracious (4:8). Do the movies you watch bring about these outcomes or do they promote foul language, glorify sexual promiscuity, glamorize violence, and pervert what it means to be a loving human being?

Listen carefully to the lyrics of the songs you enjoy because you become what you hear. Be wary of lovely rhythms and seductive beats; sometimes there is no connection between the beauty of the music and the lyrics of the song. Monitor what the music you listen to really promotes. For example, does it

- inflame your anger?
- encourage promiscuous sex?
- promote self-pity?
- endorse escapism via drugs or alcohol?
- glamorize a life of selfish materialism?
- approve of the occult?

These are all bad outcomes that pull you down and make you less of the beautiful person God created you to be. A good rule of thumb: Avoid music, movies, magazines, and television programs that produce this kind of bad fruit.

You might also examine the lifestyles of your favorite media stars. Do they deserve your support, money, and adulation? Are they loving people? Do they call forth the best in you? Would they be good role models for a younger sister or brother?

**Talk it out** ➤ ➤ ➤ ➤ ➤ ➤ ➤ ➤ ➤ ➤ ➤ ➤ ➤ ➤ ➤ ➤ ➤ ➤ ➤

- Who are your favorite musicians and actors and actresses? Are they good role models in their personal lives? Should this make a difference in whether or not we support their enterprises?
- Agree or disagree: Christians should boycott performers whose lifestyles promote sex, drugs, materialism, violence, or selfishness.
- Analyze the lyrics of at least two of your favorite songs for the values they promote.
- Check the website of the United States Catholic Conference of Bishops' Film and Broadcasting website. Read a review of a current movie.

# four ➤ ➤ ➤ ➤ ➤ ➤ ➤ ➤ ➤ ➤ ➤

*My dad's alcoholism disrupts our family life. I hate him for it. Is there anything I can do?*

Alcoholism, like drug addiction, is an insidious disease. Developed in stages, alcoholism physically and psychologically addicts the alcoholic who ends up needing a drink every day, using alcohol to reduce tension, and finally is unable to stop drinking once he or she starts.

Drinking leads to behavioral changes which include arguments, violence, and physical and emotional abuse. Left untreated, alcoholism leads to death. Unfortunately, chemically dependent people don't know they are sick, or they vigorously deny it. Their denial leads to promises they don't keep and prevents them from getting help on their own.

Knowing these basic facts can help you understand your dad's behavior. You don't really hate him, but you do hate what his *disease* is doing to your family. It is time for you to love him *now*. Include your mom and other family members in the following strategies.

- *Act now by finding a good alcoholism counselor.* Your pastor or diocesan Catholic Charities office can usually suggest a good alcoholism counselor. The counselor will probably recommend *intervention*, a technique led by the professional that involves family members, friends, employers, a parish priest, and a member of Alcoholics Anonymous. The alcoholic is confronted with the truth about his or her behavior and its effects on others. The goal of intervention is to get medical help for the abuser and psychological support to help him or her stay sober in the future.

- *Locate your local Alateen and Al-Anon groups.* Alateen is a support group for teenagers whose parents are substance abusers. Al-Anon is a group that helps spouses of alcoholics. These groups help you to discuss and effectively cope with problems, encourage one another, and learn about the Twelve-Step program that alcoholics and others apply to their relationship with God and others.

- *Pray for your dad.* He is sick. The Lord came to help sick people. Ask for his healing love to touch your family.

- *Love your dad.* His self-esteem is low. He'll need your support and encouraging words as he begins his recovery.

God bless you as you face this family problem. And remember, now is time to act. Please seek help. You can help save your father's life.

## Contact information ➤ ➤ ➤ ➤ ➤ ➤ ➤ ➤ ➤ ➤ ➤ ➤ ➤ ➤

- **Al-Anon and Alateen phone number:** 1-888-4AL-ANON
- **The National Institute on Alcohol Abuse and Alcoholism:** http://www.niaaa.nih.gov/ (Check out their Frequently Asked Questions for some basic information.)

# five ➤ ➤ ➤ ➤ ➤ ➤ ➤ ➤ ➤ ➤ ➤

*My parents seem bound and determined to dictate my future. Don't I have any say in the matter?*

Of course you do. You are an independent, uniquely gifted child of God who has rights, including the right to determine your own future. The Church teaches that your parents must respect your right to choose your profession, state in life, and your future spouse (*CCC*, 2230).

While you are under their roof, however, you must respect your parents and try to understand their concern for you. They have the right to choose a high school that reflects and respects the values and faith of the family. They also have the right and even the duty to warn you about bad companions who might mislead you or tempt you to engage in destructive behaviors.

Assuming that your parents want the best for you, they probably want you to get a good, well-rounded education. They might seem to be interested only in your academic career and thus strongly encourage you to go to college. You, on the other hand, might have other ideas. For example, you may be a good athlete who wants to play professional sports or you might be musically gifted and aspire to a career in music. College might be the farthest thing from your mind. What should you do?

First, by all means, continue to develop your athletic or musical talents. Excel at what you do. Prove to your parents and to yourself that you do indeed have the ability to make a go of it professionally.

But consider that your talents and current plans are not polar opposites of your folks' desire for you getting a college degree. Almost everyone can benefit from advanced education, as it has become almost a necessity to stay competitive in a global economy. Perhaps you can find a way to blend your talents with a suitable academic subject. Athletes do get injured and sometimes can no longer compete. Perhaps you can pursue sports medicine or train to be a physical education teacher as a backup to your dream of being a professional athlete. Or maybe you can study business to learn the ins and outs of the music industry.

Your parents don't want to control your life. Life has simply taught them an important lesson: What makes a person happy in the teen years may not be a source of true happiness and fulfillment in the future. And they have learned this by their own experiences and their own mistakes and they simply desire to help you avoid some of the pitfalls that might sidetrack you.

Be sure to keep the lines of communication open. Show through your devotion to developing your skills that you are serious about your own dreams. In the meantime, you will grow older and wiser. And so will your parents. Perhaps, as you near the time of decision, you will both think differently about your future.

# six

*Everyone seems to be better than me.
Why is that?*

I n reality, no one is better than anyone else. God loves us all equally and unconditionally. As the poster says, *God doesn't make junk.* We are different, unique sons and daughters of God. Just because your little finger is not the same as your ring finger is not to say that the ring finger is better. It is different, that's all. So it is with you.

Many teens suffer from a negative self-image, often described as an "inferiority complex," which leads them to think that everyone is better than they are. This unhealthy attitude results in a pessimistic outlook and overdue concern about one's appearance or performance. It also leads to a lack of self-confidence, shyness, bitterness, and a host of other problems.

Feelings of inferiority often come about because we received conditional love as children or people compared us to others. The "comparison game" is especially deadly because you will always discover someone who is smarter, better-looking, more socially adept, more physically endowed, and so forth, than you are.

Comparing yourself to others can also lead to pride and an inflated ego, especially if you are more skilled in one or more areas than someone you know. However, in truth, you are neither inferior nor superior to others as a *person*. You have different God-given abilities, that's all. You are God's one-of-a-kind gift to the world. Remember this: Others' gifts don't make them better than you, just as your gifts don't make you better than them.

Here are some tips for transforming a negative self-image into a positive one:

- *Remember to look at yourself from God's point of view.* God does not make mistakes. Rather, he created you as a special child from among countless other possibilities. Jesus died on the cross looking into your eyes and pouring out his love on *you.* You are so precious to him.

- *Stop comparing yourself to others.* Look to Jesus as the measure of what it means to be a "together" person. Spend time discovering the good news about his love for you by reading the gospels. He said that we can discover our true selves when we love and serve others.

- *Try something new.* Stretch your mind, your body, your emotions, your spirit. Master a new skill. By developing and discovering your gifts, you will enhance your self-image.

- *Laugh at yourself . . . often.* You are not perfect. Yet you are good, and God loves you. You'll make mistakes; everyone does. Learn from them and move on.

- *Look at the bright side of things.* Appreciate the joy of simply being alive. Take in the splendor of nature. Savor good food. Delight in the exciting competition of a sporting event. Enjoy observing the innocence of a baby.

Ralph Waldo Emerson observed, "We are what we think about all day long." Dwelling on the untruth that we are no good and everyone else is better can only lead to a poor self-image. The solution: You must ban "stinky thinking" from your mind. Resist negative thoughts about yourself or others. They make for a miserable existence. Instead, turn to Jesus and ask him to fill your heart with a joyful attitude that looks at everything as a gift from God, including yourself. This is a great first step to a fulfilling life.

## The Optimist and the Pessimist ➤ ➤ ➤ ➤ ➤ ➤ ➤ ➤

Some parents were at their wits' end over their twin boys—one an eternal optimist, the other a hopeless pessimist. Finally, they went to a psychiatrist who devised what he thought would be a sure-fire remedy.

The doctor placed the optimist in a room filled with manure and told him to dig, figuring this would cure him of his joyful nature. He put the pessimist in a room filled with toys and told him to play. This was bound to cheer the sad-faced boy.

But when the doctor returned with the parents some hours later, he was flabbergasted at the results. The little pessimist was bawling, complaining that he would hurt himself if he played with the toys. The little optimist, on the other hand, was furiously digging in the manure. When his mother asked what he was doing, the boy joyfully exclaimed, "With all this manure, there must be a pony around somewhere!"

## ? seven ➤ ➤ ➤ ➤ ➤ ➤ ➤ ➤ ➤

*It seems like people are always criticizing me. Is there anything I can do about it?*

Abraham Lincoln said this about the many criticisms leveled against him:

If I were to try to read, much less answer, all the attacks made on me, this shop might as well be closed for any other business. I do the very best I know how—the very best I can; and I mean to keep doing so until the end. If the end brings me out all right, what is said against me won't amount to anything. If the end brings me out wrong, ten angels swearing I was right would make no difference.

It takes a strong person to handle disapproval so generously. Lincoln's point is this: *Try your best and persist, despite the criticism.* Elbert Hubbard wisely said, "To avoid criticism do nothing, say nothing, be nothing."

What you should be is yourself. Don't be fake simply to avoid someone's negativity. The elderly Polonius in Shakespeare's *Hamlet* (Act 1, scene 3) gave this advice to Laertes, his son:

This above all: to thine own self be true;
And it must follow, as the night the day,
Thou canst not then be false to any man.

The point of Shakespeare's famous lines is this: Be honest with yourself so you can be a real person for others.

Fortunately, most people will be gracious enough to accept you for who you are. But not everyone will, especially other teens who put tremendous pressure on their peers to conform, to follow the crowd.

Try your best to be true to yourself and your values. But if people criticize you, investigate why. If they condemn you because they can't tolerate your effort or honesty, then *they* have a problem. *You are not at fault.* You did not come into the world to live up to their expectations.

If you are trying to be a loving person, then you are trying to be real. You are doing God's work when you love. And you are allowing God to shine through you. Anyone who criticizes you is really criticizing the God who made you his unique loving daughter or son.

Consider this quote from an anonymous author: "Don't mind criticism. If it is untrue, disregard it; if unfair, keep from irritation; if it is ignorant, smile; if it is justified, it is not criticism, learn from it." This last insight is good because valid criticism can help our growth as persons. For example, perhaps you are always late or unkempt or loud or lazy. These habits—and many others like them—are negative traits over which you do have some control. Listen to the reminders of others who care about you and accept them as helps, not hurts. With God's help and persistent effort on your part, you can work on changing these bad habits.

Finally, we all need love and understanding. We don't want constant criticism. Jesus loves you unconditionally and understands you perfectly. He accepts your limitations. He also gives you friends as gifts to accept you and allow you to be yourself. Ask your friends to evaluate any criticism directed at you. They'll know if the criticism is worthwhile or merely sour grapes. Friends can help you cope with the pettiness of other people.

Finally, pray the famous *Serenity Prayer* to gain strength:

> God, give us grace to accept with serenity the things that cannot be changed, courage to change the things which should be changed, and the wisdom to distinguish the one from the other.

# eight ➤ ➤ ➤ ➤ ➤ ➤ ➤ ➤ ➤ ➤

### Sometimes I'm not sure who my real friends are. What is true friendship?

A famous and oft-told story recounts how a soldier during World War I asked permission to leave his trench with gunfire whizzing over his head to go onto the battlefield to bring back his fallen friend.

His commanding officer said yes, but cautioned the private that it would be wasted effort and might even end with his own death.

With God's help, the soldier found his friend, lifted him onto his shoulder, and stumbled back to his trench. Immediately seeing that the rescuer was shot and that his friend was dead, the officer said, "I told you it wouldn't be worth it."

The private responded, "But it was worth it, Sir. When I got to him, he was still alive. And you know what he said? 'Jim, I knew you'd come for me.'"

This story of friendship demonstrates how true friends suffer for each other. As someone once said, "A friend is someone who walks in when everyone else walks out."

Friends are a unit. If one hurts, the other hurts. The ancient Greek philosopher Aristotle described friendship as "a single soul dwelling in two bodies." A Native American tribal expression for the word *friend* means "one-who-carries-my-sorrow-on-his-back."

It would be good to analyze how the people you consider to be friends stack up to these descriptions. Who could always depend on you through the good and the bad times? This is not always an easy question because many people you call friends are something other than committed, true friends, who really know you—your secrets, dreams, hurts, and joys.

We sometimes refer to acquaintances (like classmates) as friends, but committed friendship requires more than a superficial knowledge of someone. Likewise those we hang with we sometimes call friends, but they are not necessarily our friends. Someone correctly observed, "Pals are people I can do something with. Friends are people I can do nothing with."

Teammates and coworkers may support us in a common enterprise, but these relationships are also less than committed friendship. How, then, can you tell who your true friends are? Dedicated, close friends exhibit the following characteristics:

- *Loyalty*. Friends stick up for each other when others criticize them. They are dependable.
- *Good listeners*. Friends really pay attention to what the other is saying and feeling.

- *Time.* Friends spend time together. They make excuses for others, but they make time for their friendship. And they can be together comfortably without talking. Friends give their relationship top priority.
- *Thoughtfulness.* Friends put themselves in each other's shoes. They know how to help out in times of need.
- *Encouragement.* Friends bring out the best in each other. They care by cheering each other in bad, depressing times. They also challenge each other to try something new.
- *Honesty.* Friends lovingly tell the truth to each other. They also express their anger without being destructive.
- *Sense of humor.* They enjoy a good laugh together. And they can chuckle at their mistakes without ill will.
- *Confidence.* True friends keep secrets.
- *Acceptance.* Friends allow each other to be themselves. They give each other space in their relationship.
- *Authenticity.* Friends are down-to-earth and not phony. For example, they can talk openly about their affection for each other and not be embarrassed.
- *Forgiveness.* Friends have learned how to say, "I am sorry" and "I forgive you."

How many of these qualities do you see in you in yourself? In someone you are lucky enough to call friend?

# nine ➤ ➤ ➤ ➤ ➤ ➤ ➤ ➤ ➤ ➤ ➤

### How can I make friends?

Becoming a friend to someone is at the same time exciting, scary, fun, and challenging. The sage American writer Ralph Waldo Emerson observed, "The only way to have a friend is to be one." In general, the basic rule for making friends is simply: Be friendly! Here are some other rules to jumpstart friendships:

1. *Be yourself.* God loves you and has endowed you with many gifts. You are a unique wonder of God's creation. Accept the special person you are. Phony people attract phony friends.

2. *Be open.* Accept and respect others for who they are. Don't try to change them into your ideal. Be willing to make friends with people of different ages, genders, interests, cultures, and the like.

3. *Talk to people.* Many friendships begin with brief conversations about likes and dislikes in music, movies, sports, TV programs, or what to do on weekends. You may have to take the initiative here. Begin by asking questions. Show interest in the responses of others. Be willing to share your own thoughts and feelings if others ask your opinions.

4. *Listen.* Everyone finds a good listener attractive. Remember God gave us one tongue to talk and *two* ears to listen. Make eye contact. Notice non-verbal communication. Don't interrupt when someone is talking. Show that you are listening by occasionally rephrasing what someone said.

5. *Get involved.* Friendships often arise when people have common interests. Play sports, join clubs at school, be part of a parish youth group. You're bound to find like-minded people who want to be your friend.
6. *Smile.* People want to be with those who radiate happiness. A smile is an invitation to friendship.
7. *Be an interesting person.* Cultivate many interests—sports, politics, music, movies, hobbies. A person who has only one interest is very boring, and boring friends are not in great demand.
8. *Be persistent and patient.* Friendships take time to develop. If at first you don't succeed, don't quit. If you work at the other rules, someone will eventually discover you and cherish being your friend. As Benjamin Franklin once advised, "Be slow in choosing a friend, slower in changing."

Above all, remember that you never lose in friendship unless you refuse the friendship of Jesus. He calls you his friend (see Jn 15:15). His love for you is unconditional and everlasting. Furthermore, he proved his love by dying for you.

If you let the Lord's magnificent love touch you, then you will naturally want to love God and others. "Let us love, then, because he first loved us" (1 Jn 4:19). By being a loving friend of Jesus, you will become very attractive to other people who desperately want the love of a true Christian. Consider becoming active in your parish youth group or some service organization at school. You are bound to find other friends of the Lord who will warm up to you.

> *"A kind mouth multiplies friends, and gracious lips prompt friendly greetings."*
>
> ~ (SIRACH 6:5)

*"A faithful friend is a sturdy shelter; he who finds one finds a treasure. A faithful friend is beyond price, no sum can balance his worth. A faithful friend is a life-saving remedy, such as he who fears God finds; for he who fears God behaves accordingly, and his friend will be like himself."*

~ (SIRACH 6:14–17)

## Friendliness Quotient

Do you have the makings to attract friends? Are you easy to get to know? Rate your friendliness quotient according to this scale:

4—always  3—usually  2—sometimes  1—never

___ 1. I smile often and am usually in a good mood.

___ 2. I feel comfortable in my peer group, even if I don't know everyone.

___ 3. I make strangers (like a new classmate) feel welcome.

___ 4. I'm at ease around adults.

___ 5. I keep up with the news and can converse easily about what's going on in the world.

___ 6. I have many interests and like talking about them.

___ 7. I'm respectful of people of all ages.

___ 8. I try to listen to people when they speak to me, even if they are boring.

___ 9. I like to ask questions of people.

___ 10. I have a good sense of humor and can even laugh at my own mistakes.

Add your scores. If you have 35 points or above, you are likely to make new friends easily and often. If you have 25-34 points, you have an above-average friendliness quotient. If you are below 24 points, you have room for growth. Improving any of the above will enhance your chances of making friends.

**To Think About . . .** ▷ ▷ ▷ ▷ ▷ ▷ ▷ ▷ ▷ ▷ ▷ ▷ ▷ ▷

- Suppose you could have as a friend any one man and any one woman alive today, no matter how famous. Who would they be? Why?
- Suppose you had only a week to live. Which friends would you spend your last days with? Why? What would you do? Would you want to be alone any of the time? Why or why not?

◁ ◁ ◁ ◁ ◁ ◁ ◁ ◁ ◁ ◁ ◁ ◁ ◁ ◁ ◁ ◁ ◁ ◁ ◁ ◁ ◁ ◁ ◁

## ten ▷ ▷ ▷ ▷ ▷ ▷ ▷ ▷ ▷ ▷ ▷ ▷ ▷

*Is there anything wrong with hanging out with a certain group of people, like a clique?*

A story helps us see why cliques present problems. A religious Master was commenting that a major evil effect of religion is that it splits humanity into sects. To illustrate, he told of the little boy who asked the neighbor girl, "Are you Catholic?"

"No," she replied with self-importance. "We belong to another abomination!"

The girl meant, of course, denomination. But it is an abomination, something to detest, when we exclude others from our circle or feel superior to them for any reason.

By definition, a *clique* is "an exclusive group of friends or associates." You probably belong to groups where individuals have similar interests—for example, sports, music, drama—but your groups are not exclusive. You'll let any interested person join. This kind of group is OK and even very valuable as you grow and develop your social skills, interests, and gifts. We all need friends and companions who enjoy what we enjoy.

But when groups become exclusive, they can be destructive. True cliques exclude rather than include. The "jocks" might strut around and arrogantly look down on others. The "burnouts" might sit on the sidelines, making fun of others who don't drink or do drugs. The "beautiful people" might be so awe-struck over their wealth and good looks that they have no time for the ordinary folk. The "nerds" might bond together for self-defense against others who envy their intelligence. Every school has its cliques. What remains constant is that most cliques do not contribute to class spirit or unity.

It's fine to bond with like-minded friends. But judge the goodness of the groups to which you belong by asking these questions:

1. Does membership in this group make me look down on others?
2. Do we treat non-group members cruelly or mock them?
3. Do we exclude other classmates with similar interests from joining our circle?
4. Does our group engage in destructive behavior, like drinking and pre-marital sex?
5. Does membership in this group require me to go along with the crowd? Does it stifle my right to be myself?
6. Am I a worse person because of my membership in this group?
7. Would Jesus belong to this group?

If you answered "yes" to questions 1–6, think seriously about finding a new group of friends and associates. If you answered yes to question 7, then that is a great sign. Following Jesus means being open to others. Do the groups to which you belong have an open-door policy?

**What Do You Say** ＞ ＞ ＞ ＞ ＞ ＞ ＞ ＞ ＞ ＞ ＞ ＞ ＞ ＞ ＞

- Name five cliques at your school. Are they destructive or exclusive? Explain.
- Can you be popular at your school and not be a member of a clique? Why or why not?

＜ ＜ ＜ ＜ ＜ ＜ ＜ ＜ ＜ ＜ ＜ ＜ ＜ ＜ ＜ ＜ ＜ ＜ ＜ ＜ ＜ ＜ ＜ ＜ ＜

# eleven ＞ ＞ ＞ ＞ ＞ ＞ ＞ ＞ ＞

*How can I deal with peer pressure?*

How would you answer these questions?
- Have you ever engaged in dangerous behavior at the urging of others?
- Have you ever vandalized property, shoplifted, or experimented with drugs, alcohol, or sex because others encouraged you to do so?
- Have you ever lied to your parents to be with your friends?
- Have you ever helped a friend cheat?
- Have you ever mocked, bullied, or picked on someone just to go along with the group?
- Have you ever done something you later regretted simply to get someone to like you?

All of these questions have to do with peer pressure, one thing all teens, in fact, all people, have in common. By definition, peer pressure is the group's influence on us to conform to its outlook on life, its values, and its way of behaving.

Despite the tone of the questions above, not all peer pressure is negative. For example, peer pressure can be *positive* (like a group of classmates deciding to visit a sick classmate) or *neutral* (for example, having the same hair style or wearing the same baseball cap). *Negative* peer pressure is the problem. It is conformity that destroys a person's individuality.

A humorous story tells how a teen named Tom confessed that from the time he was a little kid he did not like being himself. He wanted to be like Bobby Smith, a popular kid who did not like him. So Tom walked like Bobby walked, talked like him, and even signed up for the same high school he signed up for.

The problem was that Bobby Smith started to change because he hung with Joe Jones. He walked like Joe and talked like Joe. This confused Tom. He began to walk and talk like the new Bobby, who was now walking and talking like Joe.

But then Tom realized that Joe Jones walked and talked like Samuel Johnson. And Samuel Johnson walked and talked like Clem Moore.

So, Tom, concluded, he ended up walking and talking like Bobby Smith's imitation of Joe Jones's version of Samuel Johnson who went around trying to walk and talk like Clem Moore. And then it dawned on Tom that Clem Moore was walking and talking like Nathan Harmon, the pesky and boring classmate who was imitating—of all people—Tom himself.

The moral of the story: Be yourself. One thing that destroys your individuality more than anything else is negative peer pressure. It may even lead you to go against your own morals. You may conclude that "everyone is doing it," that is, smoking, cheating, drinking, shoplifting, driving wildly, engaging in sex, mocking an unpopular student. "Acceptance at any cost" can make you a superficial and boring person. It also can reveal a person with low self esteem who lacks self-confidence and a clear direction in life.

Resisting negative peer pressure is tough in today's world. But to develop into a healthy adult, you have to learn how to handle it as a teen. Here are seven steps that can help you fight negative peer pressure.

1. *Be clear about your values.* How does what the peer group wants you to do clash with what you stand for? What will you feel like afterwards if you go along with the crowd? Write down your deeply-felt convictions. For example, "Because I respect my body, I will never do drugs." Frequently reread your list. Determine never to compromise your principles. With your values in mind, try to anticipate how you might be tempted to give into peer pressure in particular situations. Mentally prepare yourself ahead of time on exactly how you would react to various uncomfortable situations that might challenge your values.

2. *Resolve to be yourself always.* You have the right to do right. True friends won't make you do something you don't want to do. They will admire you for your courage and for standing up for your beliefs, especially when the group wants to put others down or make them feel bad. You don't have to be preachy. Simply by saying something like "Do we really have to do this?" you can help your peer group see the pointlessness of their character attack and help diffuse a situation meant to hurt others.

3. *Say no gracefully but firmly.* Think of yourself as a leader, not a follower. If someone challenges you on your reply, take this as a clue that he or she doesn't really respect you as an individual. Any reason you give is likely to be challenged. Simply repeat your answer. For example, "No, thanks. I don't drink and I want to keep it that way." If you can mix some humor into your reply, it's even better.

4. *Avoid tempting situations where others may pressure you to compromise your values.* There once was king who interviewed some potential chariot drivers for the job of chauffeuring him around the kingdom. He asked each driver how close he could come to the edge of a

high, winding mountain road. The first replied, "I'm so skilled, I could drive within a foot of the edge." The second boasted, "I could drive within six inches." But the third responded, "I would stay as far away from the edge as possible." The king chose the third driver who cared more for the king's safety than his driving prowess. Christians likewise avoid risky situations that can lead to trouble. To honor their king—Jesus—they stay clear of tempting and dangerous situations.

5. *Examine your peer group.* If a particular group you hang around with is constantly pressuring you to do wrong, then maybe you should start looking for new friends to spend your time with. Sometimes it's better (and easier) to avoid certain people than always trying to convince these pseudo-friends that some of their activities are simply not right.

6. *Join some organizations at school or in your parish.* You're bound to meet some good, like-minded people by getting involved.

7. *Pray.* Ask the Lord to send you some good friends who share your values. Ask the Holy Spirit to strengthen in you the gifts of fortitude and prudence. Jesus promised he would send good things to those who ask him. Why not take him up on the offer?

# twelve ➤ ➤ ➤ ➤ ➤ ➤ ➤ ➤ ➤

*I get depressed at times and even think about suicide. Is this normal?*

You are not alone if you have thoughts of suicide. About one in five high-school students stated on self-report surveys that they have considered attempting suicide in the past twelve months.[1] Many factors may contribute to these thoughts, including the abuse of drugs and alcohol, physical or sexual abuse, major stressful events like difficulties in dealing with sexual orientation or parental divorce, and depression. One way or another, depressing and distorted thoughts have you occasionally thinking about suicide.

But please don't think that occasionally being down in the dumps means that you are suicidal. It's natural to feel depressed when you're cut from a team, a boyfriend or girlfriend dumps you for no apparent reason, you go to a new school and no one seems to care that you exist, your parents are breaking up, or a close relative dies. You should be concerned, however, when the depression lasts for weeks and you're so absorbed in your problem that you have little energy for anything else.

Temporary mild depression that results in sadness or feelings of loneliness and disappointment is normal. With supportive family and friends, the well-founded belief that things will get better, and good coping skills, you will get over this common depression. For example, an antidote to the occasional blues is to get out and do something. Go exercise or play sports. Play a musical instrument. Go with friends to a movie. Moping around does not make the feeling go away. Wallowing in self-pity feeds on itself and distorts reality.

Another help to counteract gloomy thoughts is to talk over your feelings with a friend. Life has its ups and downs. Sharing your feelings with others is a proven way to improve your psychological health. The sharing process can even help you get at the reason for your hurt. And your friends can reassure you of two important truths: (1) You are worthwhile. (2) You have people you can depend on during tough times.

But if you are beyond just an occasional fleeting thought about suicide, and are actually contemplating it, please gather enough strength to seek help. Don't keep your feelings bottled up inside. Like a ticking bomb, they might explode, hurting not only you but everyone around you. There are many people to help you.

God loves you beyond what you can imagine and has given you a unique, beautiful life to live. God also loves you through other people—teachers, priests, relatives, friends. Talk to them. They will help you look at your problems more objectively. They will reassure you of their great love for you. And when you know you are loved, you will want to embrace life and enjoy all the good times worth living for.

### More Facts about Teenage Suicide ➤ ➤ ➤ ➤ ➤ ➤ ➤

- Suicide is the third leading cause of death for young people between the ages of 15–19; only accidents and homicides outrank suicides.
- Each year, there are approximately 12 suicides for every 10,000 teens.
- Firearms are the most commonly used suicide method among youths, accounting for nearly three of five completed suicides.
- The typical profile of an adolescent *nonfatal* suicide attempter is a female who ingests pills.[2]
- Adolescent females are two times as likely to attempt suicide than males, but males are four times more likely to actually commit suicide.[3]

# thirteen ➤ ➤ ➤ ➤ ➤ ➤ ➤ ➤

*Lately, my friend has been talking about suicide. I'm not sure if she's doing it for attention or what. What should or can I do?*

Talking about suicide and death is itself a warning sign. You must be a special friend if she is willing to confide in you. Here's how you can help:

- ◆ **Keep talking to her.** She needs you to listen and not judge. Give your friend your respect and attention. Praise her good points whenever you can, and don't allow her to minimize good qualities about herself, for example by saying "Other people are better" or "anyone can do that." Let her know how special she is and how you treasure your friendship. Be direct and open. Perhaps you can share an experience of when you felt down and reassure her that things can and will change. Tell her that many people think about suicide but never attempt it. Essentially, do your best to be a good friend. Some specific suggestions include:
  - Encourage her to speak with an adult she trusts.
  - Engage her in activities that she generally enjoys, like watching movies or playing sports.
  - Disarm the distorting effects depression has on her thinking. Depressed people tend to ignore any good part of their lives or good qualities in themselves, completely focusing on the bad aspects. Don't let your friend do this.
  - Remind her of good times in her past, and there is no full-proof reason to think that things won't get better. In fact, things are pretty much guaranteed to get better, and with a little perseverance and desire to seek out the good, happy times are probably just around the corner!
- ◆ **Pay attention to any of these suicide warning signs:**
  - withdrawal from you and other friends;
  - recent experience of a personal crisis, like parents divorcing or breakup with a boyfriend or girlfriend;

- extreme mood swings and anger;
- risk taking, including hurting oneself;
- failing at school;
- a change in eating patterns (including no appetite);
- loss of sleep;
- uncontrollable crying;
- heavy drinking or drug use;
- loss of interest in usual social activities;
- giving away prized possessions;
- writing a suicide note—an extremely serious warning sign.

◆ **Don't promise you'll keep it secret.** Her life is at stake. Tell her that you want to get help.

◆ **Involve an adult.** If you have even the slightest belief that your friend is suicidal, do not handle the situation alone. Tell a responsible adult (counselor, teacher, priest, parent) as soon as possible.

◆ **If you think your friend is in immediate danger, don't leave her alone.** Wait until there is no threat of danger before you go for help.

◆ **Pray.** Ask God for wisdom and strength for both you and your friend.

Is your friend's sharing these suicidal thoughts simply an attention-getting device? It could be, but you don't know for sure. Most people who try suicide are not crazy and often appear quite normal. But they really feel helpless, hapless, and hopeless. They are not thinking clearly and so turn their negative thoughts inward. Counselors are very effective in helping most suicidal persons turn their negative self-image into positive self-esteem. Play it safe. *Take any threat of suicide seriously.*

You may also wonder how God views suicide. Taking one's own life is a grave offense against self-love and a violation of the fifth commandment. If done with knowledge and consent, it is mortally sinful. But only God can know the true state of a person's soul. Certainly, many suicides result when seriously depressed, emotionally upset people act on a distorted picture of reality. Their emotions might limit their freedom to grasp fully the serious impact of the evil they are doing. And limited freedom lessens blameworthiness.

One final point: Suicide is never glamorous. It offends a loving God and wastes God's beautiful gift of life. Suicide punishes the human community by depriving it of one of its precious members. And it scars the memories of those who loved the suicide victim. Friends and relatives will often feel guilty and ask, "Could I have done something to save a life?"

Pray for your friend and all those who conclude that life is not worth living.

## Resources

**Suicide Hotline:** 1-800-SUICIDE (784-2433)

**Website:**

- SuicideHotlines.com: http://suicidehotlines.com (good source for finding counselors in every area of the country)

## Chapter Two

# WHY DO I HAVE TO GO TO CONFESSION?

Catholic Teachings about Sacraments, Sin, and Salvation

A famous coach responded to the question of how much pro football contributes to physical fitness in America. "Very little," he replied. "At a pro game, fifty thousand spectators, desperately needing exercise, sit in the stands watching twenty-two men who desperately need rest."

Some would say it is like that with the Church. Many are idle spectators on the sidelines while too few create all the action.

As you read the answers to the following questions on the Church and the sacraments, you might ask yourself whether you aim to play or merely watch. Are you part of the action or merely on the sidelines?

Certainly, Blessed Mother Teresa of Calcutta reminds us that we must be part of the action. She says that when our life's journey is over, Christ will judge us on whether we were involved or not.

> At the end of our lives we will not be judged by how many diplomas we have received, how much money we have made or how many great things we have done. We will be judged by: *I was hungry and you gave me something to eat. I was naked and you clothed me. I was homeless and you took me in.*

- Hungry not only for bread—but hungry for love.

- Naked not only for clothing—but naked of human dignity and respect.
- Homeless not only for want of a room of bricks— but homeless because of rejection.

This is Christ in distressing disguise.[1]

Will you recognize him—in your fellow Christians? In those who need your love?

# **fourteen** ➤ ➤ ➤ ➤ ➤ ➤ ➤ ➤

*What is the point of infant baptism? Shouldn't a person be old enough to be able to choose his or her faith?*

Some Christian denominations, the Baptists, for example, accept the logic of this question by refusing to baptize infants. They reason that only adults can decide to live a Christian life after a conversion experience of being "born again." Children before the age of reason are not capable of this conversion and, therefore, they should not be baptized.

The Catholic Church responds to this objection by focusing on these important truths:

1. *Salvation is God's gift, not a human achievement.* Infant baptism underscores our belief in God's unconditional love, God's own initiative and election. No one deserves God's love. God's grace, providence, and choice bring people into the Christian family. When the Church baptizes infants, it acknowledges that God is the dispenser of gifts, not humans. God gives his grace freely; we do not earn it. And God certainly does not exclude infants from his grace.

2. *Infant baptism is a traditional practice.* The Catechism of the Catholic Church puts it this way:

> There is explicit testimony to this practice from the second century on, and it is quite

possible that, from the beginning of the apostolic preaching, when whole "households" received baptism, infants may also have been baptized (*CCC*, 1252; see Acts 16:15, 33; 18:8; 1 Cor 1:16).

3. *Jesus welcomed everyone into the kingdom.* Infant baptism flows naturally from Jesus's own interactions with infants in the gospels. For example, the Gospel of Luke tells us, "People were bringing even infants to him [Jesus] that he might touch them" (Lk 18:15). And the gospels of Matthew and Mark tell how Jesus instructed his apostles to allow children to come to him (Mt 19:13–14, Mk 10:13–16) and taught all of his followers to approach the Father with childlike faith. Children are wonderful examples of the simple openness required for the gospel to take root and bear fruit in each of our lives.

4. *Parents inevitably will share their values with their children.* For example, a little boy was afraid of the dark one stormy night and called out to his mother. She said to him, "Everything is all right. God loves you and is watching over you." The little guy responded, "I know. But right now I need someone with skin on." Parents and the entire Christian community, including the godparents, are Jesus in-the-flesh to children. From the day of their birth, children meet Jesus in the love of their parents and other family members. During the liturgy of Baptism, the parents, godparents, and the assembled community promise to love the child and to model Christian faith for him or her. The child's experiences of Christ's love through these devoted Christians will serve as the foundation for their own growing acceptance of faith as they grow into adulthood.

5. *Baptism forgives original sin, adopts us into God's family, and makes us heirs to eternal life.* Baptism is the ordinary means Christ gave to his Church to bestow these graces on his followers (Jn 3:5). All persons, even infants, suffer from

the effects of original sin. The graces, or benefits, of Baptism extend to both adults and infants alike. Finally, by baptizing infants, the Church takes most seriously Jesus's command to baptize (Mt 28:19). The Lord never said not to baptize infants. The Church has always believed that Christ wants the fruits of this sacrament to be extended to everyone.

"The custom of Mother Church in baptizing infants is certainly not to be scorned . . . nor is it to be believed that its tradition is anything except apostolic" (St. Augustine, *Literal Interpretation of Genesis* 10:23:39 [A.D. 408]).[2]

# fifteen ➤ ➤ ➤ ➤ ➤ ➤ ➤ ➤

*I've always had trouble understanding how Jesus is actually in the bread and wine. How is this so?*

"What wonderful majesty! What stupendous condescension! O sublime humility! That the Lord of the whole universe, God and the Son of God, should humble Himself like this under the form of a little bread, for our salvation."

" . . . In this world I cannot see the Most High Son of God with my own eyes, except for His Most Holy Body and Blood."

~St. Francis of Assisi

This question deals with the "Real Presence" of Christ in the Eucharist. Above all else, the Eucharist is a mystery of the Lord's love. C.S. Lewis understood the depth of this *mystery* when he wrote: "The command, after all, was 'Take, eat': not 'Take, understand.'"

Catholics believe that in the Eucharist "the body and blood, together with the soul and divinity, of our Lord Jesus Christ and, therefore, *the whole Christ is truly, really and substantially* contained" in the consecrated bread and wine (*CCC*, 1374).[3]

Over the centuries, the Church has used the word *transubstantiation* to explain the change that takes place in the bread and wine when they are consecrated ("made holy") in the Eucharistic liturgy. This means that the substance (the essential reality) of the bread and the substance of the wine are changed into Christ's body and blood, though the externals (taste, appearance, etc.) remain. Thus, because of God's great love for us, the Lord himself *actually* unites with us in a most profound way at Holy Communion.

Catholics base the belief in the Real Presence on Jesus' own words. For example, after the Bread of Life discourse in John's gospel, Jesus teaches that we will have no life unless we eat the flesh of the Son of Man and drink his blood. Most of Jesus' listeners could not accept this teaching and left him. The apostles believed and stayed with him (see Jn 6:22f). And at the Last Supper, Jesus said, "This is my body, which will be given for you; do this in memory of me. . . . This cup is the new covenant in my blood, which will be shed for you" (Lk 22:19–20). The apostles took Jesus literally. So did St. Paul, the earliest New Testament writer. He warned the Corinthians: "Therefore whoever eats the bread or drinks the cup of the Lord unworthily will have to answer for the body and blood of the Lord" (1 Cor 11:27).

The mystery of the Real Presence proclaims that our Lord is alive and present in the world, transforming it and us. The Church reminds us that our loving Savior is present to us in many other ways, too. He is present in scripture; the prayer of the Church; groups gathered in his name; the poor, sick, and imprisoned; in all the sacraments; in the sacrifice of the Mass; and in the person of the minister (*CCC*, 1373).

The Eucharist is "the source and summit of the Christian life." At this celebration, we meet Jesus in the assembled community, in the priest who presides in Jesus' name, in the scriptural word, and—of course—in Holy Communion. The Eucharist is both an invitation and a challenge: We receive the Lord to become the Lord to other people.

> "The Eucharist is everything, because from the Eucharist, everything is."
>
> ~ST. PETER JULIAN EYMARD

> "The Eucharist is the Sacrament of Love; It signifies Love, it produces Love."
>
> ~ST. THOMAS AQUINAS [4]

## sixteen ➤ ➤ ➤ ➤ ➤ ➤ ➤ ➤ ➤

### Can non-Catholics receive Holy Communion at Mass?

The Eucharist is the sacrament of faith, unity, and love. Catholics believe in the Real Presence of Jesus in the Eucharist. Holy Communion celebrates our unity in the Lord and with each member of the Church. It would be false for someone to join in this symbol of unity if he or she does is not one in faith with us.

In 1996, the American Catholic bishops approved guidelines on the Church's policy for non-Catholics and Holy Communion. You can find these printed in your Sunday missalettes.

Concerning fellow Christians, the guidelines state:

> We welcome our fellow Christians to this celebration of the Eucharist as our brothers and sisters. We pray that our common Baptism and the

action of the Holy Spirit in this Eucharist will draw us closer to one another and begin to dispel the sad divisions which separate us. We pray that these will lessen and finally disappear, in keeping with Christ's prayer for us "that they may all be one" (Jn 17:21).

Because Catholics believe that the celebration of the Eucharist is a sign of the reality of the oneness of faith, life, and worship, members of those churches with whom we are not yet fully united are ordinarily not admitted to Holy Communion. Eucharistic sharing in exceptional circumstances by other Christians requires permission according to the directives of the diocesan bishop and the provisions of canon law (canon 844 § 4).[5]

The guidelines also welcome non-Christians to the celebration, but do not extend permission for them to receive the Eucharist. However, they are invited to be united with us in prayer.

In general, then, those who are not Catholic may not be invited to receive Holy Communion. However, some circumstances would allow some Christians who share our belief in the Real Presence of Christ in the Eucharist to receive Holy Communion. For example, Eastern Orthodox Christians not in union with the pope may receive if they ask to receive the sacrament of their own accord and if they are properly disposed.

Also, the local bishop or bishops' conference can give permission for non-Catholics to be given the Eucharist in grave circumstances like the danger of death. But in such cases, the non-Catholic Christian must:

- believe the same as Catholics do about the Eucharist,
- be in the state of urgent necessity (for example, in danger of death, facing persecution),

- be unable to go to their own minister,
- and request the sacrament on their own initiative.

Finally, anyone—Catholic or not—must have the right disposition to receive the Eucharist. This means that we should be in the state of grace. We should be free of any conscious mortal sins that separate us from the Blessed Lord. Because the Eucharist is a banquet of love, everyone who receives it should do so worthily.

May a Catholic go to a Protestant service? The answer is yes. However, in general, a Catholic cannot receive the bread and wine at a Protestant service because it would imply a unity of belief that does not fully exist. Efforts to repair and reconcile beliefs—known as *ecumenism*—are ongoing between Catholics and Protestants. For now, unfortunately, differences in belief remain.

Finally, only the bishop of the local diocese has the authority to judge if intercommunion can take place. Some bishops have given permission for non-Catholic parents to receive Holy Communion at the marriage of their Catholic children. Others have allowed non-Catholic spouses to receive at the funeral of their Catholic husband or wife. These bishops have judged these events (and ones like them) as "urgent needs."

# seventeen > > > > > >

### I find Mass boring. Can't I worship God on my own? Why do I have to go?

First, yes, you can worship God on your own. And you should. Praise him each day for his goodness. Thank him for the gift of life that he has given you and all the other gifts and talents that make you the special person that you are. Ask him for forgiveness and what you need to live a loving life.

Second, yes, Mass is boring sometimes. But so is eating breakfast, taking a daily shower, washing clothes, practicing music, memorizing formulas, and playing with your little sister. Much of the daily routine of life *is* boring, but also necessary for our physical, mental, and spiritual survival.

But, third, although you can worship God alone, you should also worship him with others. And there are things you can do to overcome boredom, for example, by realizing that Mass is not meant to be a rock concert, or by learning more about the Mass so you can understand what is really going on, or by changing your mindset that has told you that you are only at Mass "to get something" and not there to give something back. Instead of being passive at Mass, be active: Listen actively to the beautiful and timeless words of the Eucharistic prayer.

For us Catholics, going to Sunday Mass is essential for our spiritual survival and health as a Christian community. Just as we need food to live, we need the Bread of Life—Jesus—to thrive as God's children. Catholics believe that we have a *serious* duty to participate in the Sunday liturgy, a word that mean's "public work" that is done in the service of others. This belief comes from Jesus himself. At the Last Supper, Jesus told his friends to "break bread" in his name. When we celebrate the Eucharist, we *obey, honor,* and *love* our friend and savior, Jesus Christ.

Consider the title of the autobiography *I Am Third,* which tells the life of Gale Sayers, a great running back for the Chicago Bears of the 1960s. Gale explains the meaning of the title: "The Lord is first; my friends are second; and I am third." Faithful Mass attendance shows where our priorities are. *Is the Lord first in our lives? Is the community around us second?*

Thinking of Mass attendance as work that we are doing to serve the Lord and others also teaches us that we not only go to Mass "to get something out of it," but to give something back as well. First, we are giving God one hour of our time (out of a 168-hour week) to thank and praise him for all his blessings. We are worshiping God by offering the sacrifice of Jesus that has won us salvation and eternal life. This world-shaking event is worth celebrating!

Second, Mass attendance not only demonstrates our love to the Lord we receive in Holy Communion, it also shows our commitment to our fellow believers. Building community was essential for Jesus in his earthly ministry. He prayed that we might all be one. He wants his followers to build community by coming together in his name. The poet John Donne stated it so well when he said, "No man is an island, entire of itself." As Christians, we go to God together. We find Christ in our fellow believers assembled in the Lord's name at Mass, just as we find him in the Eucharist that strengthens us to live a Christian life for others, in his scriptural word that speaks to us today and guides us on how to live our lives, and in his priestly minister. Celebrating the Eucharist is *the* primary way for Catholics to build and celebrate community.

True, we may not get an emotional high, be entertained, or meet interesting people at Mass. Most people there are ordinary believers just like you and me. Don't forget, however, that Christ, the divine physician, came for the sick. And we are all sick and in need of divine healing. Yes, some Mass-goers are phony. Yes, some Mass-goers are less-than-perfect. Yes, some Mass-goers are boring. But in truth, all of us are phony, imperfect, and boring people . . . at least sometimes.

The essential truth, though, is this: They are our brothers and sisters in Christ. They need us, and we need them. And our Lord loves us ordinary people so much that he comes in our midst to join us and give us life. Externally, this may seem quite humdrum. Internally, it is a marvelous miracle of love.

The question is: Are you a *faithful* Catholic Christian? Do you apply the same standard of fidelity to Mass attendance that you do in other areas of your life? Wouldn't you be upset if your car only started three times a week, or the water heater unpredictably dispensed ice-cold water, or your computer crashed several times a month? We expect things and other people to be dependable. Doesn't God expect the same from us?

## The Catechism of the Catholic Church teaches:

The Sunday Eucharist is the foundation and confirmation of all Christian practice. For this reason the faithful are obliged to participate in the Eucharist on days of obligation, unless excused for a serious reason (for example, illness, the care of infants) or dispensed by their own pastor. Those who deliberately fail in this obligation commit a grave sin (CCC, 2181).

## Who's Who of Catholic Church Members

Check the kind of Catholic you expect to be as an adult.

____ **Annuals** can be seen in church in their "Sunday best" on Easter and Christmas only.

____ **Leaners** use church for baptisms, weddings, and funerals.

____ **Pillars** are regular Mass attendees; give support, time, and selves.

____ **Specials** help and give on only those occasions that appeal to them.

____ **Sponges** take all the Church has to give, but never return the favor.

____ **Whiners** stay on the outside and criticize and complain about everything.

____ **Hypocrites** think they are better than everybody, even the Pillars.

## What Do You Say? ➤ ➤ ➤ ➤ ➤ ➤ ➤ ➤ ➤ ➤ ➤ ➤ ➤

- Should anyone be excluded from the Church? Explain.
- What would you establish as minimum requirements to be a Catholic?

# eighteen ➤ ➤ ➤ ➤ ➤ ➤ ➤ ➤

*Why do I have to confess my sins to a priest? It's embarrassing.*

Have you ever wondered how a worm gets inside of an apple? From the outside? Not really. Botanists tell us that the worm comes from the inside. It does so when an insect lays its egg in the apple blossom. Weeks later, the worm hatches in the heart of the apple, then eats its way out. Sin is like the worm. It begins in the heart and works its way out of a person's thoughts, words, and actions.

How do we Christians deal with sin that eats away at us, disfiguring the person Christ meant us to be? He's given us a great way to undo the damage of sin in our lives—the sacrament of Reconciliation. When we go to confession we are saying to ourselves and to our fellow Christians: "I want to be good—right now! I want to be a good apple and bear good fruit for Christ. I want to get rid of sin that is disfiguring me."

The sacrament of Penance, also known as the sacrament of Reconciliation, is Jesus' gift to his Church to assure us of his forgiveness of our sins and to lighten our hearts.

Unless we confess our sins, they will continue to eat away at us. Sacramental confession is medicine to the soul. It attacks the evil in our hearts and allows the Divine Physician to heal our spiritual ills.

How often should you go to confession? Church law (known as *canon law*) requires Catholics to confess once a year, if they are consciously aware of committing a mortal sin. The *Catechism of the Catholic Church* states:

> Individual and integral confession of grave sins followed by absolution remains the only ordinary means of reconciliation with God and with the Church (*CCC*, 1497).

The *Catechism* also teaches that if we are conscious of mortal sin, we must receive the sacrament of Reconciliation before receiving Holy Communion (*CCC*, 1385). These teachings support the regulation that Catholics must receive the Eucharist at least once a year, during the Easter season. This is a bare minimum for being a practicing Catholic. To receive the Eucharist worthily, we should be in a friendship relationship with Jesus, free of mortal sin.

Strictly speaking, if we have not committed mortal sin, we don't have to go to confession. But the Church recommends regular celebration of this sacrament—for example, during Advent and Lent, on a school retreat, during times of renewal, even every month or so. It is a great means to grow in holiness by practicing the virtue of humility, a first step to repentance and a way to fight pride, the root of all sin.

Why go to confession? Here are some excellent reasons.

- **To experience Christ's love firsthand.** Jesus forgave sin. He continues to do so today through his Church and his representatives—bishops and priests—to whom he gave power to forgive in his name: "Whose sins you forgive are forgiven them, and whose sins you retain are retained" (Jn 20:23). It is very human to want some assurance of love and forgiveness when we have sinned, and yet repented. Jesus left us this great sign of love to lift our burdens and comfort us.

- **To tell the truth about ourselves.** We all sin. We carry guilt. The New Testament instructs: "If we say, 'We are without sin,' we deceive ourselves, and the truth is not in us. If we acknowledge our sins, he is faithful and just and will forgive our sins and cleanse us from every wrongdoing" (1 Jn 1:8-9).

When we confess our sins aloud to Christ's representative, the priest, we overcome self-deception. We've named our sins, a sure sign of contrition and true repentance. Modern psychology tells us that confession is "good for the soul." It lifts burdens, relieves guilt, forgives sin, and starts you on a new path on the spiritual journey. The priest, who acts in the person of Christ, says "I absolve you." We need to hear this to be assured of God's forgiveness and love for us.

Don't be afraid to be honest in confession. Sure, you might be embarrassed at some of your sins. But father has heard them all. And he, too, is a sinner. If you are unduly anxious, find a sensitive priest and tell him you are nervous. Ask him to help you make a good confession. He'll take it from there. And he will rejoice that you came to him. Remember always that the sacrament of Reconciliation is a sacrament of love.

- **To reconcile with others.** Sin is never an isolated affair. It alienates a person from God, self, and others. We are a family. We are the body of Christ. When one members sins, other members of the body suffer. Confession acknowledges that we need to reconcile ourselves not only to God but to our Christian brothers and sisters as well, those we have harmed by being less than what we should be. The sacrament of Reconciliation heals my sinfulness, repairs my relationship with the Christian community, and challenges me to transform the sinful world in which I live.

- **To grow in holiness.** The sacrament of Reconciliation intensifies our love of Jesus. It gives us a more sensitive conscience, so we can look at reality with the eyes of Christ. Going to confession can counteract spiritual laziness and combat bad habits and attitudes. It can draw us closer to God and our brothers and sisters. It can teach us to detest venial sin, strengthen us to resist all mortal sin, and love virtue.

If you have been away from confession for a while, check the times the sacrament is scheduled for your parish. You'll really be glad you did.

# nineteen ➤ ➤ ➤ ➤ ➤ ➤ ➤ ➤

### Will God still love me no matter what I do?

Three devils-in-training came up to earth to practice their wiles. Their teacher asked them to describe how they planned to get people to sin. The first said, "I'll use the old method of telling them there is no God, so sin to your heart's delight." The second devil said, "I'll convince them there is no hell, so sin all you want." The third novice, the cleverest of all, responded, "I'll be subtle. I'll tell them, 'Why worry? Sin all you want *now*. You can always repent and be good *later*.'"

Yes, God will love you no matter what you do. God's nature is love. He cannot ever stop loving you—the daughter or son he made in his own divine image. He proved his immense love by sending his only Son, Jesus Christ, to suffer and die for your sins. What a supreme act of love! With arms stretched out wide on the cross, Jesus, in effect, was saying, "I love you this much."

Does this mean you can do whatever you want and then just assume God will forgive you? No it doesn't. There are two issues here. The first is that you may develop the attitude that you can sin and not worry about it because God will forgive you some time in the future. This attitude is the sin of *presumption*, that is, presuming that God will forgive us despite our disregard of his commandments. You may get in habit of thinking that he will never let you down regardless of what you do.

This is faulty thinking because God's forgiveness depends on our repenting of our sins. To repent means to turn from our sins, to be genuinely sorry for them, to avoid what leads us to commit them, and to have a firm purpose of amending our lives and doing all we can to avoid sin in the future. Sin is often addictive. It becomes so attractive that we may end up thinking we are not even sinning. We may be duped to think we have all the time in the world. But we don't. We never know when our life will end, or whether we will have repented of our sins beforehand. This is why we pray in the Hail Mary, "Holy Mary, Mother of God, pray for us sinners, now and at the hour of our death." We want to make sure that our heavenly mother is always looking out for us, especially at the time when we need her help the most.

The second danger with this attitude of doing whatever I want and God will forgive me is that I am really using God. And to use God in this way is to mock him. We are almost daring him to forgive us because he is so loving and compassionate. However, don't forget this important point: God can only forgive us if we are *truly* sorry for our sins. And to state it once again, true sorrow or *contrition* for our sins means we must turn away from our sins and what leads us into sin. We must also have a "firm purpose of amendment" of not sinning again. This means we must make our best effort to keep his commandments and to love as he taught us to love.

True, God's love is unconditional. But our salvation has a condition attached to it: We must freely respond to his love by turning from our sins—right now!

The Christian writer C.S. Lewis, wrote, "St. Augustine says 'God gives where He finds empty hands.' A man whose hands are full of parcels can't receive a gift." This means we must drop our sins to accept God's forgiveness. If we hold on to them, we won't be able to receive this wonderfully divine gift.

# twenty ➤ ➤ ➤ ➤ ➤ ➤ ➤ ➤ ➤

*My mom and dad have been divorced for over five years. My mom has been miserable ever since. She told me that she can never be married in the Church again. Is this true?*

omeone once observed rather cynically that sixty years ago parents tended to have a lot of kids, but today kids are likely to have a lot of parents. This speaks to the reality of divorce that touches the lives of almost everyone in our society to some degree. (Recent statistics reveal that there are around one million children in new divorces each year in the United States.) You yourself know well the pain divorce causes because you experienced it firsthand. May the Lord bring you comfort through your friends, relatives, and even your parents. They still love you despite their problems.

The understanding of Jesus and his Church is that sacramental marriage is a lifelong covenant of love and life between a man and a woman. Fidelity and devoted, unconditional love mark this union, one that is fertile ground for raising a Christian family. The Church sees in Christian marriage a reflection of Christ's unconditional love for the Church and each Christian.

It is true that the Church cannot give permission to a divorced Catholic couple to remarry if they have entered a true, sacramental marriage. This teaching is in obedience to Christ's command not to divorce (see Mt 5:31–32, 19:1–12; Mk 10:11–12; and Lk 16:18) and St. Paul's warning that separated spouses must remain single or reconcile.

You probably know from experience that sometimes it is wise for a couple to separate. Church authorities might even recommend that a couple seek a *civil divorce* to settle child support, custody, property, and alimony issues. But please note: A legal (civil) divorce does *not* "dissolve" a valid Christian marriage blessed by God through the Church.

Christian marriage is a *lifelong* commitment. Jesus taught this, and the Church—even out of motives of compassion—does not have the authority to change this teaching. Christian marriage is about faithfulness—both of the spouses to each other and of Christ to the Church. The sacrament represents this fidelity. The Church cannot turn its back on this essential dimension that the Lord intends for marriage. If the Church approved divorce *and* remarriage, it would be denying the unconditional, lifelong commitment of marriage. To do this would betray Jesus Christ and his clear teaching.

The vital question in some marriage cases is whether it was a valid Christian sacramental marriage from the beginning. If the answer is no, the couple can petition for a declaration of nullity (popularly called an *annulment*). In a decree of nullity the Church declares that some essential quality was lacking when a couple exchanged marriage vows and therefore no true sacramental marriage ever existed. Grounds for annulment include "lack of form," that is, the marriage did not take place according to Church law. Others include lack of knowledge about or reflection on what true Christian marriage requires, as well as psychological immaturity. Pretending to give true consent, hiding an intention never to have children, or inability to complete sexual intercourse are still other grounds for annulment. If a marriage is annulled, then the persons are free to marry again in the Church.

Having a marriage declared "null and void" is very different from divorce, that is, dissolving a true, Christian marriage. The Church, following the teaching of Christ, cannot authorize the dissolution of a valid, consummated, sacramental marriage. If a couple did indeed enter a true Christian marriage, then they are *not* free to remarry while the other spouse is alive.

Unfortunately one common understanding in years past was that divorced people were not permitted to receive the sacraments. This is completely untrue. The Church encourages your parents and other divorced Catholics to stay close to the Lord and his Church. They remain in full communion and can still fully participate in the Eucharist and the sacraments of healing (the sacraments of Reconciliation and the Anointing of the Sick). In addition, the Church sponsors support groups for the divorced and separated to help them deal with the suffering they are experiencing.

Pray for your mother and father and all who have been touched by divorce. They need your support, love, and understanding.

> *Love is patient, love is kind. It is not jealous, [love] is not pompous, it is not inflated, it is not rude, it does not seek its own interests, it is not quick-tempered, it does not brood over injury, it does not rejoice over wrongdoing but rejoices with the truth. It bears all things, believes all things, hopes all things, endures all things. Love never fails.*
>
> ~1 CORINTHIANS 13:4–8

# twenty-one ➤ ➤ ➤ ➤ ➤ ➤

*Some people say all religions are basically the same. On the other hand, my grandfather insists that the Catholic Church is the only true religion. Who is right?*

This question suggests a couple of attitudes we should avoid. First, it is wrong to hold that it doesn't make any difference what religion one belongs to, that we can attain salvation through any of them. Second, it is wrong to conclude that *all* religious truth belongs to Catholics or, for that matter, any Christian denomination. Most religions contain some truth; it's just that some contain much more than others.

A famous story from India illustrates this second point. Three blind persons are in a dark room touching an elephant. One describes the trunk, another the tail, and a third the feet. All are describing the same reality, but none has a grasp of the entire truth. Religions are like this. According to this fable, every religion has a grasp of part of the truth, but none can claim to know everything.

Christians would agree with this story up to a point. But the story does not go far enough. From a Christian perspective, Jesus—the Light of the World—enters the dark room and brings light as well as offering the gift of sight to those who believe in him. The gift of the Holy Spirit and the virtue of faith enable Christians to see Christ Jesus as "the Way, the Truth, and the Light" (Jn 14:6). Through this gift of faith, Christians recognize that Jesus Christ is the *fullest* truth that God has revealed to humanity. He is God's only Son, the one and only Savior who came to redeem all humans whether they know it or not. "No one comes to the Father except through me" (Jn 14:6).

We must ask a fundamental question about the Christian faith: "Is it true or not?" In the words of C. S. Lewis, is Jesus a "liar, lunatic, or Lord?" Is he only *a* representative of God, or is he *the* representative? Is Jesus the Savior, the only Son of God, God's unique Word? If you believe that Jesus Christ is God's ultimate revealer who saves us, then you *must* conclude that Christianity is true. Logically, you'd want to be a Christian.

But which community of Christians should you join? Catholics believe that Jesus founded a Church—the Catholic Church—to continue his work, to be "the sacrament of salvation, the sign and the instrument of the communion of God and men" (CCC, 780). Historically, we can trace the Catholic Church in an unbroken line all the way back to the time of the apostles. This is why the Second Vatican Council taught that the Church Christ intended to found subsists in the Catholic Church, meaning that it has the fullness of the means of salvation, that is, the correct and complete confession of faith, full sacramental life, and ordained ministry in apostolic succession

(CCC, 830). The traditional "four marks" of the Church help reveal this fullness. Briefly, they show that the Church is:

- **One.** The Church "acknowledges one Lord, confesses one faith, is born of one Baptism, forms only one Body, is given life by one Spirit" (*CCC*, 866). Jesus prayed for unity in his Church. Unfortunately, due to human sin, there is a fractured unity in the body of Christian believers. All Christians must work and pray for the call of the Holy Spirit for unity in Christ's Church.
- **Holy.** The Catholic Church is holy because of Christ's presence in it. He and the Holy Spirit work to sanctify its members through *all* seven sacraments—especially the Eucharist. The Church also possesses the Bible, the example of countless saints, many rich prayer styles, and so forth, to help a Church of sinners strive for holiness.
- **Catholic.** The word *catholic* means "universal." The Church is catholic because Christ is present in her, sending her on a mission to the whole human race. The Catholic Church has in herself and administers all the means of salvation to all people, in all places, at all times. It is not an exclusive club or limited to certain races, sexes, national, or ethnic groups. It is open to *everything* Jesus taught, and it contains the fullness of a faith relationship to him.
- **Apostolic.** Jesus founded the Church on the apostles, who in turn appointed successors. The pope and bishops can trace their offices of teaching back to the apostles. Christ governs his Church through these leaders who profess the same basic truths of faith and morals taught and lived by the Church of the apostles.

The Catholic Church has the fullness of Christ's truth. Therefore, we believe it is the one true Church that Christ intended to found. However, the Church also teaches that other Christian faith communities have varying degrees of sanctification and truth, for example, the Bible, the life of grace, the theological virtues, and various gifts of the Holy Spirit (CCC, 819). The Holy Spirit sheds his light and love on other Christian denominations, religions, and all people.

**What Do You Say?**

> "And so I say to you, you are Peter, and upon this rock I will build my Church, and the gates of the netherworld shall not prevail against it. I will give you the keys to the kingdom of heaven. Whatever you bind on earth shall be bound in heaven; and whatever you loose on earth shall be loosed in heaven" (Mt 16:18–19).

How important do you think this saying of Jesus is for determining the identity of the "true" Church of Christ?

# twenty-two

*What about non-Catholics or non-Christians, will God save them? After all, most people are not Catholic and may have never heard about Jesus or his Church.*

There's a story about a little boy who was taking a walk with his father one clear night. With great wonder, he looked up at the stars and joyfully observed, "Wow, Daddy! If the wrong side of heaven is so beautiful, what must the right side be like?"

It is the hope of all followers of Jesus that every good person will eventually find out how beautiful heaven is. The Lord left his Church the task to bring the good news of salvation to every person on earth. Before his ascension into heaven, Jesus instructed his followers to

> "Go, . . . and make disciples of all nations, baptizing them in the name of the Father, and of the Son, and of the Holy Spirit, teaching them to observe all that I have commanded you. And behold, I am with you always, until the end of the age" (Mt 28: 19–20).

Jesus is the savior of all people (Acts 4:12). He is also the head of his body, the Catholic Church, which he uses to be the "the sacrament of salvation, the sign and the instrument of the communion of God and men" (CCC, 780). As we saw in the previous question, the Lord left his Church with all the means necessary for us to attain our final goal of salvation. Those who know this truth—namely that the Catholic Church was founded as necessary by God through Christ—yet "refuse to enter her or to remain in her could not be saved" (*Dogmatic Constitution on the Church*, #14).

But what about all those who do not know this great truth? What about those who are not Catholic? Does the Lord save them? First, the Church acknowledges that she is joined to Christians who have been baptized and yet are not fully united to the Catholic Church—like Orthodox Christians and Protestant Christians. There are many key elements of salvation to be found in these communities, including the work of the Holy Spirit. Likewise, the Church finds a strong link with the Jewish People, a common belief in monotheism with the Muslims, and the search for God in so many other religions. The Church finds goodness and truth in these religions and considers them as "a preparation for the gospel. . . . given by Him who enlightens all men so that they may finally have life" (*Dogmatic Constitution on the Church*, #16).

Second, it is important to stress that God loves everyone, even those who have not heard the gospel or perhaps only have received an incomplete picture of Jesus. "This is good and pleasing to God our savior, who wills everyone to be saved and to come to knowledge of the truth" (1 Tm 2:3-4). In ways unknown to us, the Spirit moves in the hearts of all. He moves in the depths of their consciences, calling them to do good and avoid evil, and to salvation.

Third, the Church teaches that God does indeed extend his salvation to all people who are trying to live a good life as best they can. In an eloquent passage, the Second Vatican Council sums up the Catholic position:

> Those also can attain to everlasting salvation who through no fault of their own do not know the gospel of Christ or His Church, yet sincerely seek God and, moved by grace, strive by their deeds to do His will as it is known to them through the dictates of conscience. Nor does divine Providence deny the help necessary for salvation to those who, without blame on their part, have not yet arrived at an explicit knowledge of God, but who strive to live a good life, thanks to His grace (*Dogmatic Constitution on the Church*, #16).

# twenty-three ➤ ➤ ➤ ➤ ➤

*I have a Protestant friend who says unless I am born again, I can't be saved. What does she mean?*

This question comes from an exchange between Jesus and his secret follower, the Pharisee Nicodemus. Jesus had instructed Nicodemus: "No one can see the kingdom of God unless he is born again" (Jn 3:3, *Good News Bible*).

Nicodemus did not understand this teaching. He asked, "How can a person once grown old be born again? Surely he cannot reenter his mother's womb and be born again, can he?"

Jesus answered, "Amen, amen, I say to you, no one can enter the kingdom of God without being born of water and Spirit. What is born of flesh is flesh and what is born of spirit is spirit" (Jn 3:4–6).

Catholics interpret this being "born again" as a spiritual rebirth. We believe this takes place at Baptism. Baptism bestows on us the new life of Jesus and the gift of the Holy Spirit, who empowers us to live Christ-like lives.

Various Christian denominations, however, interpret "born again" to be a personal *experience* that guarantees someone his or her salvation. They often explain this as a *specific* emotional or spiritual event or an individual private revelation. Often, they believe this takes place at a revival where the preacher invites the person to come up and proclaim his or her faith in Jesus Christ. This highly emotional experience convinces the person to accept Jesus Christ as a personal Savior. This pivotal event also marks the day on which the person commits his or her life to the Lord. According to this interpretation, if you have this experience, you are saved; if you have not had it, salvation is not yours.

The Church rejects the interpretation that you *must* have this earth-shattering experience to be born again. Certainly, some Christians, like St. Paul, do experience the Lord in a way that turns their lives completely around. But having this single experience is *not* a necessary condition for salvation. Rather, the Church teaches that Baptism begins a new life of spiritual growth. Most often, the Holy Spirit gently leads God's people. Over time, most Christians gradually turn their lives over to Christ. Spiritual rebirth to a life in Christ is another name for Christian conversion. It begins at Baptism and signals a lifelong journey of growth. It is not simply a one-time event.

# twenty-four ➤ ➤ ➤ ➤ ➤ ➤

*I'm not sure that I know the difference between the various kinds of sin like original sin, mortal sin, and venial sin. Can you explain them?*

"What's wrong with the world?" a newspaper editorial once asked. The brilliant Catholic convert G. K. Chesterton wrote in reply, "I am." Chesterton's insightful reply shows that the root of the world's problems is human sin.

The *Catechism of the Catholic Church* defines sin "as an offense against reason, truth, and right conscience; it is a failure in genuine love for God and neighbor caused by a perverse attachment to certain goods" (*CCC*, 1849). Sin results in wounding our human nature, which was meant to love, and it ruptures our unity with God and others.

St. Augustine says that when we sin, we love ourselves even to contempt of God. He wrote, "Sin is believing the lie that you are self-centered, self-dependent, and self-sustained."

When we sin, we take a "good" and make it our "god." This distortion of reality causes hurt. We can see this easily when we misuse drink, sex, money, power, and the like. Drunkenness, for example, harms our bodies, minds, and spirits. It closes us in on ourselves, debases us, and injures our relationship with God and others. All sin is like this.

There are different types and degrees of sin. Theologians distinguish between *original* and *actual* sin. Original sin refers to our first parents' deliberate act of disobedience against God, described in the book of Genesis as the deliberate act of disobedience of Adam, the first man.

> "Man, tempted by the devil, let his trust in his Creator die in his heart and, abusing his freedom, disobeyed God's command. . . . All

subsequent sin would be disobedience toward God and lack of trust in his goodness" (*CCC*, 397).

By choosing self over God, Adam's original sin had numerous consequences: The harmony humans originally had with God was destroyed, the union of man and woman would be subject to tensions, harmony with creation was broken, and death entered human history. All humans are implicated in Adam's sin. Each person is born a sinner, prone to choose evil over good. All humans must die. But, thank God, after the fall of our first parents, God did not abandon humans once and for all to the power of original sin. Jesus' redemptive sacrifice has conquered the power of original sin. He offers us forgiveness and a rebirth into a new life of grace through the gift of Baptism.

Yet, though Christ's life, death, resurrection, and glorification conquered original sin and its worst effect—death—humans still sin in thoughts, words, deeds, and failures to act. This type of sin is *actual* sin, that is, personal, individual sin. There are two degrees of actual sin.

- *Venial sin* involves slight matter or does not include full consent. A person who commits a venial sin (like disobeying one's parents) partially rejects God, but does not destroy a friendship relationship with him. Nor does venial sin result in the loss of love or eternal happiness. The danger with venial sin is that it can dull a person's resolve to the point that his or her relationship with God is neglected. As someone once commented, "The bad thing about little sins is that they grow up too fast."
- We should be concerned about venial sin because it drags us down. A medical journal reported how a young teen had an operation to remove the pericardium, a paper-thin lining around his heart. It had grown so large that the function of the heart

muscle was restricted. The operation was successful and the young person's heart immediately
began to function about twice as fast as it had
before. Venial sin in our life is like an enlarged
pericardium. It restricts our spiritual functioning.
With the help of the Holy Spirit, when we work to
cut sin out of our lives, we will become much
more alive disciples of our Lord Jesus Christ.

- *Mortal sin* destroys love in us and cuts us off from
others and God. It is also called "deadly sin"
because it results in the loss of charity and sanctifying grace. "If it is not redeemed by repentance
and God's forgiveness, it causes exclusion from
Christ's kingdom and the eternal death of hell"
(*CCC*, 1861).

For a sin to be mortal (deadly), it must involve serious matter (for example, murder, adultery, blasphemy). The person
must also have full knowledge of the seriousness involved and
give complete consent of the will. To return to a state of grace
and friendship with God, a person who has committed a mortal sin must repent and confess his or her sins in the sacrament
of Reconciliation.

Chesterton is right in saying that sin is the bad news of
what's wrong with the world. The good news to counteract it is
God's forgiveness. Despite our weakness and even our vicious-
ness at times, God's love for us in Christ Jesus remains stead-
fast. We need to acknowledge the truth that we are sinners and
turn to the Lord, who will certainly welcome us back. To help
remember this, think of this story:

A teenager told her parish priest that Jesus was
appearing to her. To see if the visions were true,
the priest said, "Next time Jesus comes, ask him
what was my worst sin." Two weeks passed
before the teen returned. The priest asked,
"Well, what sin did Jesus say I committed?" The
young lady answered, "Jesus said he forgot it."

Jesus forgives and forgets. That is the true sign of love for repentant sinners.

## More Chesterton

Gilbert Keith Chesterton (1874–1936), a convert to Catholicism, is considered by many to be one of the greatest thinkers and writers of the twentieth century. He wrote over a hundred books and contributed to two hundred more, and he wrote hundreds of poems, five plays, five novels, and over 4,000 essays! He was known for many things, including his defense of the poor, the common person, common sense, Christianity, and the Catholic faith. Learn more about this brilliant thinker at the website listed below. It provides a good sampling of some of his more insightful quotations, including the following:

"Love means loving the unlovable—or it is no virtue at all."

—*Heretics, 1905*

"The first two facts which a healthy boy or girl feels about sex are these: first that it is beautiful and then that it is dangerous."

—*Illustrated London News,* January 9, 1909

"The Bible tells us to love our neighbors, and also to love our enemies; probably because they are generally the same people."

—*Illustrated London News,* July 16, 1910

"The Christian ideal has not been tried and found wanting; it has been found difficult and left untried."

—*What's Wrong With The World, 1910*

"There are some desires that are not desirable."
—*Orthodoxy*

**The American Chesterton Society:**
www.chesterton.org

# twenty-five ➤ ➤ ➤ ➤ ➤

*How do I know I am doing right?*

A dishonest businessman, who put up a front of acting virtuously, told the famous author Mark Twain, "Before I die, I want to go the Holy Land. While there, I want to climb up to the top of Mount Sinai and read the Ten Commandments aloud."

"I have a better idea," replied Twain. "Concerning the Ten Commandments, why don't you stay at home here in Boston and keep them."

If you keep the Ten Commandments, you are on the road to doing right.

There is a story about prince who was traveling in the care of his tutor. "How should I act in various circumstances?" he asked.

"Always remember that thou art a king's son," replied the tutor.

This is also pretty good advice, not only for a prince, but also for a Christian. "Remember who you are as a child of God and a brother or sister to Jesus." If you act as the beautiful child of God that you are, then you will act morally. Christians accept the responsibilities of being God's children.

Here are some other aids to doing right. Pause for a minute and think about some moral decision you want to make. Then

ask yourself these questions based on the following categories.
They'll help you do right.

*The Jesus Test*

Is the act loving? Does it serve others or is it self-serving?
Will it bring you a sense of joy? Would a follower of Jesus do
this?

*The Mother Test*

Would you be proud to do this in front of your mother?

*The Children Test*

Would this action give good example to those younger than
you?

*The Universal Test*

What would happen if you permitted everyone to do this?

*Practicality Test*

What will be the results if you do this? Will the consequences be good or bad? Do you have any alternatives to
this action? Do you have to do evil to achieve good? (A good
end does not justify evil means to attain it.)

*The Integrity Test*

Will this make you more honest? Will it strengthen or weak-
en your character? Will you respect yourself more or less
because of this action?

*People Test*

Will your action treat people as means or ends? Will it isolate
you from others or result in frayed relationships?

*The Bible Test*

Does the Bible outlaw this action? Specifically, do the Ten
Commandments or Christ's law to love God, neighbor, and
self forbid it?

*The Reality Test*

Would a reasonable person do this? If someone asked your
advice about this same issue, what would you say?

*The Sinner Test*

Do you admit that you are weak and may not be thinking
clearly? Is it possible that what you want to do might be

wrong? Are your passions getting in the way? Will this bring you closer to God?

*Prayer Test*

Have you asked Jesus for his help? Have you asked the Holy Spirit to enlighten you?

*Church Test*

Have you asked a wiser, holier Christian for advice? Have you consulted Church teaching on this issue?

Apply these tests and then follow your conscience. If you are honest in how you answer these questions, you are likely to do the right thing.

## What Would You Do? ➤ ➤ ➤ ➤ ➤ ➤ ➤ ➤ ➤ ➤ ➤ ➤

Apply the tests you just read about to these situations:
- stealing supplies from work;
- gossiping about a classmate's sexual orientation;
- cheating on a quiz;
- consuming a couple of beers before going to a football game;
- making racist comments to a member of a minority;
- pressuring a date for sex;
- using obscene language.

# twenty-six ➤ ➤ ➤ ➤ ➤ ➤ ➤

*Must I always follow my conscience?*

"Right is right, even if everyone is against it. Wrong is wrong, even if everyone is for it."
~William Penn (1644-1718)

A man went to his psychiatrist and told him that he was engaged in some immoral behavior. He confessed to the doctor that his conscience was troubling him.

The psychiatrist asked, "Do you want some strategies to strengthen your willpower?"

"Not really, Doc," replied the man. "I was hoping you would give me some tips that would weaken my conscience."

Contrast this insincere person with President Abraham Lincoln. He was president during the Civil War, a time that scarred our nation. At times, he was subjected to severe criticism and even admitted that he would make mistakes in the conduct of the war. However, he resolved that he would never compromise his integrity. His wise words echo down to us today and serve as a model of righteousness:

I desire so to conduct the affairs of this administration that if at the end, when I come to lay down the reins of power, I have lost every other friend on earth, I shall at least have one friend left, and that friend shall be down inside of me.[6]

That friend for Lincoln was a peaceful conscience. The *Catechism of the Catholic Church* defines conscience this way:

Conscience is a judgment of reason whereby the human person recognizes the moral quality of a concrete act that he is going to perform, is in the process of performing, or has already completed (*CCC*, 1778).

Conscience is the practical judgment about the rightness or wrongness of an action or attitude. It is the ability to discover God's will for your life. It enables you to hear God's voice speak to your heart.

The late great woman golfer, Babe Didrikson Zaharias (1911–1956), exemplified a mature conscience. She once disqualified herself from a tournament because she hit the wrong ball out of the rough. "But nobody would have known," a friend told her. "I would have known," she replied. The measure of a person's real character is what he or she would do if no one would ever find out.

The Catholic Church teaches two important rules about conscience.

1. **Always form your conscience.** "Conscience must be informed and moral judgment enlightened. A well-formed conscience is upright and truthful. It formulates its judgments according to reason, in conformity with the true good willed by the wisdom of the Creator" (*CCC*, 1783).

2. **Always follow your conscience.** "In all he says and does, man is obliged to follow faithfully what he knows to be just and right" (*CCC*, 1778).

Forming one's conscience is a *serious* responsibility. For a Catholic, this is a lifelong task that takes place in the Christian community. The scriptures and the Church's *Magisterium* ("teaching office") are two key sources of authentic truth about right and wrong. Jesus empowered Peter, the apostles, and their successors (the pope and bishops) to teach and interpret his word and truth in the area of faith and morals. When we listen to the Church's official teachers, we are listening to Christ (Lk 10:16).

Everyone must obey conscience. It is the subjective norm of morality. Note, though, that conscience is one's *own* judgment. Thus, it can be wrong. People can make mistakes because, through no fault of their own, they may not know that certain actions or attitudes are destructive. Ignorance in cases like this is not blameworthy. But negligence, selfishness, prejudice, or laziness cannot excuse an ill-informed conscience.

In the end, you must follow your conscience. But to do so well you must always form it by learning from and assenting to Christ's teaching as it comes to us in the Church. This is a lifelong task (*CCC*, 1784).

# twenty-seven ➤ ➤ ➤ ➤ ➤

*What's so wrong about me drinking a few beers or smoking pot? I can handle it.*

C onsider the lesson of an old story: "Alcohol makes you more colorful. It gives you a red nose, a white liver, a yellow streak, and a blue outlook." Alcohol, though, is not evil in itself. Jesus himself drank it. His first miracle was to change water into wine at a wedding (Jn 2). He used wine, along with bread, when he gave us the Eucharist.

The trouble with alcohol is not with its use, but its misuse. It is especially easy to abuse alcohol because it is an addictive substance. Hence, it is hard to be a person who only "occasionally gets high." The same reasoning is true of marijuana, a hallucinogenic drug. The body builds up a tolerance as a person uses it more often, leading one to require stronger doses to get high as well as to a psychological dependence on the drug.

The pattern for many teens who become dependent on alcohol or other drugs usually goes like this: Peer pressure leads a teen to get high for a first time. An alcohol high lowers inhibitions. Marijuana often causes giddiness. This "fun" leads the person to try the experience again. A pattern has been established, even if the experience of being high never again meets the person's expectations and leaves the person depressed once the effects of the drug wear off.

Alcohol and drug abuse leads to tragedy. This is why parents and schools make so much effort to dissuade you from using them. You are likely aware of many of the facts. Here are some recent ones:

- More than ten million current drinkers in the United States are between the ages of 12–20. Of these young drinkers, 20% engage in binge drinking and 6% are heavy drinkers.

- By the time they are high school seniors, more than 80% have used alcohol and approximately 62% have been drunk.

- Due to heavy or binge drinking, one out of every six teenagers (16%) has experienced "black outs," after which they could not remember what happened the previous evening.

- Alcohol is an important factor in the four leading causes of death among persons ages 10 to 24: (1) motor-vehicle crashes, (2) unintentional injuries, (3) homicide, and (4) suicide.

- Young people who begin drinking before age 15 are four times more likely to develop alcohol dependence than those who begin drinking at age 21.

- Teens under 15 who have ever consumed alcohol are twice as likely to have sex as those who have not. Nearly four in ten (39%) sexually active teens who use alcohol have had sexual intercourse with four or more individuals.

- Researchers estimate that alcohol use is implicated in one- to two-thirds of sexual assault and acquaintance or "date" rape cases among teens and college students.[7]

Nationally, 50% of all driving fatalities involve alcohol, 40% of criminal offenders were under the influence of alcohol when they committed their crime, and 75% of spousal abuse cases involved alcohol use by the offender. In addition, 43% of Americans have been exposed to alcoholism in their families.[8] Add in other drugs and the figures are even higher. There are other dangers of alcohol and pot use, including:

- *Physically,* alcohol damages the liver, stresses the heart, impairs memory, and often creates the need for a greater amount or tempts one to try a stronger drug. Marijuana use leads to lung cancer and prevents the proper formation of DNA, proteins, and other essentials for cell growth and cell division.

- *Emotionally*, alcohol and marijuana use cause guilt, a poor self-image, and embarrassment over stupid behavior done under their influence.
- *Socially*, alcohol is a factor in family problems like domestic violence, broken homes, assaults, and even murder. Marijuana use causes people to lose interest in things that were once important to them. Both can also make a person a mindless conformist.
- *Legally*, especially for teens, the use of alcohol and marijuana involves deception and disregard for the law.
- *Psychologically*, any drug use encourages immaturity and immediate gratification. Although drinking alcohol or smoking pot may seem to provide a temporary escape from problems, one learns quickly that the problems never go away by themselves, and frequently are compounded by the use of drugs and alcohol.
- *Spiritually*, alcohol and marijuana use limit freedom and dull one's ability to think. They make it hard to distinguish between right and wrong, for example, in the area of sexual morality.

One can say that misuse of these substances is suicide on the installment plan. Please consider all these factors of alcohol and marijuana *before* endangering yourself and others. Besides having a network of like-minded friends to support you in a sober and healthy lifestyle, here are five healthy alternatives to alcohol and pot use. They can safely add some spice to your life.

1. Learn how to relax by mastering techniques of meditation.
2. Pursue beauty in nature, film, music, art, and the like.
3. Get involved in sports or exercise vigorously.

4. Try something new. This could be joining the school play or musical, writing for the school newspaper, taking up a new outdoor activity such as skiing, or joining the parish youth group.
5. Commit to meaningful sharing with your friends. Go to a café or late night diner and talk about things that are meaningful to you (God, faith, what you want to do with your life, or what kind of world you want to help create).

## The Bible on Alcohol

> Wine is arrogant, strong drink is riotous;
> none who goes astray for it is wise.
> —Proverbs 20:1

> Therefore, do not continue in ignorance, but try to understand what is the will of the Lord. And do not get drunk on wine, in which lies debauchery, but be filled with the Spirit.
> —Ephesians 5:17–18

## What Do You Say?

Write out a realistic strategy to resist peer pressure to use alcohol or other drugs. Compare it with a friend who does the same thing.

# twenty-eight

*Where does the Church stand on abortion in cases like rape and incest or when the pregnancy threatens the life of the mother?*

Would you support abortion in the following situation? A teenage girl is pregnant. She's not married. Her fiancé is not the father of the baby, and he's very upset.

If you said yes, you would have allowed the killing of Jesus Christ. The bottom line is that it is not right deliberately to kill an unborn child under any circumstances. Each human being, made in God's image and likeness, is a precious person of dignity. No human life, even unborn human life conceived in the worst of circumstances, is ours to do with as we please. Human life is God's. Helpless, unborn human beings especially need reverence and protection.

Ask yourself the question, "Was the baby at fault for the rape or incest?" Though the baby comes into the world through tragic circumstances, it is not to blame for those circumstances. The baby and victim of rape or incest are innocent. Each deserves our complete support, protection, and love during this emotionally devastating time. Christians do what is right when they care for innocent babies as well as the female victims of male violence.

Next, consider the case of a difficult pregnancy that threatens the life of the mother. Note that these cases are extremely rare in modern medicine. Modern medical skills and procedures have developed to such a degree that doctors can almost always save both mother and baby. The past president of the Catholic Medical Association, George Isajiw, M.D., in an interview with Fr. Frank Pavone of Priests for Life, said he had never heard of a case of where there was a direct abortion needed to save the life of the mother. It is not needed. And furthermore, it is not right because it is *never* right to kill directly an innocent baby, no matter what the motive.

The confusion arises when the baby loses his or her life *indirectly* as the result of a mother and baby experiencing a life-threatening medical situation. Catholic theology would permit an operation as a last resort to save the mother's life, even knowing that the *unintended* consequence would be the loss of the baby's life. Note well: There is no *direct* abortion of the baby. Dr. George gives examples:

There are really only three situations like this that I can think of and that's ectopic pregnancy, cancer of the uterus, and perhaps trauma, or an accidental traumatic injury to the uterus. And if you don't do anything then both mother and child will die. Now if you treat the mother for whatever needs to be treated, the uterus is bleeding, and you remove the uterus and the baby is still in there, and you do nothing to kill the baby, that is if you had a means an artificial incubator, some day we will have it, I'm sure, you could put that baby in there, so in no way do you directly attack the life of the baby. But you can foresee that that baby will lose its life, but it will lose its life anyhow but without directly attacking. Those are the three instances, very rare, very rare, but those are not abortions. If you look at the five ways that abortions are done, which is the only purpose is to kill the child, none of these techniques are the methods used in these operations. So there is no such thing as a necessary abortion.[9]

In conclusion, the Church's position on abortion is extremely clear. In the words of the *Catechism of the Catholic Church*:

Human life must be respected and protected absolutely from the moment of conception. From the first moment of his existence, a human being must be recognized as having the rights of a person—among which is the inviolable right of every innocent being to life (*CCC*, 2270).

Since the first century the Church has affirmed the moral evil of every procured abortion. This teaching has not changed and remains unchangeable. Direct abortion, that is to say, abortion willed either as an end or a means, is gravely contrary to the moral law (*CCC*, 2271).

It is our moral right and duty to protect the life of innocent unborn human beings, no matter how they were conceived. Abortion—the deliberate killing of unborn human life—is wrong regardless of the circumstances. Pope John Paul II reminds us in his encyclical *The Gospel of Life*, "As far as the right to life is concerned, every innocent human being is absolutely equal to all others" (#57).

**Pro-life quotes to think about**

"Cowardice asks the question, 'Is it safe?' Expedience asks the question, 'Is it politic?' Vanity asks the question, 'Is it popular?' But conscience asks the question, 'Is it right?'"
~Martin Luther King, Jr.

"First they [the Nazis] came for the communists, but we were not communists, so we said nothing. Then they came for the trade unionists, but we were not trade unionists, so we said nothing. Then they came for the Jews, but we were not Jews, so we said nothing. Then they came for the mentally deficient, but we were not mentally deficient, so we said nothing. Then they came for me, and no one bothered to say anything either. We did not know what was going on. Maybe we did not want to know."
~Lutheran Pastor Martin Niemoller (1945)

"When the time comes, as it surely will, when we face that awesome moment, the final judgment, I've often thought, as Fulton Sheen wrote, that it is a terrible moment of loneliness. You have no advocates, you are there alone standing before God—and a terror will rip your soul like nothing you can imagine. But I really think that those in the pro-life movement will not be alone. I think there'll be a chorus of voices that have never been heard in this world but are heard beautifully and clearly in the next world—and they will plead for everyone who has been in this movement. They will say to God, 'Spare him, because he loved us!'"[10]

~Congressman Henry Hyde

**What Can You Do to Promote Life?** For some great ideas, check out "Resources for Students" at the excellent Priests for Life website: www.priestsforlife.org

# twenty-nine ➤ ➤ ➤ ➤ ➤

*A girl I know had an abortion. Is she kicked out of the Church forever? What should she do?*

Your question reveals that you realize the seriousness of abortion. The Church emphasizes the gravity of certain sins by imposing automatic excommunication. According to canon law, these sins include desecrating the Eucharist, violence against the pope, violating the seal of confession, giving absolution to an accomplice in a sin against the sixth commandment, consecrating a bishop without authorization, committing the sins of apostasy, heresy, or schism, and participating in an abortion. The abortion penalty applies to any person who is an accomplice in the abortion, for example, the doctor and nurses who perform the procedure as well as the person having the abortion. Other accomplices might include friends or family members who directly aided in the abortion, like paying for it or driving the woman to the clinic.

A person who has been excommunicated cannot have any ministerial part in the celebration of the Eucharist or other ceremonies of public worship, cannot receive the sacraments or sacramentals, and cannot exercise any ecclesiastical offices, functions, or acts of governance. Christ gave the Church the power to excommunicate to the apostles and their successors (see Mt 16:17–19, Jn 20:22–23) for three purposes: (1) to deter certain actions; (2) to help people recognize their error; and (3) to call sinners to repent and reconcile with the Church.

In the case of abortion, however, certain conditions must be present for an automatic excommunication to take place. Canon law holds that a person cannot be excommunicated if he or she has not reached the age of 17, was unaware of the penalty, did not freely choose to abort her baby as in the case of physical force, compulsion, or grave fear, or lacked the use of reason.[11] All too commonly teens (and others) who have abortions are afraid, confused, and under severe pressure (from family, the man, and friends) to abort their child. If any of these conditions is present at the time of abortion, then she does not incur excommunication.

Thus, a teenage girl who secured an abortion is unlikely to have been "kicked out of the Church." But she has committed an offense that objectively involves the most serious matter—the taking of innocent human life. Depending on the degree of freedom and knowledge of wrongdoing, she may be guilty of mortal sin.

Her first step is to admit that she has sinned. Pope John Paul II offered some sensitive and consoling words to women who have had abortions:

> Certainly what happened was and remains terribly wrong. But do not give in to discouragements and do not lose hope. Try rather to understand what happened and face it honestly. If you have not already done so, give yourselves over with humility and trust to repentance. The Father of mercies is ready to give you his

forgiveness and peace in the sacrament of Reconciliation. You will come to understand that nothing is definitively lost, and you will also be able to ask forgiveness from your child, who is now living in the Lord (*The Gospel of Life* #99).

Repentance is the beginning of the healing process. The Lord Jesus forgives all repentant sinners, no matter how grave the offense. If the girl you know asks for your help or advice, remind her of God's great desire to forgive all people of their sins. Share with her the parable of the Prodigal Son (Lk 15:11-32), which stresses his unconditional love for those who have strayed. Those who repent of the taking of innocent life need to hear loud and clear that with genuine repentance our Lord forgives all.

Encourage her to reconcile with God and the Christian community in the sacrament of Reconciliation. A sensitive confessor will repeat the message of God's love and advise her on what to do next. For example, he will probably recommend that she receive some follow-up counseling because many women who have aborted their babies experience guilt and regret. The Church sponsors counseling through a group called Project Rachel.

Like a loving mother, the Church has open arms for this girl. May you help her to feel willing and able to seek reconciliation and healing.

**For Reference** > > > > > > > > > > > > > > >

Contact a local Catholic parish for the phone number and address of the Project Rachel ministry near you, or you may contact the national office:

**Hope After Abortion**
www.hopeafterabortion.com
*National Office of Post-Abortion Reconciliation and Healing*
www.noparh.org
P.O. Box 07477
Milwaukee, WI 53207-0477
1-800-5WE-CARE

# thirty > > > > > > > > > >

## Why is the Church against birth control?

This question is a common misstatement of the Church's position. The Church is against *artificial* birth control. On the other hand, the Church does support and encourage Natural Family Planning because it cooperates with God's intention for human sexual sharing by observing and using a wife's infertile periods to regulate births.

Parents must exercise human and Christian responsibility in planning and raising a family. A husband and wife, in dialogue with each other and with God, will consider their physical and psychological health, family finances, and present family size in responsibly planning their family. God does not require a couple to have as many children as possible. In most cases, this would be irresponsible. The *Catechism of the Catholic Church* teaches:

For just reasons, spouses may wish to space the births of their children. It is their duty to make certain that their desire is not motivated by selfishness but is in conformity with the generosity appropriate to responsible parenthood. Moreover, they should conform their behavior to the objective criteria of morality (CCC, 2368).

Therefore, the Church does encourage family planning out of unselfish motives using natural means of birth control that are consistent with God's law and the natural law written on human hearts ("the objective criteria of morality"). This is why the Church approves the *natural family planning* (NFP) method of birth control to determine the spacing and number of children in a family. These methods are natural because the couple does not use anything mechanical or artificial (e.g., a condom or birth control pills). NFP depends on the wife charting her fertility cycle and the couple abstaining from sexual intercourse during those days of the cycle when she can conceive a child. Besides being up to 99% effective in regulating pregnancy when properly observed, NFP improves communication between the husband and wife, fosters mutual respect, and helps them grow closer to God and each other.

The definitive teaching on responsible transmission of human life appears in Pope Paul VI's encyclical *Humanae Vitae* (1968). The pope noted that marriage has two purposes: *unitive* (the sharing of love) and *procreative* (the giving of life). In order for sexual intercourse to conform to God's plan, it must be in harmony with *both* purposes: "*Each* and every marriage act must remain open to the transmission of life" (*Humanae Vitae,* #11). The couple must not introduce any artificial means of regulating conception (contraception) into the act. These artificial means (pills, condoms, diaphragms) unnaturally frustrate one of the purposes of marriage, the procreative dimension. Thus, they are wrong.

In a society that promotes self-indulgence, it is a challenge for Catholic couples to live in harmony with God's design for sexual intercourse in marriage. The Church, however, offers its compassion and concern to couples struggling to do right in the area of family planning. Couples are reminded to celebrate the sacraments of Penance and the Eucharist frequently and to engage in honest self-reflection, prayer, and meditation on the reasons behind Church teaching.

## Learning More

*Couple to Couple League*
An interfaith organization dedicated to teaching Natural Family Planning (NFP) to married and engaged couples. www.ccli.org

*LifeIssues.net*
Clear Catholic Thinking on Life Issues, including contraception. www.lifeissues.net

*ThinkChastity.com*
This website gives some good answers to frequently asked questions about Natural Family Planning and Church teaching on contraception. www.thinkchastity.com/Homex.html

# thirty-one

People say honesty is the best policy. But it's tough not to cheat on tests and schoolwork because everyone else is doing so. I don't want to fall behind. What's so bad about a little cheating?

"An honest man is the noblest work of God."
                    ~Alexander Pope

There's an old proverb that contains much wisdom:

For want of a nail, the shoe was lost.

For want of a shoe, the horse was lost.

For want of a horse, the rider was lost.

For want of a rider, the battle was lost.

For want of a battle, the kingdom was lost.

The lesson of the proverb is clear: Little things mean a lot. A little bit of cheating makes a difference. Cheating has certainly rocked our society to its core. Corporate scandals like insider trading on the stock market, marital infidelities among prominent politicians, steroids in sports, stretching the truth to push particular agendas, price fixing, and similar moral failings have wrought untold harm to civic welfare. Just one example of the cost of cheating: "The National Insurance Crime Bureau (NICB) estimates that all Americans pay $200 to $300 in increased insurance premiums each year just to cover the cost of insurance fraud."[12] This example and all the others have one thing in common: They all began with "just a little cheating."

A recent national survey by Rutgers University's Management Education Center of 4,500 high school students found that 75 percent of them engage in serious cheating. More than 50 percent of those in the survey admitted to using the Internet to plagiarize. Sadly, half of the respondents did not think copying answers on a test was even cheating. The students in the survey claim they cheat because of academic pressure and the poor example of adults in the "real" world. Furthermore, students admit that their schools don't do a very good job of teaching about integrity.[13]

Students cheat for many reasons including laziness, the fact that "everyone else is doing it," and the lack of consequences if they get caught. Many teachers ignore cheating because they don't want the hassle with parents who often claim that "their child" would never cheat. Some parents even threaten lawsuits.

The current situation has led many observers to conclude that there is a serious "hole in the moral ozone." How prevalent is cheating at your school? Do you cheat? Simply stated, cheating is wrong because it violates God's law. It involves deception and theft. Cheaters take what doesn't belong to them (a violation of the seventh commandment, which forbids stealing). Then, they pass it off as their own (a violation of the eighth commandment, which forbids false witness).

The trouble with even "a little cheating" is drawing the line. If you cheat in little things often enough, you next are likely to cheat in bigger things. You become what you do; you become a cheater. Soon your conscience dulls and you will think nothing of making excuses for cheating in all areas of your life. Sin is like that. It starts small, pokes a hole in the "moral ozone," and then gradually allows for the justification of anything.

Honesty is the touchstone of a person's character. To the degree that you are honest and willing to stand alone, you are a person of integrity. In a world that tolerates deception in politicians, infidelity in marriage, and inferior workmanship, it takes moral courage to be honest and resist the crowd.

Jesus can help you be a person of integrity. There is a story about the local butcher whose life turned around when he decided to follow Jesus. "I stopped weighing with my thumb," he said. "Before I met Christ, I placed my thumb on the scale in a way that added an ounce to the weight of the meat. Now that I am following Christ, who is Truth, I use the scale correctly. I am also making restitution to all the customers I have cheated in the past."

Just say no to cheating. It will take strength. It will take character. You will need the Lord's help. But you will be an example for others and help break out of the cycle of dishonesty. Perhaps you can adopt for your own West Point's "Cadets Prayer."[14] The cadets recite it every Sunday.

> Make us choose the harder right instead of the easier wrong, and never be content with half truth when whole truth can be won. Endow us

with courage that is born of loyalty to all that is noble and worthy, that scorns to compromise with vice and injustice and knows no fear when right and truth are in jeopardy.

## What Do You Say?

- Right or wrong? I tell people what they want to hear rather than what I truly believe. Explain.
- Right or wrong? I have my mom call me in sick when I really am staying home to finish a term paper. Explain.
- Right or wrong? I see a classmate cheat and I do nothing about it. Explain.
- Right or wrong? A store clerk gives me $10 more in change than I am owed. I say nothing. Explain.

## Chapter THREE

# GOD WRITES
# STRAIGHT WITH
# CROOKED LINES

### Mysteries of the Bible, Jesus, and Life

L ife is full of mysteries. Some are pleasant, for example our wonderment as we ponder a life of peace and joy in eternity. Others are more confusing; we may question how a good and loving God can allow evil and suffering. We simply don't know everything because we can't see everything from his perspective.

Perhaps you have seen this famous prayer penned by an anonymous author.

## Footprints

> One night a man had a dream. He dreamed he was walking along the beach with the Lord. Across the sky flashed scenes from his life. For each scene, he noticed two sets of footprints in the sand; one belonging to him, and the other to the Lord.
>
> When the last scene of his life flashed before him, he looked back at the footprints in the sand. He noticed that many times along the path of his life there was only one set of footprints. He also noticed that it happened at the very lowest and saddest times in his life.

This really bothered him and he questioned the Lord about it. "Lord, you said that once I decided to follow you, you'd walk with me all the way. But I have noticed that during the most troublesome times in my life, there is only one set of footprints. I don't understand why when I needed you most you would leave me."

The Lord replied, "My precious, precious child, I love you and I would never leave you. During your times of trial and suffering, when you see only one set of footprints, it was then that I carried you."

We won't know the answers to all of life's mysteries until we meet our Lord in eternity. But we can be sure of one thing: He is carrying us through the tough times of our life right now, whether we know it or not. He is the one true friend who has proved his love.

This chapter will discuss some of the tough questions about life, God, Jesus, and the Bible. Although we cannot perfectly grasp every mystery these questions raise, we can surely come to know as a friend the One who lent a hand and who led the way to our salvation.

# thirty-two ➤ ➤ ➤ ➤ ➤ ➤ ➤

*Why does God allow for evil and suffering in the world? For example, why does God let little babies suffer and die?*

This question has challenged all religions, including Christianity, from time immemorial.

In the Old Testament, the book of Job is entirely concerned with this very problem. In this book, God allows Satan to afflict his upright servant Job with all manner of evils in order to test his faith. Therefore the innocent Job loses all his children and property and eventually contracts a horrible disease. Always trusting God despite his setbacks, Job's sufferings reveal one partial answer to why there is suffering: Good can come from it. As the proverb goes, "God writes straight with crooked lines." Job becomes a holier man, a better friend, and more trusting of God because of his sufferings. The story of Joseph in Genesis 37–45 also points this out. Joseph was shoved into a ditch and left for dead there by his jealous brothers. Yet from suffering he emerged as the pharaoh's assistant in Egypt, in charge of dispensing food during a worldwide famine. In this position he was able to save his own family from starvation.

A key insight came to Job toward the end of his trials. Job says to God:

> I have dealt with great things that I do not
> understand; things too wonderful for me, which
> I cannot know. I had heard of you by word of
> mouth, but now my eye has seen you. Therefore
> I disown what I have said, and repent in dust
> and ashes (Jb 42:3, 5–6).

Job admits that God's ways are mysterious and that ultimately we can't understand them. It takes humility and trust to admit that we can never understand the mystery of innocent suffering and evil in the world. We are not God, and we don't see things from his perspective. We need to know that we are totally dependent on him and not in control of everything. Therefore, we can never adequately explain all the evil that befalls us.

But we can explain some of it. Consider these points:

- *God's created world is on a journey to perfection.* God could have created a "perfect" world where there would be no physical evil, but in his goodness and wisdom he decided to create a world that is in a process of becoming. It is *not* yet perfect. Nature's constructive and destructive forces exist side-by-side. The more perfect exists alongside the less perfect. "With physical good there also exists *physical evil* as long as creation has not reached perfection" (*CCC*, 310).

Just as the star athlete must experience the pain that is a byproduct of training to hone his or her skills, so the world undergoes pain to achieve the perfection God has in store. We cannot now appreciate the pain involved in this growth process because innocent people suffer at the hands of nature. But we believe that in God's wisdom this growth is good both for individuals and humanity as a whole as we journey to perfection.

- *The misuse of freedom is the cause of much moral evil.* Out of divine goodness, God created humans (and angels) as *intelligent* and *free* creatures, not mindless robots or unthinking puppets. The gifts of intellect and free will are what make us beings of tremendous dignity and not mere automatons. But these two gifts require responsibility. We must freely choose to love God and others on our journey toward eternity. When we refuse to love, we sin. And sin brings about incredible evil and suffering.

  Christian revelation tells us that when some angels chose to sin, they (the fallen angels, or devils) unleashed evil in the world in opposition to God. This is one explanation of some of the natural evil in the world (e.g., tornadoes, earthquakes, and the like).

  Human sin leads to moral evils like war, rape, abortion, drug abuse, prejudice, and greed. God does not cause this moral evil. Humans, by misusing their freedom, are the cause. God permits moral evil, however, because he loves and respects the free creatures he has made. And in a way known only to God (as Job eventually admits), God knows how to derive good out of all evil.

- *Christian faith announces the good news of Jesus Christ, who conquered the forces of evil.* Certainly, the worst moral evil in the world was for humans to put to death the innocent God-man. Like any normal person, Jesus abhorred suffering and even asked his Father to remove it. But Jesus freely embraced the sufferings that unjustly came his way by submitting to his Father, "May your will be done."

  God heard Jesus' prayer, not by saving Jesus from death, but by saving him *out* of death. Jesus' suffering, death, and resurrection have conquered the worst evil: death and separation from God. If we love as Jesus teaches us to do and join our sufferings to him, we will share forever in the Lord's blissful, superabundant, joy-filled life. This is "good news" that can help us cope with the mystery of evil and suffering.

*Consider the work of God. Who can make straight what he has made crooked? On a good day enjoy good things, and on an evil day consider: Both the one and the other God has made, so that man cannot find fault with him in anything.*

~ECCLESIASTES 7:13–14

*We know that all things work for good for those who love God.*

~ROMANS 8:28

## What Do You Think? ⟩ ⟩ ⟩ ⟩ ⟩ ⟩ ⟩ ⟩ ⟩ ⟩ ⟩ ⟩ ⟩

Think of a time the Lord carried you and you did not realize it until after the fact.

When was a time some good came out of an "evil" that befell you?

# thirty-three ⟩ ⟩ ⟩ ⟩ ⟩ ⟩

*How can a good and loving God send someone to hell? This doesn't sound very loving to me.*

A man died and found himself in the next world. He saw there beauty and luxury beyond describing. He also discovered that every wish and whim he had were immediately fulfilled. Merely thinking about something gave him what he wanted. It didn't take too long before he became incredibly bored. He thought to himself, "If only once I would not get what I wanted." The monotony almost drove him crazy. So, he eventually called on an attendant and said, "For once, I would like something given to me but only if I earn it." "Can't be done," said the attendant. "It's your only wish that we cannot grant here." "Fine," replied the man. "Then let me out of here. I'd rather be in hell." The attendant smiled and hissed a reply, "And where do you think you are?"

Those in hell get what they want—themselves for eternity. But God doesn't want it that way. Our loving God has created us with freedom to choose, to love or not to love, to choose a path that leads either to heaven or perdition. Here are three points of explanation.

1. God *"wills everyone to be saved"* (1 Tm 2:4). As the New Testament teaches, the Lord is "patient with you, not wishing that any should perish but that all should come to repentance" (2 Pt 3:9).

2. God *gives all people countless opportunities to repent of their sins, to accept truth and love.* The Lord is free with his gifts. The graces to live a good life are always present to everyone throughout life. We can accept these graces or reject them; everyone is free to make his or her own choice.

   Thus, there won't be surprises at judgment time. We will know what kind of life we chose and what we deserve as reward. As a loving Abba, God is not "out to get us," to catch us in some failing, zap us, or condemn us to eternal hell. He is the loving Father of the parable of the Prodigal Son, always awaiting the return of repentant sinners with open arms. Why is God to blame if people choose themselves over loving him and other people?

3. A true sign of love is that it allows people freedom, even if the possibility exists that the freedom will lead the person to do harmful, even self-destructive things. God so loves us that we are entrusted with that kind of freedom. G. K. Chesterton knew this when he said, "Hell is the greatest compliment God has ever paid to the dignity of human freedom." Freedom and intelligence give us dignity. If there were no consequences to what we do (the existence of heaven, hell, and purgatory), then there would no freedom.

Consider this: Is it more loving for God to create free, intelligent beings who can respond in love or mere robots or automatons who have no freedom? Compare God to your parents. As you mature, they risk giving you increasing amounts of freedom so you can responsibly become an adult. Would they love you if they never allowed you to do anything? Would you ever be your own person?

In truth, God does not condemn anyone to hell. People themselves choose their own destiny by the decisions they make. Some people say to God, "Thy will be done." They go into a heaven of eternal union with God. Other people say, "My will be done." With heavenly tears that respect human freedom, God allows them to walk into the darkness of eternal separation from him, the source of all joy and life.

**Heaven or Hell?** ➤ ➤ ➤ ➤ ➤ ➤ ➤ ➤ ➤ ➤ ➤ ➤ ➤ ➤ ➤

Heaven and hell are the same place—a wonderful banquet hall where people gather around a table overflowing with the most delectable food. They can't wait to enjoy the feast.

However, there is one condition. Each person must eat with an eight-foot spoon. The people in heaven are deliriously happy while those in hell are frustrated and eternally unhappy. Why? Well, those in hell are accustomed to going it alone that they unsuccessfully try to feed themselves—an impossible task with an eight-foot spoon. Those in heaven, in contrast, eat to their hearts' content because they feed each other with their oversized spoons. They've learned to care for others. And their reward is eternal happiness.

# thirty-four ➤ ➤ ➤ ➤ ➤ ➤

### How can I be truly free if God knows everything that is going to happen to me in the future?

et's say you are standing at a crosswalk waiting for a light to change green so you can cross the street. You know the light will change in five seconds. And it does. Did your *knowing* it was going to change *cause* it to change? No.

Now, lets turn to God, a God of mystery whose ways are not our ways. One of his attributes is his *omniscience*, derived from the Latin for "all-knowing." God always was, is, and always will be. He is eternal. He knows all that has happened, is happening right now, and will ever happen. In other words, God knows all things all the "time." Why? Because he exists outside of time as well as in time. After all, God created time at the beginning of creation. But be careful: Don't confuse God's perfect and timeless knowledge of future events ("future" from our perspective, always "present" from his perspective) with his timeless *determining* these events.

What God did was to create a being who can make free choices, a being who exists in time, a being whose choices determine the future. This being is the human being, endowed with an intellect and free will. Our free will enables us to make real choices in the present that determine our futures. God has perfect knowledge of these choices, but he did not make them. We did—freely.

Let's turn again to our fundamental point: God's knowledge of everything does *not* take away your freedom. For example, he knows you will sin. Sin is contrary to his will. But he permits you to sin because God respects your use of free will, his great gift that gives you dignity. Obviously, he desires you to choose love, the life of God. But he doesn't force you to love. The nature of love is to allow the other to be free. And God is Love.

Two examples can help you see how God's omniscience interacts with your gift of freedom.

In the first, a group of teens, out drinking all night, decides to drive home. The driver, under the influence of alcohol, crashes the car into a tree. Did God *know* this would happen? Yes. Did God *permit* this to happen? Yes, because he respects our free will and ordinarily does not suspend the laws of nature (for example, by moving the tree to avoid the car). Did God *cause* the accident? No, an abuse of human freedom caused it— getting intoxicated, driving under the influence of alcohol, and driving recklessly. God did not foreordain the teens to drink. His knowledge did not take away their power to act freely. They could have chosen otherwise.

In the second example, you are looking out of a window on the fifth floor of a building. You see a car speeding to an intersection. You know it will hit a pedestrian who is looking in the opposite direction. Unfortunately, the car does strike the inattentive person. Your foreknowledge did not *cause* the accident. God's omniscience works like this.

# thirty-five ➤ ➤ ➤ ➤ ➤ ➤ ➤

### The Church teaches that Mary was "ever virgin," yet the Bible says that Jesus had "brothers or sisters." How can both be true?

This question arises out of passages in the New Testament (most notably, Mt 13:55–56, Mk 6:1–6) that refer to certain "brothers and sisters" of Jesus. Catholics have always believed that these so-called brothers and sisters of Jesus were actually his cousins or other close relatives. Hence, the Church continues its long-standing belief in the perpetual virginity of the Blessed Mother.

Many prominent Scripture scholars present convincing arguments to back up this belief. For example, they show how neither Hebrew nor the western Aramaic language that Jesus spoke had a special word meaning "cousin." The word available to them—*ah*—was used for various types of relations. The patriarchal family dominated Jesus' world. His society considered the oldest living male—the patriarch—the father. In such a family, relatives, like cousins, referred to themselves as brothers and sisters.

Patriarchal families exist even today. A Jesuit friend of mine told me of his missionary days in Nepal. He would often have in class two students with the same surname. When my friend asked the boys if they were brothers, they often said yes. Only after some months did my friend learn that most of these "brothers" were really cousins. In reality, their fathers were brothers. And because of the closeness of their families, the two boys—actually cousins—considered themselves brothers and referred to themselves that way.

Scripture gives even more support to the Church's teaching. For example, two of the men Matthew's gospel names as brothers of Jesus—James and Joseph (Joses in some versions)—could not have been the sons of Mary, Jesus' mother, because Matthew (27:56) and Mark (15:40) mention them as the sons of another Mary. This Mary was one of the women who witnessed Jesus' crucifixion and who later went to anoint him on Easter Sunday morning.

Consider this question: If Jesus had blood brothers, why would he entrust his mother to John, the beloved disciple, and not to one of his so-called siblings (Jn 9:26)? This is especially true when we consider that James the "brother of the Lord" was the leader of the Jerusalem Christian community after the resurrection and martyred in the year AD 62 (Gal 1:19). If he were Mary's natural child, would it have not made a lot more sense for him to take responsibility for his mother, if indeed, she was his mother?

Finally, there is an interesting ancient tradition that came from a Christian writing not held to be divinely inspired, yet it was believed by several important early Greek Church Fathers. This tradition held that Joseph was a widower and that he was considerably older than Mary when he took her as his wife at the time of Jesus' birth. According to this theory, Joseph had children from this first marriage, children that would have been Jesus' stepbrothers and stepsisters.

## thirty-six ➤ ➤ ➤ ➤ ➤ ➤ ➤

*I heard that the novel* The Da Vinci Code *claims that Jesus was married. Is this true? Did Jesus at least experience sexual desires like other people?*

Dan Brown's controversial and extremely popular novel-turned-movie, *The Da Vinci Code*, was a commercial phenomenon that generated television documentaries and numerous articles and books that both support and debunk its theses. Before we start discussing it, it is important to point out that the claims of the novel cannot merely be written off as poetic license. First, the rich tradition of historical fiction generally strives for historical accuracy, making characters in the book and events in history match the actual historical characters and events. Second, where the fiction takes license, it generally is obviously flagged as fiction. However, Dan Brown has repeatedly stated that through his "research" he was convinced of the truth of his alternative history of Christianity that he presented in *The Da Vinci Code*. Therefore, the claims of novel are not mere fiction, but something the author has actively promoted as true, and therefore deserve a serious rebuttal.

Written in the style of an exciting mystery story, the novel claims that the Holy Grail was really the body of Mary Magdalene who became Jesus' wife and bore his child. She was supposed to be the head of the Church but was displaced by

Peter and other men, and it even holds that the bloodline of Jesus exists in France today. The novel further asserts that the Church has been involved in a cover-up since the first century. The title comes from the claim that Leonardo Da Vinci knew this when he painted the *Last Supper* because he depicted Mary Magdalene (not the beloved John) sitting on the right side of Jesus.

At its core, *The Da Vinci Code* is anti-Christian, anti-Catholic, and riddled with serious errors of every kind. It charges, for example, that first-century Christians did not believe in the divinity of Christ and that the New Testament was fabricated in the fourth century. These are patently false claims accepted by no reputable scholar. Part of the book's appeal, no doubt, is that it plays into our scandal-obsessed age that preaches that an active sex life is the be-all and end-all of human existence. But consider what the New Testament says. There, we see that Jesus rarely speaks about sex. He cares more about respect in human relationships. In first-century Palestine, men looked on women as objects they owned, as outlets for their own pleasure. They could toss their wives aside for virtually any reason. Jesus' own example and teaching elevated the role of women: He condemned lust, adultery, and divorce.

Scripture and the early Church councils teach that Jesus is like us in everything but sin. Therefore, as a teen and a young man, Jesus learned to integrate his maturing sexuality into his personality as anyone else would. However, unlike most, he did so without disrespecting self or others.

Remember an important truth: The sex drive is good, not dirty or sinful. It is both normal and healthy to have sexual feelings. God made us with these urges so males and females can unite in love and bring forth new life, thus beautifully sharing in God's own creative activity. Having said this, in our Lord's day and in our own day, for various reasons some people do not marry. What about Jesus himself?

The Church has *always* taught that Jesus *never* married, despite what modern novelists might claim to increase the sales of their books. What can a modern historian see as evidence of the truth of the Church's teaching? First, nowhere in the gospels is there any mention of a wife or children for Jesus. The gospels have no trouble mentioning by name Jesus' mother, his foster father, his so-called brothers, his close male apostles and disciples, his cousin John the Baptist, and various women disciples like Salome, the sisters Mary and Martha, and others, including, of course, Mary Magdalene. Yet there is no mention of a wife for Jesus. But the most powerful evidence comes from Paul's first letter to the Corinthians, where he defends the fact that he, as an apostle of Jesus, still can marry by writing, "Have we not every right . . . to be accompanied by a Christian wife, like the brothers of the Lord, and like Cephas (Peter)?" (1 Cor 9:4–5). It is basically unthinkable that, were Jesus married, Paul would not have cited Jesus to validate his right to marry rather than the chief apostle, Peter. (By the way, if you are wondering why Paul mentioned Jesus' "brothers," make sure to check out the previous question!)

We can speculate that Jesus did not marry because taking a wife and worrying about raising a family would have distracted him from his passionate, all-consuming vocation to proclaim and spread God's kingdom. In Matthew 19:12 Jesus refers to those who make themselves eunuchs for the sake of God's kingdom. Jesus calls this a gift that some will freely choose to further God's work. Undoubtedly, Jesus himself chose this path. And as we know, his total commitment for others led ultimately to his death.

One final point: In the wake of the popularity of *The DaVinci Code*, ABC news did a special on its claims. Interestingly, it found no serious scholar today who believes that Jesus was married, thus supporting the long-held tradition of the Church.

**What Do You Think?** ➤ ➤ ➤ ➤ ➤ ➤ ➤ ➤ ➤ ➤ ➤ ➤ ➤ ➤

If you could ask the teenage Jesus one question, what would it be? What do you think he'd say in reply?

◄ ◄ ◄ ◄ ◄ ◄ ◄ ◄ ◄ ◄ ◄ ◄ ◄ ◄ ◄ ◄ ◄ ◄ ◄ ◄ ◄ ◄ ◄ ◄ ◄

# thirty-seven ➤ ➤ ➤ ➤ ➤ ➤

### How can Jesus be both God and human?

I magine, if you can, a mere thimble holding all the oceans of the world. This is incredible when you think about it. How could a mere thimble contain an almost infinite amount of water? But this example pales compared to our belief in the Incarnation, the doctrine that in Jesus Christ the immensity and boundlessness of God took human form in order to save us.

An important gospel passage that proclaims the doctrine of the Incarnation, of God becoming human, occurs in John's gospel:

> In the beginning was the Word,
> and the Word was with God,
> and the Word was God.
> All things came to be through him . . .
> And the Word became flesh
> and made his dwelling among us (Jn 1:1, 3, 14).

Christians proclaim that Jesus of Nazareth, a historical person who lived among us, walked the earth, died, and rose from the dead, is also the second person of the Blessed Trinity, the Word of God. He is both the Son of Man and the Son of God. Jesus is God in human flesh ("the Word became flesh" and lived among us). Jesus is not half God and half human, but fully divine and fully human. Thus, Christianity professes that Jesus Christ is one divine person who has both a divine nature and a human nature. He is completely God; at the same time, he is completely human.

*How* this can be is a mystery of love beyond human comprehension. If we could understand how Christ could be both God and human, Jesus would be no greater than us. But we accept it as true because God has given us the gift of faith and the grace to believe it. We thank him for the gift of the Incarnation because it helps us understand so many other truths about God and our own human destiny.

For example:

- *We have been created precious in God's sight.* We can proclaim with great pride, "He was one of us." Jesus is our Lord, our Savior, and our brother. St. Athanasius said, "The Word was not degraded by receiving a body. . . . Rather he deified what he put on; and, more than that, he bestowed this gift upon [us]."

  "God does not make junk," the poster proclaims. How could any human be junk if God became one of us? On the contrary, the Incarnation teaches that we are beings of tremendous worth and dignity. Jesus, our brother, adopts us into the divine family.

- *Jesus shows us the way to live.* His life is the model for all to follow. His suffering and death graphically demonstrate the meaning of love. He practiced what he preached. Because he is one of us, he completely understands what we are going through and is thus completely willing to lend us his support and grace. He exemplifies the meaning of friendship and will forever stand at our side.

- *God loves us with an infinite love.* Not only did God take human form, but also he gave his life for us. An early Christian hymn puts it this way:

> Who, though he was in the form of God,
> did not regard equality with God something to be grasped.
> Rather, he emptied himself,
> taking the form of a slave,
> coming in human likeness;
> and found human in appearance,
> he humbled himself,
> becoming obedient to death,
> even death on a cross.
> — Philippians 2:6–8

Jesus' death and resurrection bring forgiveness for our sins and make it possible for us to live forever! Is there greater love? Is there better news?

## Faith Checklist

Check any statements about Jesus that you agree with.

_____ Jesus is the Messiah.

_____ Jesus is my best friend.

_____ Jesus is my brother.

_____ Jesus is fully human.

_____ Jesus is fully God.

_____ Jesus is my personal Savior.

_____ Jesus is Truth.

_____ Jesus lives!

_____ Jesus is the second person of the Trinity.

_____ Jesus is my Lord.

Why do you respond the way you did to each item?

# thirty-eight ➤ ➤ ➤ ➤ ➤ ➤

*How can God be one yet three at the same time? I'm confused.*

After all the people had been baptized and Jesus also had been baptized and was praying, heaven was opened and the holy Spirit descended upon him in bodily form like a dove. And a voice came from heaven, "You are my beloved Son; with you I am well pleased."

~Luke 3:21–22

This scripture quote is related to your question because all three persons of the Blessed Trinity are mentioned: Father, Son, and Holy Spirit. Another important Trinitarian passage comes from Matthew 28:19 where Jesus instructs his disciples: "Go, therefore, and make disciples of all nations, baptizing them in the name of the Father, and of the Son, and of the holy Spirit." Notice here that the Father, the Son, and the Spirit share *one* name (the name of God, that is, *Yahweh*, a name revealed to Moses). Three persons yet *one* God. Yours is one of the great questions of theology because it goes to the very heart of the mysteries of our faith. The *Catechism of the Catholic Church* tells us that

> The Trinity is a mystery of faith in the strict sense, one of the "mysteries that are hidden in God, which can never be known unless they are revealed by God." To be sure, God has left traces of his Trinitarian being in his work of creation and in his Revelation throughout the Old Testament. But his inmost Being as Holy Trinity

is a mystery that is inaccessible to reason alone
or even to Israel's faith before the Incarnation of
God's Son and the sending of the Holy Spirit
(*CCC, 237*).

In other words, we would never know that God is a Blessed
Trinity unless God himself revealed this central truth to us. God
did so when the Son of God, the second person of the Blessed
Trinity, became man in Jesus Christ. Jesus revealed to us that he
was God, "The Father and I are one" (Jn 10:30). He also
promised that he and the Father would send the Holy Spirit to
be with his followers:

"And I will ask the Father, and he will give you
another Advocate to be with you always, the
Spirit of truth, which the world cannot accept,
because it neither sees nor knows it. But you
know it, because it remains with you, and will
be in you" (Jn 14:16–17).

The Holy Spirit came in power on Pentecost Sunday to
teach, guide, protect, and comfort Christ's Church until the end
of time.

In brief, we believe the Trinity is one God in three persons
because God himself revealed this profound mystery to us. The
dogma of the Trinity is the central mystery of our Christian
faith and Christian life. We believe that the Father, Son, and
Holy Spirit are not three gods, but one God. They share the
same being, the same "essence," the same substance. Each
divine person is God whole and entire: "The Father is that
which the Son is, the Son that which the Father is, the Father
and the Son that which the Holy Spirit is, i.e., by nature one
God."[1]

Yet, we also believe that the three persons are really distinct
from each other, not just three ways of talking about how God
works. God is one, but not alone. God is a community. Think of
the three persons as three relationships: The Father is related to
the Son, the Son to the Father, and the Holy Spirit to both.

Are you confused? You are in good company because the mystery of the Trinity is beyond human comprehension. Great minds have used analogies, comparisons, to try to explain how God can be one yet three. One example you might be familiar with is the image of the shamrock of St. Patrick. He would hold up a shamrock and ask his potential converts: "Is it one leaf or three?" "It is both one leaf and three," was their reply. "And so it is with God," Patrick argued. The three divine persons all have the same essence, that is, the same single divine nature.

Another example comes when we try to explain "the missions" of the Blessed Trinity. The missions refer to their roles. For example, we attribute creation to God the Father, salvation to God the Son, and sanctification to God the Holy Spirit. Yet, recall that the three persons are inseparable. They all share together in the common divine work or missions. For example, the Son as well as the Holy Spirit were also at work at the time of creation. You play roles, too. For example, at the same time you are a son or daughter, a student, and a friend. You are the same person, yet you play three different roles. It is something like that with God. There is one God, but three relations.

God is a unity-in-community. St. Augustine suggested thinking about the Trinity as the Lover (Father), the Beloved (Son), and bond of Love between them (Holy Spirit). In short, God is love.

Reflect on what love does. A major quality of love is that it unites. It creates community. We humans are made in the image of the loving God. That means we were made for love. This is a great insight for Christian living that we can gain from reflecting on this great mystery of the Trinity. We are most like God when we love. "Beloved, let us love one another, because love is of God; everyone who loves is begotten by God and knows God. Whoever is without love does not know God, for God is love" (1 Jn 4:7–8).

# thirty-nine ➤ ➤ ➤ ➤ ➤ ➤

### What makes the Bible so special? Where did it come from?

T he Bible is a one-of-a-kind book. We read most books for *information*, but we look to the Bible for *transformation*. The following story illustrates this well.

A South Sea Islander proudly showed his Bible to an American soldier during World War II. "We stopped reading that long ago," the soldier said.

The native, once a cannibal, smiled back, "It's good *we* haven't. If it weren't for this book, you'd have been a meal by now."

"Bible" comes from the Greek *biblion* meaning "the book." The plural form was *ta biblia*, "the books." This is a good description of what the Bible is—a library of books. But these are no ordinary books since God is the author of the Bible. As the *Catechism of the Catholic Church* teaches:

God inspired the human authors of the sacred books. "To compose the sacred books, God chose certain men who, all the while he employed them in this task, made full use of their own faculties and powers so that, though he acted in them and by them, it was as true authors that they consigned to writing whatever he wanted written, and no more" (CCC, 106).[2]

Therefore, the Bible is special because it is the inspired word of God. It contains the "greatest story ever told," the story of his love affair with the human race despite its sins and betrayals. Love oozes from its pages, from the first verse to the last. Genesis 1:1 says, "In the beginning, when God created the heavens and earth." Thus, the Bible opens with a ringing affirmation of a loving Creator. God gives existence to all creatures, especially to those made in his image and likeness—human beings.

The last two verses of the Bible read: "Amen! Come, Lord Jesus! The grace of the Lord Jesus be with all" (Revelation 22:20–21). This prayer concludes the written record of revelation by commending us to Jesus. Jesus Christ is God's supreme gift of love, the key to our salvation and eternal life.

The various individual books of the Bible were composed over the course of approximately one thousand years. Most books of the Bible came into being through this process: *experience, reflection, oral tradition, written book.*

1. *Experience.* God touched the daily lives of the Israelites and the early Christians in many different but consistently loving and reconciling ways. These experiences were powerful, affecting the very identity of the people. God's involvement in their lives changed them and their way of thinking.

2. *Reflection.* Over time, the religious leaders and people deepened their understanding of God's presence in their midst. Prophets, for example, helped explain how God worked through events, persons, ordinary life, miracles, and the like, to instruct and guide the people.

3. *Oral tradition.* The custom of people in the ancient world was to tell of God's work in their history through word of mouth. Our ancestors in the faith were storytellers whose memories were outstanding. Generation after generation would hear and then repeat the stories of God's saving action in their history. Only after time, and often during periods of crisis, would they commit anything to writing.

4. *Written Book.* Eventually, the Israelites wrote down parts of their heritage. First came the Ten Commandments and parts of the Mosaic Law. After the nation came into being under a king, court histories and chronicles appeared.

During the Exile, scribes preserved the history of the people and wrote down the words of the prophets.

A similar process took place in the New Testament. At first, early Christians retold the Jesus story, focusing especially on the events of the passion, death, and resurrection of Jesus. Key preachers like Paul wrote letters (from around AD 50-64) to support the faith of their early converts and instruct them on how to live a Christian life. The early churches circulated these epistles (letters) for reading at the Sunday celebrations of the Lord's Supper.

The gospels came into being from around AD 65 to as late as AD 100. Eyewitnesses to Jesus' life were dying and distortions were setting in. Consequently, the authors of Mark, Matthew, Luke, and John composed orderly accounts of Jesus' life, his teaching, his miracles, and the saving events of his last days. These evangelists relied on the oral traditions, selecting and arranging their material to bolster the faith of the communities for whom they were writing.

One final point about the Bible: Though its books offer a rich written record of God's work in human history, it is only a *partial* record. Recall the closing words of John's gospel:

There are also many other things that Jesus did, but if these were to be described individually, I do not think the whole world would contain the books that would be written (Jn 21:25).

The Church holds that *Sacred Tradition* includes other revealed truths handed down from the apostles, truths the Bible does not spell out. It, like the Bible, has as its common source God's revelation in Jesus Christ. This Sacred Tradition is the living transmission of the Gospel in the Church carried on by the successors of the apostles.

Through Tradition, "the Church, in her doctrine, life and worship, perpetuates and transmits to every generation all that she herself is, all that she believes" (CCC, 78).[3]

One example of a revealed truth preserved by Sacred Tradition that is not explicitly contained in the Bible is the doctrine of the Immaculate Conception of Mary.

**Check Up**  ➤ ➤ ➤ ➤ ➤ ➤ ➤ ➤ ➤ ➤ ➤ ➤ ➤ ➤ ➤ ➤ ➤ ➤ ⋁

> **Factoid:** In a recent year, researchers found that 55% of Protestants read the Bible in the past week versus 27% of Catholics.[4]
>   • *Do you own a Bible? Do you use it?*

◄ ◄ ◄ ◄ ◄ ◄ ◄ ◄ ◄ ◄ ◄ ◄ ◄ ◄ ◄ ◄ ◄ ◄ ◄ ◄ ◄ ⋁

# forty  ➤ ➤ ➤ ➤ ➤ ➤ ➤ ➤ ➤ ➤ ➤

## Is the Bible true?

Yes, the Bible conveys God's truth. According to the Second Vatican II, the Bible teaches "firmly, faithfully, and without error that truth which God, for the sake of our salvation, wished to see confided to the Sacred Scriptures" (*CCC*, 107).[5]

But if what you mean by your question is whether everything in the Bible is *scientifically* or *historically* true, the answer is no. Not everything in the Bible is science or history. Think of the Bible as a library of books with many different literary forms. These include poetry, allegories, fables, speeches, fictional short stories, census lists, historical accounts, and many other types of literature. To discover the religious truth of the Bible, we must first identify what kind of literature we are reading. For example, is it a fictional short story or an historical account or poetry or something else? Then we must ask what the biblical author meant to communicate to us about God and salvation by using this particular literary form.

Take, for example, the parable of the Prodigal Son. Was there historically a younger son like the one Jesus described in his story, one who squandered his inheritance? Most likely, there is no real, historical person behind this passage. Jesus told this vivid short *story* to reveal in a graphic way God's forgiving love for sinners.

Similarly, in the Old Testament, it is highly doubtful that a large fish swallowed Jonah. Rather, this is a story that contains the powerful truth that God loves everyone and wants all people saved. In this story, God wanted Jonah to preach to the Ninevites despite Jonah's unwillingness to do so. The story shows that God's will cannot be thwarted: God found a way for Jonah to get to Assyria and its capital city of Nineveh, despite Jonah's protests. Another lesson we can learn from this story is that no matter how we might resist what God wants, he will have his way.

On the other hand, much in the Bible is historically true, including the chronicles of the Israelite kingdom, the gospel stories of Jesus Christ, and the missionary travels of St. Paul.

The Church teaches that we must always interpret the Bible in light of the Holy Spirit by whom it was written. This means we must be attentive to both the content and unity of the whole Scripture. For example, we can understand more clearly the meaning of Old Testament passages in light of what Jesus accomplished for us in the New Testament. Second, the Bible should always be read within the living Tradition of the Church. And third, those who interpret Scripture must do so by being attentive to the analogy of faith, that is, how the various truths of the faith are related among themselves and to God's whole plan of salvation (see *CCC*, 1123–114).

It always takes prayerful reflection to understand the truth of the Bible. Furthermore, it is helpful to refer to a good Bible commentary for further insight. Finally, Catholics should always look to the Church's Magisterium for help to understand the controversial passages. This is what it means to read the Bible within the living Tradition of the Church since Jesus entrusted the Holy Father and the bishops to interpret authentically the word of God.

A final thought: People do not reject the Bible because it contradicts itself, but because it contradicts them.

## The Bible in Fifty Words

> God made
> Adam bit
> Noah arked
> Abraham split
> Joseph ruled
> Jacob fooled
> Bush talked
> Moses balked
> Pharaoh plagued
> People walked
> Sea divided
> Tablets guided
> Promise landed
> Saul freaked
> David peeked
> Prophets warned
> Jesus born
> God walked
> Love talked
> Anger crucified
> Hope died
> Love rose
> Spirit flamed
> Word spread
> God remained.
> —Source Unknown[6]

**Fun Story** ➤ ➤ ➤ ➤ ➤ ➤ ➤ ➤ ➤ ➤ ➤ ➤ ➤ ➤ ➤ ➤ ⋎

A second-grade class was asked about our first parents. Here are two students' unedited responses:

Billy: "Adam and Eve were created from an apple tree."

Emily: "The first commandment was when Eve told Adam to eat the apple."

◄ ◄ ◄ ◄ ◄ ◄ ◄ ◄ ◄ ◄ ◄ ◄ ◄ ◄ ◄ ◄ ◄ ◄ ◄ ◄ ◄ ◄ ◄ ⋎

# forty-one ➤ ➤ ➤ ➤ ➤ ➤ ➤ ➤

### What do Catholics believe about evolution? Did a "real"Adam and Eve exist?

In a letter to the Pontifical Academy of Sciences, Pope John Paul II observed that due to remarkable and converging evidence from a variety of scientific fields, the theory of evolution is now regarded as "more than a hypothesis." Some observers took this to be an admission of the Church of overturning some long standing teaching against evolution. That is not the case. According to the 1909 Catholic Encyclopedia, the theory that present forms of life other than humans had evolved over long periods of time according to natural laws was "in perfect agreement with the Christian conception of the universe" and noted also that the evolution of the human body was "*per se* not improbable." One hundred years later, Church leaders by and large consider the evolution of the body *per se* probable.

This follows the long standing Church tradition to allow scientists the space for genuine scientific inquiry, and respect for the resolutions that scientists come to within their proper sphere. The Church teaches that no truth of science can contradict a truth of revelation. One set of problems occurs when scientists start jumping from legitimate scientific inquiry into religious inquiry, claiming for instance that the process of evolution definitively excludes the action of God. But this is nonsense that no scientific experiment could demonstrate, and should be rejected.

Thus there are always questions and problems that science will never answer or solve. For example, to speak of the evolution of the human body does not explain the human soul nor does it explain our unique relationship to the God that is love. Nor does the discussion of a singularity exploding in a Big Bang explain where that singularity arose from. With this type of speculation, we engage what the International Theological Commission, headed by the future Pope Benedict XVI, mentioned as the Christian duty to "to locate the modern scientific understanding of the universe within the context of the theology of creation."[7] When we turn to the Bible, we find definitive truths about God's creation of the universe, the goodness of creation, and God's immediate creation of each human soul.

These truths are revealed in Chapters 1–3 of the book of Genesis and are connected to the story of Adam and Eve. Recall that Genesis was written only a few centuries before the coming of Christ. Its first eleven chapters are a masterfully written account of human origins, of primeval history. They are classified as a form of literature known as "religious myth," that is, a literary genre that employs a poetic writing style of stories, parables, allegories, and so forth to communicate cosmic truths.

Religious myth as a form of literature is *not* the same as a legend or a fairy tale. The authors of Genesis used figurative language to convey important religious *truths* that God wants us to know. These truths include the following:

- Human beings are created in the image and likeness of the one, true, and loving God.
- God created humans in friendship and in harmony with him and creation.
- God created men and women as equals who were to care for and love each other.

- God alone creates each human soul, the spiritual principle in humans. The human soul is immortal.
- The world God made is good and for the benefit of humans.
- The misfortunes of humans, including death, resulted from the prideful sin and disobedience of the first man. This is what we call original sin, an essential truth of Catholic faith. In the words of the *Catechism of the Catholic Church*:

    By yielding to the tempter, Adam and Eve committed a *personal sin*, but this sin affected the *human nature* that they would then transmit *in a fallen state*. It is a sin which will be transmitted by propagation to all mankind, that is, by the transmission of a human nature deprived of original holiness and justice. And that is why original sin is called "sin" only in an analogical sense: It is a sin "contracted" and not "committed"—a state and not an act (CCC, 404).

- Despite human failure, God still loved humanity. He did not abandon us. From the beginning, God had a plan to rescue humans from their sins. In Genesis 3:15, which has been called the "first gospel," we see "the first announcement of the coming Messiah and Redeemer, of a battle between the serpent and the Woman, and of the final victory of a descendant of hers" (CCC, 410).

Genesis is *not* a scientific treatise. It does not address the issue of whether humans descend from one set of parents or many sets of first parents. Nor does Genesis intend to tell us the historical names of our original parents. The name *Adam* means "man" or "from the earth"; *Eve* means "helpmate." These symbolic names are the prototypes of humanity.

In the end, much of the confusion and controversy over evolution results from misreadings by two groups: rabidly atheistic scientists and fundamentalist Christians. The first group misuses the discoveries of biology and physics to make a claim that simply does not follow: that God does not exist. The second group rely on a method of biblical interpretation that the Church has never endorsed, claiming that the plain and literal meaning of the Bible is available to anyone reading the words on the page. This leads them to adding up the years in biblical genealogies and claiming that the world is only six thousand years old. On the view of both, faith and reason clash. In the Church, the two exist in harmony.

## forty-two ➤ ➤ ➤ ➤ ➤ ➤ ➤

*The book of Revelation seems impossible to understand. It's almost like a dream, what with trumpets sounding and strange beasts appearing. Also, I hear so much about the number "666" in Revelation 13:18. What does this number mean?*

The book of Revelation is the last book in the Bible. Mysterious and difficult to comprehend, yet simultaneously fascinating, the book of Revelation draws us in because it deals with humanity's fate, the end of the world, and the beginning of Christ's heavenly reign. St. Dionysius of Alexandria observed, "The darkness of this book does not prevent one from being astonished at it. And even if I do not understand everything in it, that is only because of my incapability. I cannot be a judge of the truths which are contained in it or measure them with the poverty of my mind, being guided more by faith than by understanding. I find them only surpassing my understanding."[8]

We find Revelation difficult to grasp because much of it is written using a highly symbolic form of writing known as *apocalypse*. Like the Old Testament book of Daniel, Revelation uses a weirdly imaginative writing style to disguise its contents should it fall in the wrong hands. At the time of its composition around AD 95, the Roman emperor Domitian was fiercely persecuting Christians for refusing to acknowledge the divinity of the emperor as the state religion required. Christians believed then, as they do now, that Jesus Christ alone is God. Thus the book of Revelation is in code, with numbers and animals, for example, assigned a specific meaning. An ancient scholar commented that studying the book of Revelation will either find us crazy or make us crazy. St. Jerome wrote that it contains more secrets than it does words.

The main purpose of the text was to strengthen the hope and determination of those suffering in the infant Church. Its basic message is that God controls history and the outcome of events, not any earthly rulers or forces of evil. Eventually God will usher in a golden age of justice and peace. Until that time, Christians should patiently endure suffering and live like Jesus Christ.

In Revelation 13, the author describes a vision of a beast from the sea and a beast from the earth who is also a false prophet. The prophet-monster from the land has two horns like a lamb and speaks like a dragon. It forces people to worship the first beast and kills those who do not. In verse 18, the author assigns this beast-prophet the number **666.**

Biblical scholars have noted that in the Hebrew and Greek languages, letters have a numerical value and that the letters *NRWN QSR* (Nero Caesar) in Hebrew add up to 666. Nero was an Emperor who viciously persecuted Christians after the fire in Rome in AD 64. Many believed that the evil of Nero was being inflicted once again on Christians in the person of the current emperor, Domitian.

# forty-three ➤ ➤ ➤ ➤ ➤ ➤

*A Protestant friend has told me about some novels she is reading in the Left Behind series. She mentioned the "rapture" and that the world is going to end soon. Is it? With all the violence and terrorism in our world, do you think the Lord is coming soon?*

The very popular *Left Behind* series of twelve novels has sold millions of copies. The authors of the books are Tim LaHaye and Jerry B. Jenkins who, unfortunately, also promote anti-Catholic sentiments through the treatment of certain Catholic characters in their books. For example, in some books in the series, the pope is an agent of the anti-Christ.

The series began with a book telling how Christ came to lift up millions of "good" people and took them to heaven in an event known as the Rapture. Those "left behind" had to contend with the Antichrist and his battle for their souls in the next seven years. The last book in the series rewrites the book of Revelation as a thriller about the end of the world and the sudden disappearance of millions of Christians.

These novels are the product of biblical fundamentalist theology that is severely at odds with Catholic teaching about the end of the world and the coming of Jesus. (One characteristic of fundamentalism is to read the Bible literally with little regard to literary types.) Catholic teaching sees the book of Revelation as a beacon of hope to Christians under persecution. Its basic message is that if we remain faithful to Christ, we will share in his heavenly kingdom. Catholic theology, therefore, looks with hope to the day of our Lord's return. In contrast, the *Left Behind* novels present a harsh and judgmental God at odds with scripture.

As you read in the last question, the book of Revelation was written in highly symbolic language; when this language is taken literally, distortions set in. This is the case with "Rapture Theology," which relies on St. Jerome's Latin translation of a word in 2 Corinthians 12:4 and 1 Thessalonians 4:17. *Rapio* means "to snatch" and this is how some fundamentalist Christians have used this term when they read Revelation literally. According to their theology, Christ really comes to the earth three times: at his birth over two thousand years ago, his secret coming to snatch away the just before the trials that will take place before the world ends (the Rapture), and then at the end of the world to become king of heaven and earth.

In reality, though, the so-called seven-year tribulation between the "rapture" and Christ's *second* coming is *not* found in the Bible. What Scripture *does* teach is that Christ will come after a period of trial. His second coming will be the end of the world at which time he will take all believers to heaven with him. There will be no previous "snatching."

Some good advice: Be wary about fundamentalist interpretations about the end of the world. Distrust claims of sects like the Jehovah Witnesses who periodically try to predict when the final battle between good and evil will take place. And ignore groups that make scary predictions about the world's end. Some people, consciously or not, exploit the natural fear we have of the unknown. Their "secret" knowledge of the future gives them a type of control over others.

Catholic teaching holds that, yes, Christ will come again to judge the living and the dead (Mt 12:36). But since Jesus is a loving savior, we should not fear this day (Jn 3:17). We should, however, prepare for judgment day by serving others (Mt 24:42-44). The Church does not pretend to know *when* the world will end *or* the nature of the events preceding it.

The Church directs us to the teaching of Jesus himself. When the apostles asked him when the world would end, Jesus replied, "But of that day or hour, no one knows, neither the angels in heaven, nor the Son, but only the Father" (Mk 13:32).

Jesus teaches that we should always be ready by living a Christian life *right now* (Mk 13:33). Needless worry about the future is pointless, accomplishing nothing. Jesus instructs us to set our hearts on God's kingdom first and to trust in God's saving justice. Everything else will take care of itself (Mt 6:33–34). It is hard to improve on this formula for a happy, productive, Christian life.

# forty-four ➤ ➤ ➤ ➤ ➤ ➤ ➤

### What does the Church teach about extraterrestrial intelligent life?

Interestingly, the Catholic Church has never made an official statement one way or another about the existence elsewhere in the universe of other intelligent beings. Basically, this is a question for science to answer, not theology.

But we can still think about the theological implications if there were other intelligent beings in our universe.

First, some Catholic astronomers have commented on the vastness of the universe and how strange it would be if we were the *only* intelligent creatures God made. Strange, yes, but that still does not prove that there is extraterrestrial intelligent life. And so far, we have not found any.

Second, we acknowledge that Jesus Christ is the Word of God spoken once and for all to humanity. He is our unique Savior, the Son of God who became man to redeem us. Although the Bible records the history of human sin and Christ's redemption, it does *not* record the history of all the civilizations that might exist elsewhere in the universe and how Jesus saves them. We simply do not know how God dealt with or deals with them, if in fact they do exist. If they do, and if we meet ET, the first thing we should ask is, "How has God revealed himself to you? How has the Son of God shown his love to you?" Christian theology would hold that God would want all his creatures to share in his Trinitarian love and that his saving plan touches them all in some way. How? We simply don't know because we don't even know if they exist or not. (On the question of how God might save other intelligent beings, you would probably greatly enjoy C.S. Lewis's science fiction Space Trilogy, especially the first title in the series, *Out of the Silent Planet*.)

Third, the Church teaches that science and religion should not be at odds. If life on other planets were to be discovered, it would simply strengthen our belief in a marvelous, Creator-God who is much greater than we can possibly imagine. Fr. George Coyne, the long-time director of the Vatican Observatory, makes an interesting point. He thinks we should look on the stars as God's sperm. From your biology class, you know how sperm has the potential to produce life, but most never realize that goal. According to Fr. Coyne, like sperm, "each star is fired with a propensity for life, but there is no reason to think any of them have achieved this."[9] It could simply be that there is nothing there. But in God's wisdom, perhaps there is. What do you think?

One final point: This question assumes that we are talking about material beings who have spirits, yet exist in space and time like we humans do. Certainly the Church teaches that God created other spiritual, immortal creatures, beings we call angels (and the fallen angels known as demons).

> As purely *spiritual* creatures angels have intelligence and will: They are personal and immortal creatures, surpassing in perfection all visible creatures, as the splendor of their glory bears witness (CCC, 330).

# forty-five ➤ ➤ ➤ ➤ ➤ ➤ ➤

### Do Satan and demons really exist?

"So submit yourselves to God. Resist the devil,
and he will flee from you."

~James 4:7

The word *Satan* means adversary. Both the Bible and
Church teaching hold that Satan, also known as the devil,
does indeed exist.

Satan, along with other demons, was at first a good angel,
made by a loving God. (Recall that angels are spiritual beings
created by God before the world began. They have free will and
intellects naturally superior to ours.) Scripture reveals that
these angels freely sinned against God (2 Pt 2:4). They radically
and irrevocably rejected God and his reign. A hint of their sin
appears in Genesis when the "father of lies" told our first parents, "You will be like gods" (Gn 3:5). By trying to make themselves God, the evil angels rebelled against a loving, gracious
Creator. Filled with hate and unwilling to repent, Satan and the
other devils were driven from God's presence.

The sin of Satan and the devils turned them into vengeful,
hateful, bitter creatures who oppose God and his plan for
humanity. The gospels present Satan as Jesus' prime enemy
who even tried to turn Jesus away from his divine mission.
Jesus spoke often of Satan, calling him a "murderer from the
beginning." But Jesus came to defeat Satan, saying that he saw
him fall from the sky like lightning. Jesus' many exorcisms pre-
viewed Satan's downfall.

Jesus' passion, death, resurrection, and ascension definitively overpowered the forces of evil and the demons. These saving

events reversed the effects of the disobedience of our first parents. Through this Paschal Mystery of divine love, Jesus Christ conquered sin, death, diabolical power, and our alienation from a loving God.

It is a mystery to us why God permits the devil to tempt us and to work against the kingdom of God. "The power of Satan is, nonetheless, not infinite. He is only a creature, powerful from the fact that he is pure spirit, but still a creature. He cannot prevent the building up of God's reign" (*CCC*, 395). The Risen Lord, through the Holy Spirit, is in charge of human history, gently guiding it until that day of his Second Coming. On that day, everyone will recognize the sovereign divinity of Jesus Christ.

Satan does indeed exist. But if you stay close to Jesus you need never fear the work of the Devil.

# forty-six ► ► ► ► ► ► ► ►

## Do miracles happen today?

"Although he had performed so many signs in their presence they did not believe in him."

~Jn 12:37

I believe miracles happen today, and so does my wife. To be brief, my wife and my oldest child are alive today because they survived an extremely life-threatening situation years ago during childbirth.

The attending physician, a non-Catholic, told me that it was a "miracle" that both survived the emergency procedure. He said he never saw anything like it in the twenty years he was chief obstetrician in a large hospital. He claimed it was God's intervention that saved them both. I fervently believe he was right, though I could never "prove" it to another person beyond a shadow of a doubt. But in my heart I *know* that our Lord did something extraordinary to spare my wife and child.

I'm not the only one who believes that God performs miracles today. A Harris poll of 2,201 adults, entitled "Religious and Other Beliefs of Americans 2003," found that 93% of the nation's Christians believe in miracles, while a FOX News/Opinion Dynamics Poll conducted in 2003 revealed that 82% of American adults believe that God performs miracles.[10]

Many miracles have been verified by teams of scientists and doctors. For example, Catholics and others have claimed that God has performed miraculous cures of sick people—many of them terminally ill—at Lourdes, France. (This is the site of the shrine where Mary appeared to St. Bernadette Soubirous in 1858.) More than 7,000 individuals reported cures to the Medical Bureau at Lourdes. An objective commission of scientists and medical personnel, using the most stringent criteria, examined the cures and led the Lourdes Bureau Médical to declare that sixty-seven cases should be officially acknowledged as miraculous, from 1858 to today.[11]

Biblical scholar Fr. John P. Meier provides an up-to-date, comprehensive definition of *miracle*: [12]

- It is an unusual, startling, extraordinary, and observable event.
- Human abilities or known forces that operate in space and time cannot explain this event.
- It results from a special act of God, doing what no human person can do.

Certainly, Catholics and Christians believe that miracles happen. After all, God became human in Jesus Christ! Jesus performed many miracles during his ministry.

> The signs worked by Jesus attest that the Father has sent him. They invite belief in him. To those who turn to him in faith, he grants what they ask. So miracles strengthen faith in the One who

does his Father's works; they bear witness that
he is the Son of God (*CCC*, 548).

Jesus' resurrection from the dead is the greatest miracle of
all. It is the ground of our Christian faith. God has indeed intervened in human history through this extraordinary person—
Jesus Christ.

The Lord continues his work through the ages. Church history is full of examples of God's miraculous intervention in the
lives of people. This is true even in our own day. For example, it
is possible to view the incorrupt bodies of some saints (their
bodies were not mummified at death). Science cannot explain
this phenomenon. At Fatima, Portugal, where our Lady
appeared in 1917, more than seventy thousand people saw the
sun dancing. Holy persons like Saint Pio of Pietrelcina (Padre
Pio, died in 1968 and canonized in 2002) bore the stigmata (the
wounds of Christ) and cured many people during his lifetime,
including a lady he cured of blindness. Incredibly enough, she
has no pupils, yet she sees!

Many miracles are associated with the saints. Catholics
believe in the doctrine of the communion of saints, our spiritual union with Christ. The Lord gives us favors through his
friends, extraordinary gifts that we don't deserve. In his
acclaimed book *Making Saints*, Kenneth L. Woodward describes
the exhaustive, "very severe," and carefully thought-out procedure the Vatican uses to determine if a candidate for canonization has worked a miracle.[13] A doctor, whose job it is to
determine if these medical wonders attributed to saints are
really miracles, calls them "fantastic, incredible, and well-docu-
mented." Science fiction does not compare to the works God
sometimes accomplishes through his friends, those holy people
we call saints.

Modern skeptics, influenced by the belief that it is impossible for God to intervene in the natural world, claim that miracles don't happen. But this opinion often does not square with
the facts. For those who believe in the good news of Jesus

Christ, we know that the world is full of grace. Wonders do take place.

Like a wise mother, however, the Church is not gullible. Church authorities always try to find a natural explanation for marvelous events brought to their attention. But after careful and exhaustive examination, there are times when the Church is willing to state that God has intervened miraculously in our world. Why? Because miracles do happen.

## What Do You Think?

"To those who believe, no proof is necessary; to those who don't believe, no proof is possible."

The Bible's concept of miracle includes the idea of a marvelous event that signals God's presence in a person's life. An example is how a person narrowly escapes a fatal car accident in an unexplainable way. This happened to a former student whose car wondrously stopped from plunging down a cliff. The police said that it was a miracle he survived.

- Have you ever personally witnessed a sign ("miracle") like this or heard about one from a friend of family member?
- Is it more reasonable to believe or not believe in miracles?

# forty-seven

### Are apparitions taking place today?

In our troubled world, it seems that the number of people reporting having visions of the Blessed Mother, Jesus, and other supernatural persons is on the rise. What does the

Church say about all of these? And why does the Church seem so slow in approving them?

First, the Church acknowledges that with God all things are possible. He is the almighty Creator and nature's Lawgiver. So he can intervene and allow visions to take place to help people on their faith journey. This is why Church authorities have approved some major Marian apparitions over the centuries, including three famous ones: Our Lady of Guadalupe (to Juan Diego in Mexico in 1531), Our Lady of Lourdes (to Bernadette Soubirous in France in 1858), and Our Lady of Fatima (to Lucia de Santos, and Francisco and Jacinta Marto in Portugal in 1917). After rigorous examination of these apparitions, the Church found that these were not the product of fraud or hallucination and that the messages associated with the apparitions were helpful to living an authentic Christian life.

However, the Church cautions against too easily accepting people who claim to be having visions. For one thing, it is a matter of Church doctrine that all we need to know for our salvation has been revealed in the gospel of Jesus Christ. Nothing can be added to it.

> "The Christian economy, therefore, since it is the new and definitive Covenant, will never pass away; and no new public revelation is to be expected before the glorious manifestation of our Lord Jesus Christ." . . . Throughout the ages, there have been so-called "private" revelations, some of which have been recognized by the authority of the Church. They do not belong, however, to the deposit of faith. It is not their role to improve or complete Christ's definitive Revelation, but to help live more fully by it in a certain period of history (CCC, 66–67).

Jesus himself rebuked people who sought out extraordinary signs yet made little effort to live their faith. Typically, we find that our faith is strengthened if we follow Christ's commandments in ordinary life. Going around looking for special signs is not the sure-fire formula for holiness.

Third, the Church is pretty exacting when it examines alleged apparitions because of the danger of superstition and the manipulation of believers. Historically, many who claimed to have had visions were doing so to build themselves up rather than to glorify Christ and his Church. Today, in our country alone, there are people in Ohio, Georgia, Arizona, Colorado, Illinois, Arkansas, New York, Texas, California, Connecticut, and Maryland who are claiming to have apparitions. Are they? How does the Church decide what is authentic or not?

The Church heeds well the advice of Scripture:

> Beloved, do not trust every spirit but test the spirits to see whether they belong to God, because many false prophets have gone out into the world. This is how you can know the Spirit of God: every spirit that acknowledges Jesus Christ come in the flesh belongs to God (1 Jn 1:1–2).

In testing the "spirits," the Church proceeds cautiously and with prudence so that people are not deceived and that it does not make any errors in approving an alleged apparition. It calls in specialists in blessed causes who examine and study the credibility of the vision. These experts try to answer questions like these:

- Is this a truly exceptional occurrence? Is there some human explanation for it? For example, if the visionary has claimed that the vision was responsible for a cure of his or her illness, is there some other medical explanation? Did a miracle really take place? Is there proof?

- Does the message associated with the apparition teach something contrary to Church doctrine, for example, by telling people to reject a Church teaching? (If so, then it is clearly false.)

- Is the visionary, or those associated with him or her, profiting financially? (If so, then their motives have to be seriously questioned.)
- Is the visionary leading a moral life? Is the person sincere and humble?
- Is the visionary mentally stable or is the person suffering from some psychotic delusion?
- Does the visionary accept the authority of the local bishop and submit to his commands while the case is being examined?
- Does the apparition promote healthy devotion and strengthen people's belief and the practice of the Catholic faith?

Today, of all the many private revelations and apparitions that you may hear about, realize that none has been officially approved by the Holy Father. A few have been examined on the *local* level and approved by the bishop, for example, at Betania, Venezuela. Others have been found to have no supernatural basis, for example, at Medjugorje, in the former Yugoslavia. Still others have been condemned as frauds, for example, at Bayside, New York. But the vast majority of alleged apparitions have not been examined by Church authorities at all.

You have no obligation to put any belief in someone claiming to have visions. Your duty as a Catholic is to receive the sacraments frequently, pray, read and study the holy scriptures, and try your best to live a good life by following the teachings of the Church's official teachers.

# forty-eight ➤ ➤ ➤ ➤ ➤ ➤

## Why do we have to die?

"Take care of your body as if you were going to live forever, and take care of your soul as if you were going to die tomorrow."

~St. Augustine

When we die we leave behind us all we have, and take with us all we are.

~Author Unknown

Death is all around us. The National Center for Health Statistics reported that about 2,444,000 Americans died in 2003.[14] This averages to about 6,700 persons each day! These facts make death seem very natural, and it is.

Though our nature is mortal, death—the separation of the soul from the body—was not in God's plan for us. Death entered the world because of sin, the original sin of the first man. Humans would have been immune from death had not Adam proudly disobeyed God and put his will first. Death is a result of Adam's sin. And this sin has resulted in all humans being subject to bodily decay and, eventually, death, our enemy. The book of Job calls it "the king of terrors."

But our Christian faith helps us to face it. Jesus himself transformed the meaning of death. In fact, in the Incarnation, Jesus freely accepted death as part of the human condition. Like any normal person who would face a painful death, Jesus anguished over it. But he accepted death in obedience to his Father's will. And because of this act of obedience, God raised Jesus up. Jesus' resurrection has conquered sin and death, once and for all. Through our Lord's resurrection, we, too, will conquer death.

Every person who has ever lived walked a road that ended in the grave. Fame, personal wealth, power, influence, prestige, earthly success—none of these can ever take us through the valley of death. Only our Lord Jesus can do that. As St. Paul proclaimed:

> For just as in Adam all die, so too in Christ shall all be brought to life. . . . The last enemy to be destroyed is death (1 Cor 15:22, 26).

Faith and trust in Jesus Christ and living in conformity with his Father's will put us on the right road. Death then becomes, in the words of St. Bernard of Clairvaux, "the gate of life."

### "I Need Jesus Now"

Once a missionary preached to an old Indian chief about Jesus Christ, describing Jesus as God's only way to heaven. "The Jesus road sounds like a good road," the chief observed. "But I have always followed the Indian road, and I don't want to change now."

A year later, the chief was dying of a fatal disease. He called the missionary to his side and asked for baptism. "I need Jesus now," the dying chief said. "The Indian road stops here. It cannot take me through the valley."

# forty-nine

## What will heaven and hell be like?

A recent Harris Poll® reported that 70% of those polled believe that there is a heaven, while only 59% believe in hell.[15] Our Christian faith holds that both heaven and hell exist. We can only speculate what each is "like" based on divine revelation and the teachings of Jesus Christ. The famous

Christian author C.S. Lewis compared heaven and hell in these graphic images:

> In hell they talk a lot about love. In heaven they just do it.

> Hell is an unending church service without God. Heaven is God without a church service.

> In hell, everything is pornographic and no one is excited.
> In heaven everything is exciting and there is no pornography.

> In hell there is sex without pleasure.
> In heaven there is pleasure without sex.

> Hell is a bad dream from which you never wake.
> Heaven is waking from which you never need to sleep.

These images provoke thought, but St. Paul wrote that we cannot begin to imagine the joy in store for us in heaven.

> What eye has not seen, and ear has not heard, and what has not entered the human heart, what God has prepared for those who love him (1 Cor 2:9).

In a series of three widely reported addresses given in the summer of 1999, Pope John Paul II reminded us that heaven, hell, and purgatory are *states* of being, rather than *places* as described in ordinary human speech.[16] Thus, according to the *Catechism of the Catholic Church*, heaven is perfect life with the Blessed Trinity, a state of supreme, definite happiness. "To live in heaven" is to be with Christ where we will find our true identity (*CCC*, 1024–1025). Being forever in the presence of a God who is love, joy, peace will make us happy and fulfilled to the utmost. We will see and know God as God really is. We will be one with God and all his other beloved friends, including our own family members and friends who are there with us.

Scripture uses images like a shining, crystal city with gates of pearl and streets of gold or an incredibly delightful, joy-filled banquet to describe heaven. But these images pale in comparison to the reality. Imagine describing a beautiful sunset to a blind person or the kiss of a loved one to a person who cannot feel. You can only hint at the reality, just like heaven.

Just the opposite, hell is a "state of definitive self-exclusion from communion with God and the blessed" (*CCC*, 1033). Jesus himself referred to hell often in his own instructions to his contemporaries (for example, Mk 9:43–48 and Mt 25:46). The New Testament also reveals that hell is a place of consciousness and torment (Lk 16:23–24, 28) and a place of darkness (Mt 8:12). Hell involves eternal separation from loved ones (Lk 13:28), with no hope of release (Mt 25:46, Hb 6:2).

God does not send us to hell; he wills the salvation of everyone. Yet, God respects a person's free, stubborn decision to say "no" to the gift of salvation. If one dies in the state of alienation from him (mortal sin), then the result is hell.

Though writers often use fire to describe hell, the Church reminds us that this is only an image. Christ reveals that hell is eternal separation from God, the worst fate that could befall us. And though we believe hell exists, the Church has never defined how many people are actually there.

Writers through the ages have come up with their own images of what hell is: For example,

Hell is "the suffering of being unable to love."
~Fyodor Dostoevski

Hell is to be completely alone.

Hell is eternal homesickness.

"Hell is truth seen too late."
~Thomas Hobbes

God made us to be with him in heaven—forever. We should resolve to live a faith-filled, loving, Christ-like lives to get there. As the famous French writer Victor Hugo wrote, "Good actions are the invisible hinges of the doors of heaven."

# fifty ▸ ▸ ▸ ▸ ▸ ▸ ▸ ▸ ▸ ▸ ▸

*Speaking of heaven and hell, what is purgatory?*

P urgatory is the spiritual state of purification of those souls who die in God's grace and friendship, yet are not free from all the imperfection of sin (*CCC*, 1030–1032). In the state of purgatory, these souls endure punishment for unforgiven venial sins and already forgiven mortal sins. Since nothing that is imperfect can go before God (see, for example, Wis 7:35 and Hb 1:13), this purification prepares souls to meet the all-holy Lord face-to-face in heaven.

The Church has wisely not defined the time, intensity, or quality of the punishments which the souls in purgatory experience. Once we die, we enter eternity—God's time. Thus to talk about purgatory in human terms like time is not very helpful. All we know is that through this process a person becomes perfectly unselfish and capable of loving God fully. Thus, a transformed friend of the Lord can meet God with a pure heart. Any pain associated with this process is the pain of wanting to become worthy of union with a perfect, all-loving God.

Scripture teaches that prayers for the dead can help deliver them from the remnants of their sins (2 Mc 12:38–46). This underscores the doctrine of the communion of saints, the bond of unity that exists between God's people on earth and those who have died.

The Church has always offered prayers for the dead, especially at the Eucharist. Almsgiving, works of penance, and indulgences are other practices that the Church has supported as valuable helps to our departed ancestors in purgatory.

## Chapter FOUR

# LET'S TALK ABOUT SEX

## What We Believe about Love, Dating, and Sexuality

T wo little boys, at first strangers, were getting to know each other. The first asked the second how old he was. The second said he didn't know. The first then inquired, "Do you like girls?" The second responded, "No." "Then you must be five," replied the new friend.

Something happens to boys between the ages of five and the teen years. They discover girls. And girls start having their eyes on the guys as well. It has been this way ever since our first parents came on the scene. People and sex have gone together since the dawn of our existence.

The Bible tells us the first truth about sex: It is good because it is about love, companionship, life, caring, and closeness. The second creation account in Genesis explains how God made the first human—Adam. God made him from the mud of the earth, that is, with flesh and bones, and breathed his spirit in him, thus endowing him with an immortal soul. God gave Adam a beautiful garden to live in which was a heaven on earth.

However, God saw that Adam was incomplete. He put into the garden animals and birds of the air. But none of them was a suitable companion for Adam. So Scripture poetically relates how God created woman—Eve—from the rib of Adam, and Adam's enthusiastic response to the lovely creature:

"This one, at last, is bone of my bones
and flesh of my flesh;
This one shall be called 'woman,'
for out of 'her man' this one has been taken."
That is why a man leaves his father and mother
and clings to his wife, and the two of them
become one body. The man and his wife were
both naked, yet they felt no shame (Gn 2:23–24).

This beautiful, vivid story has much to tell us. First, before sin entered the world, man and woman were comfortable and unashamed in each other's presence. They took delight in their being and, with God, saw that everything he made was very good, including their own sexual nature.

Second, Genesis states that woman is the equal of man, having been created from his rib. The rib was close to Adam's heart, a symbol for love. From the beginning Adam yearned for love and companionship, as we all do. So God made a creature like him—but different—who could fulfill his heart's desire. God purposely made humans sexual beings. Some scholars believe the word *sex* might be derived from the Latin *secare*, which means "divide." God made us two so we can become one. "'Be fertile and multiply; fill the earth and subdue it.' . . .God looked at everything he made, and found it very good" (Genesis 1:28, 31).

The Bible is absolutely clear about the goodness of the beautiful mystery of sex. By nature, each of us is a sexual being— male or female—who was created this way by God. Because we are sexual beings created by a loving God, we should be neither fearful nor ashamed. On the other hand, sex is not a plaything or mere biological function that should be satisfied whenever or with whomever we want, as so many in our culture try to tell us. No, sex is so much more precious than this. Sex is at the heart of what it means to be a human person.

This chapter will examine some of the questions teens ask that deal with relationships and sexual issues. Perhaps you know all this stuff already. But then again, maybe there's still something to learn about this great mystery that makes human life such a challenge. Like a wise mother, the Church has learned a lot through the ages about what happens when people misuse their sexuality in ways contrary to God's plan. You may find that some of the Church's experience and teaching will be a great help to weather the storms of teenage angst in this area of your life.

# fifty-one ➤ ➤ ➤ ➤ ➤ ➤ ➤ ➤

### My girlfriend dumped me. Now she's dating someone else. What can I do to get over her?

Breaking up will naturally bring hurt simply because you cared for another person and she cared for you. You may have expressed your love verbally, shared your deepest thoughts and feelings and dreams, and exchanged various signs of affection. You took a risk in getting close to her. Love requires a letting go and commitment. So now you are feeling a tremendous sense of loss and may be confused as to why your relationship ended. You may be experiencing other symptoms of lost love, including:

- disordered thinking and attention (for example, you can't concentrate at school);
- undesirable behavior (for example, you have flashes of violent anger);
- persistent negative emotions (depression, anxiety, and persistently listening to sad music);
- physical complaints (for example, a poor appetite).

Whether what you had with your girlfriend was simply an intense infatuation or whether it was a taste of true love, there is no denying that a breaking-up experience is tough and that your pain is real. What can you do about it? Try the following:

1. *Stop contact.* If you've tried to rekindle the relationship, and it is not going anywhere, accept the fact that the relationship has ended. Stop finding excuses to call her or "accidentally" run into her. And don't keep tabs on her through a friend.

2. *Keep busy.* Develop new interests. Meet new people. Go out with your friends, especially in mixed groups. The old adage, "there are plenty of fish in the sea" really is true. You will begin dating again. And if you are a good person with a variety of interests, young ladies will find you fun to be around. But make sure to slow down. Jumping into a new relationship right away is generally not a good idea. Give yourself some time to get your emotions in order again.

3. *Stop blaming yourself.* If it was not your fault that the relationship broke up, why get down on yourself? If it was your fault, then learn from the experience. Remember, "the only mistake is not to learn from our mistakes." Love is a mystery. Romantic relationships require a type of "chemistry" of attraction that is beyond our conscious control. It could be no one is to blame for the breakup. The relationship was simply not meant to be.

4. *Trust the Lord.* Ask for God's help in getting over the hurt and learning from the experience. He will help you focus on your good and loving qualities and will help you to get through this in time. The Lord's love heals all.

# fifty-two ➤ ➤ ➤ ➤ ➤ ➤ ➤ ➤

*Is there such a thing as an ideal person to date? What should I be looking for in a date?*

Two not-too-helpful lines if you want to ask someone for a date:

- "You wouldn't want to go out with me, would you?"
- "I have nothing better to do Saturday night. Want to go to a movie with me?"

Let's face it, many of today's young ladies like the following when they go looking for guys: good looks, athletic prowess, and popularity. And guys? They hunt for good-looking, popular, fun-loving girls who make them feel important. Certainly there is wide variety in what girls and guys look for, but even with the variety these desired types certainly have a strong pull.

These qualities, some superficial, initially cause sparks to fly between teens. However, it is best to date people who you like first as true friends. That means sharing the same interests, having compatible personalities, and holding the same important core beliefs and values.

Trust, respect, and care are the building blocks of healthy, loving relationships. Ask yourself, is this person:

- considerate? (Does the person ever ask about *you* and *your* interests?)
- honest? (Does the person look you in the eyes and tell you the truth?)
- loyal? (Will this person stand by your side in times of trouble?)

- intelligent? (Does the person have a lively, creative mind that helps you stretch your own?)
- kind? (Is this person thoughtful and loving?)
- dependable? (Does this person follow through on his or her commitments?)
- interesting? (Is this person fun to talk to? Does he or she have a variety of interests?)
- affectionate? (Can this person accept and give compliments? Does he or she smile and laugh? Is the person warm and approachable?)

## What Do You Say?

- Design your own list of desirable traits for the ideal date. How many traits on your list are physical traits? Intellectual traits? Personality traits? Spiritual traits?
- Discuss qualities that the media push as most desirable in a male or female teen. For example, analyze the articles in some magazines targeted for teens. Are the media selling an impossible, unrealistic, or superficial ideal? Are they encouraging bad or reckless behavior? Explain.

# fifty-three › › › › › › › ›

### What's the difference between love and infatuation?

Infatuation is usually based on a strong physical or sexual attraction. When you instantly fall in love with another, you are probably infatuated. This "love at first sight," "blinding" attraction to someone is emotional rather than rational. You cannot build a lasting relationship on infatuation. As a wise person once said, "To marry a person for physical beauty is like buying a home for its paint."

Because it is superficial, instantaneous, and emotionally charged, infatuation won't last. It is, however, possible for infatuation to evolve into true romantic love where the feelings of the other person are more important than your own. But you need time to get to know and care for the other person. True love, in contrast with infatuation, is mature, stable, and rooted in reality. So what to do if you are infatuated with another from time to time? "Puppy love," as infatuation is often called, certainly doesn't make the world go around, but it can make the trip worthwhile as long as it is understood for what it is.

Also, try to help the other person understand infatuation just in case your beauty and charm are blinding him or her. Deepen your "mutual admiration society" by getting to know each other as you *really* are. Don't have unrealistic expectations for yourself or the other person. Finally, do not let the feelings of infatuation lead you to disrespect yourself or the other person, especially in the area of sexuality.

## What's the Difference Between Love and Infatuation?

| The Fantasy of Infatuation | The Reality of Love |
|---|---|
| Fall in to and out of quickly; fickle | Grows slowly with time; faithful |
| Based on superficial knowledge of a person | Rooted in a deepening knowledge of the other |
| Is fleeting | Is lasting |
| Lives in a dream world, always expecting the other to help create a perfect world | Is realistic, practical, accepting the other's imperfections and limitations |
| Emotional roller coaster | Stable and consistent, building self-confidence |
| Driven by suspicion and jealousy; possessive | Allows the other person freedom to develop; mutually supportive |
| Wants immediate gratification | Is patient and respectful of the other |
| Impressed with externals; looks, status, money | Unconditional acceptance of another |
| In love with the idea of love | In love with a person |
| Takes | Gives |
| Self-centered | Other-directed |
| Can be fake to get the other to accept | Always honest |
| Instant desire—"I want you now." | Chaste friendship: "I am waiting for the one who is waiting for me." |

## What Do You Think? ➤ ➤ ➤ ➤ ➤ ➤ ➤ ➤ ➤ ➤ ➤ ➤ ➤ ➤

- Do you agree or disagree with psychologist Erich Fromm when he wrote:

  Immature love says: "I love you because I need you."

  Mature love says: "I need you because I love you."

◁ ◁ ◁ ◁ ◁ ◁ ◁ ◁ ◁ ◁ ◁ ◁ ◁ ◁ ◁ ◁ ◁ ◁ ◁ ◁ ◁ ◁ ◁

# fifty-four ➤ ➤ ➤ ➤ ➤ ➤

*What does sex have to do with religion? Why is the Church always getting involved with people's sex lives?*

Headlines bombard us with facts and figures concerning the prevalence of AIDS and other sexually transmitted diseases, teen pregnancies, the number of abortions and divorces, incidences of adultery, and crimes like pedophilia and rape. With the pervasive availability of pornography in all types of media, a person might just get the impression that sex is bad. On the other hand, one might get the impression that sex is the be-all and end-all of human existence.

But sex isn't bad. What can be bad is what people do with their sexuality. They distort and misuse it for selfish motives. For example, some treat others as objects for pleasure. In the process, they disfigure their own personal dignity and hurt another person.

People often misuse sex because they think it is the greatest good to which they can achieve. As Chesterton put it, "Every man who knocks on the door of a brothel is looking for God." The point is that humans often believe the intimacy and pleasure of sex will result in their happiness. But this is just smoke and mirrors. Sex always takes place in the context of a relationship with another person and God. If there is not happiness in these relationships already, sex will not put it there.

This is where the Church comes in—to teach in areas of sexual morality because the misuse of sex hurts people and causes unhappiness. Jesus cared about the happiness of people and their well-being. As his representative and presence in the world, the Church—often called a wise mother—has seen the damage people suffer when they distort God's will. It has a Christ-given duty to call people to faithful observance of God's laws, including laws in the area of sexuality.

Like any good and loving mother, the Church speaks out on behalf of our interests in many different areas, including:

- **Emotionally.** Sex outside of marriage almost always results in emotional pain. Premarital or extramarital sex is usually associated with feelings like guilt, regret, and anxiety. Self-esteem always suffers. For example, premarital sex affects relationships. One study revealed that "the average high school relationship will last only twenty-one days once the couple has sex."[1] The guilt and regret after the relationship ends is often crushing, and leaves teens vulnerable to the pursuit of further sex as a way to gain approval and companionship. This strategy never works. As for extra-marital affairs, the tensions within the family caused by the deceit of the affair, and the gossip and rumor mill that result when affairs end, as well as the catastrophic impact on the parents' relationship, ends in emotional disasters for many teens.

- **Physically.** There are more than fifty sexually transmitted diseases that cause many physical problems, including death. Here are some statistics which should concern every thinking person:

◆ The estimated total number of people living in the US with an incurable STD is over 65 million.

◆ Every year, there are approximately 15 million new cases of STDs.

◆ Two-thirds of all STDs occur in people 25 years of age or younger. One in four new STD infections occur in teenagers.

◆ Hepatitis B is 100 times more infectious than HIV.[2]

In addition, almost one million teenage women become pregnant; 78% of those pregnancies are unplanned.[3] Slightly over half of these pregnancies will be terminated by abortion.[4]

• **Spiritually.** Sex is meant to involve one's whole being—body, mind, soul. St. Paul warns us that when we misuse sex, we hurt our relationships with God and others. For example, how would a future marriage partner feel knowing you had sex with several other people? Will he or she be able to trust you? Does it diminish the gift of your whole self—body, mind, soul—to the spouse? Sociological studies have found, for example, that the more people engage in premarital sex, the more likely they will be unfaithful in their marriage and have less satisfying marriages. Other studies have shown how those who live together before marriage are more likely to divorce.

When we use our sexuality as God intends, it can enhance our happiness. When we misuse it, it can tear us apart and bring us misery. Why does the Church get involved in sexual issues? Primarily to remind us—against the propaganda of the day—that following God's way, not our own urges for self-indulgence, is the true path to happiness.

# fifty-five ➤ ➤ ➤ ➤ ➤ ➤ ➤ ➤

*I think about sex quite often. Is that wrong? What is meant by "impure thoughts"?*

exual thoughts, like sexual desire and passion, are natural and normal. It is difficult for any healthy person *not* to have these thoughts. This is especially true of young people whose bodies are raging with hormones and who are discovering the beauties and the mysteries of members of the opposite sex. And it is doubly true in a society that bombards us constantly with suggestive or explicit sexual imagery.

The phrase "impure thoughts" usually refers to *lust*, a vice contrary to the virtue of *chastity*. Chastity is purity of heart that empowers us to use our gift of sexuality according to God's intent. Lust, the *inordinate* desire for sexual pleasure, begins in the mind and the imagination; its goal is to make a god out of sex. Jesus condemns lust because he knows how it deliberately inflames one's sexual desires by going beyond the boundaries God has set for healthy and moral sexual attraction. He knows how lust leads to looking at others not as persons to respect, but as mere objects for one's own sexual pleasure. Thus Jesus teaches, "Everyone who looks at a woman with lust has already committed adultery with her in his heart" (Mt 5:28).

How can you tell the difference between normal sexual thoughts and lust? Consider the following:

> Let's say a good-looking person walks by and catches your eye. Because God made you a sexual being you are attracted to this person and have warm feelings for this person. You find this person desirable. These are natural and normal feelings. Neither your thoughts nor feelings are lustful.

> Lust, however, enters the picture when you *deliberately* entertain impure thoughts about this person. The problem isn't your first glance, but the second and third when you continue to fantasize sexually with the *sole* purpose of inflaming your passions. For example, you begin to imagine what he or she would look like undressed. Or you try to picture what the person would be like in bed. You stay with these thoughts, take delight in them, and allow them "to turn you on." Sometimes, you might even allow them to lead you to masturbate.

Lust, like any vice, is wrong and sinful. But lust is a sin of weakness. It is *not* the worst sin in the world. Pride, arrogance, greed, prejudice, and hatred are worse. All of these are cold, heartless sins that transform us into uncaring, unloving, inhuman persons.

Our emotional life can contribute to lustful thoughts. When we lack tenderness, love, and acceptance in our real "outer" lives, we sometimes escape into sexual fantasy that may lead us away from God. But having these thoughts does not make us bad persons. They do not become sinful unless we consent to and indulge in them. If you are struggling with impure thoughts, you are not alone. Even the great saint St. Augustine of Hippo fought a lifelong battle to gain mastery of his passions.

To counteract impure thoughts, think wholesome thoughts when tempted to dwell on sexual fantasies. Root out the sources of temptation that lead to sexual temptation. A good example is to make sure that you stay away from online pornography, a major source of sexual temptation in today's world. Also, if you can admit that your "inner life" of sexual fantasy might be caused partly by feelings of loneliness or insecurity, then put some effort into developing healthy friendships and pursuing activities that will help build up your self-confidence. Lust is a vice, which is a bad habit; chastity is the virtue or good habit that counteracts it. Develop chastity by placing in your mind good thoughts. In the words of St. Thomas More, "Occupy your minds with good thoughts, or the enemy will fill them with bad ones."

Also, turn to Jesus and the Blessed Mother for their help in times of temptation. And if you slip, don't get down on yourself. Remember that Jesus left us the sacrament of Penance to hear his loving words of forgiveness and encouragement. And the Lord gave us his very self in the Eucharist to give us strength to live the right way.

# fifty-six ➤ ➤ ➤ ➤ ➤ ➤ ➤ ➤

### I heard that masturbation is wrong. Is it?

By definition, masturbation is the deliberate stimulation of the genital organs to get solitary sexual pleasure.

Note that the person who masturbates is concerned only with him or herself; that is, seeking pleasure for its own sake. This behavior is wrong because God intended sexual activity to be relational. God gave human beings sex organs—and the pleasure associated with them—to share with a member of the opposite sex to whom we have totally committed our lives. He intended that we use our sexual faculties to communicate our deep, unconditional love for another and to cooperate with him in the conception of new human life.

Many people masturbate to escape problems. But note the word *escape*. Masturbation does not cure one's problems, and it quickly becomes habit-forming. After masturbating, people often feel spiritually empty and psychologically depressed. They still have problems and their self-esteem suffers worse than it was before.

Another downside to this habit is that one who masturbates quickly gets used to immediate self-gratification. When dating starts, the habit of immediate gratification can easily translate into using another merely as an object for personal pleasure. True love for another demands discipline and control, patience, and the ability to say no.

How serious of a wrongdoing is masturbation—an action that is contrary to both aims of God's design for sexual activity: the giving of life and the sharing of love? The Church teaches the following: "Both the Magisterium of the Church, in the course of a constant tradition, and the moral sense of the faithful have been in no doubt and have firmly maintained that masturbation is an intrinsically and gravely disordered action" (*CCC*, 2352). Actions and attitudes that are gravely disordered constitute serious matter. And if we freely, willingly, and with full knowledge do something that is seriously wrong, then we are guilty of mortal sin.

But the Church wisely teaches certain factors can *lessen* or even erase one's guilt or moral blameworthiness in the case of masturbation. These include immaturity, anxiety, the force of an acquired habit, and other social or psychological factors (like compulsion).

For teens and even adults, a major factor in the area of masturbation is the force of habit and the difficulty of overcoming ingrained behavior. If, for example, you have acquired the habit of masturbation, the last thing you want to do is to get discouraged and down on yourself. Always remember that God—who made you a sexual being with strong feelings—still loves you. It takes time, self-discipline, and the graces of our dear Lord to help you mature in all aspects of your life, including in the area of sexual self-control. A healthy dose of honesty and self-reflection can help you if you are struggling with this habit. For example:

- Are you making an honest effort to avoid those situations that in the past have led you to fall?

- Are you avoiding Internet pornography (and other forms of it) at all costs? In our sex-obsessed culture, sexual imagery is all around us tempting us to be self-indulgent. Do you go out of your way to look for pornography? If so, stop. Pornography seriously offends against the virtue of chastity, degrades the dignity of everyone involved in it (the participants as well as those who sell and view it), and offers an escape into a fantasy world of distorted "love-making" that goes against God's beautiful intent for sexuality. Using pornography as an outlet for your sexual feelings will, in the last analysis, be an unrealistic escape that will distort your view of what people are—beautiful persons of dignity made out of love for *true* love.
- Are you honestly trying to live an upright and loving life, caring for others? Making a strong effort to help others will draw you out of yourself and help form you into a more loving person with better self-esteem.
- Are you trying to gain self-control by using some of the spiritual helps available to you? For example, do you ask for the Lord's help in prayer? Do you receive him frequently in Holy Communion? Do you regularly celebrate the sacrament of Reconciliation, asking for spiritual advice from the priest who knows very well how many good people struggle daily to master their sex drive?

A "yes" to these questions is a good sign that your acts of masturbation may not be completely free or deliberate. You have not given up; you are trying to gain self-mastery; you care about others and are not a selfish person.

A final word of advice: Remember that every adult known to you is struggling to live a chaste life. They were young once, too, and they remember very well the storms of the teen years.

Today's world is sex-saturated. It scoffs at Christ's command to reserve sexual activity for marriage. It ridicules Church teaching in this area and so many other areas that touch the human heart and the human spirit. Each of us needs help to live as Christ intends us. Please, don't be afraid to approach a priest-friend, a trusted teacher, a parent, or another adult you love to discuss your struggles in this area. He or she will understand. And this person will profoundly respect you for asking for advice and help. God bless you.

# fifty-seven ➤ ➤ ➤ ➤ ➤ ➤

### How far can I go sexually?

Teens (and adults) have been asking this question from time immemorial. What they often mean is "How much pleasure can I get from playing with another's body (and he or she playing with mine) before I break God's law?" If this is what is meant, then what the person is only concerned with is using the other person as an *object* for his or her own gratification. If this is what is being asked, then one needs a change of heart to fight the battle for sexual purity, which always treats others as persons to respect, not objects to use.

Sex is not a plaything. Sex is the language of love between totally committed persons. Real love seeks true commitment and is unconditional. God gave us our sexual powers to say "I love you forever" to someone with whom we will procreate new life—our own children—whom we will lovingly raise and educate. Sexual intimacy without the true love commitment found only in marriage leads to rejection. In our day, we have also seen how it often results in the tragedies of abortion, disease, destroyed relationships, and damaged people.

Sex is beautiful, exciting, passionate, and *progressive*. Once the sexual passion gets started, its natural outcome is greater intimacy and eventual union with another. God intends this union, of course, for a husband and a wife in the sacrament of Marriage. The term for premarital sexual intercourse is *fornication*; the term for extramarital sex is *adultery*. In many places in scripture, any form of fornication or adultery is condemned (see: Dt 5:21, Mt 5:27–30, Hb 13:4, 1 Thes 4:3–5, and 1 Cor 6:9, 18).

Premarital sex is like the TV commercial about a certain brand of potato chips. The advertisement says, "You can't just have one." Once a person has entered the danger zone of premarital sex, it is difficult indeed to draw back. The Book of Sirach says it well concerning "sins of the flesh,"

> For burning passion is a blazing fire,
>
> not to be quenched till it burns itself out (23:16).

Going near the fire almost always means you will get burnt. Alcohol can provide fuel for the fire, so avoid it on dates. And draw some lines to help you avoid inappropriate and sinful behavior. The first line should be drawn in your head: Stop the minute you lust after someone. Ask, what if this were your future daughter or future son? Would you want them to be used in this way *before* marriage?

Here are some over-the-line actions that should be avoided because they can lead to sexual sin:

1. Prolonged kissing which leads to French kissing, including the last stages of "necking," nibbling on the ears and the neck.

2. Any type of *petting*. Petting is intimate touching (sexual foreplay) of another's private parts. It arouses the passions and leads to sexual intercourse. Light petting includes the touching of covered or bared breasts. Heavy petting includes the touching of genitals either covered or bared. At the most serious end it includes oral sex and genital-to-genital contact.

3. Sexual intercourse. Prolonged kissing and petting lead naturally to "going all the way" which is fraught with many physical, emotional, and spiritual dangers for unmarried teens.

A guideline that can answer your question and keep you in the safety zone: *Before marriage, limit yourself to handholding, hugs, and light kissing as ways to show affection.*

## Positive Tips for Handling Sexually Tempting Situations ➤ ➤ ➤ ➤ ➤ ➤ ➤ ➤ ➤

- Kiss only with the lips closed.
- "Don't touch what you don't got." (Beware of roaming hands. Don't touch another's private parts. Don't allow someone to touch your private parts.)
- Keep your clothes on.
- Don't lie down together on a bed.
- Stop when genitalia are aroused.
- Stop immediately when you feel yourself losing control.

# fifty-eight ➤ ➤ ➤ ➤ ➤ ➤

*Isn't it hateful toward gays not to support gay marriage?*

C atholic teaching on marriage is rooted both in human reason, which can discover truth, and in divine revelation. For example, obviously men and women are complementary beings endowed with the ability to transmit life in cooperation with God. Genesis elaborates on this common-sense observation. There we learn how God created humans in his image, making male and female equal in dignity (Gn 1:27–28).

Thus, at creation, God instituted marriage. From the beginning, he intended it to be a faithful, exclusive, lifelong union of a man and woman joined together into a community to share both life and love. In this union of marriage, the husband and wife commit themselves completely to each other and are open to the possibility of bringing children into the world and helping to raise them in a caring and loving community.

The marriage of man and woman is a natural institution, experienced by humans since the dawn of creation. It is also a sacred union because it reflects God's plan for creation. Finally, for Christians, a valid marriage is a sacrament, a union that brings holiness because it reflects the superabundant love Christ shows for his Church. A couple involved in Christian marriage filled with love, forgiveness, sacrifice, and generous giving is a powerful sign of God's love at work in the world.

Only the union of a man and a woman expresses the sexually complementary partnership God intends to transmit human life. A same-sex union is, simply put, not marriage, nor can it ever be.

> It is not based on the natural complementarity of male and female; it cannot cooperate with God to create new life; and the natural purpose of sexual union cannot be achieved by a same-sex union. Persons in same-sex unions cannot enter into a true conjugal union. Therefore, it is wrong to equate their relationship to a marriage.[5]

Marriage between a man and a woman has always been the foundation of the family. And the family is the basic unit of society. A stable marriage between a loving mother and father is the best place for raising children. Governments have recognized this reality legally because a natural family headed by a man and a woman makes a unique and essential contribution to the common good.

If governments were to recognize same-sex unions as marriages, they would be saying that homosexual activity is officially recognized as OK and is equivalent to God's perfect plan for human sexuality. This would weaken and devalue marriage, and potentially threaten the very fabric of society.

Does not recognizing "gay marriage" mean persons with a homosexual orientation are evil? No, it does not. Christian teaching simply affirms that sexual sharing should take place only in marriage. In that sacred bond, a man and woman unite as one, sharing their unconditional love and remaining open to any new life God graces them with.

God's intent is for us to use our sexual faculties according to the divine plan—openness to the sharing of life and of love. This is why it is morally wrong to engage in sexual practices that make the generation of new life impossible. And therefore sexual activity between two persons of the same sex cannot be in accord with God's plan; it is objectively wrong. St. Paul condemns homosexual practices as "against nature" (Rm 1:27). Same-gender sexual acts are unnatural because they do not bring about the natural male/female bonding of body and spirit God intended when he made us sexual beings.

Homosexual, genital *acts* are wrong because they misuse the sexual faculty as God intended it. Like pre-marital and extra-marital sexual activity, homosexual acts deny the life-giving and unitive nature of sexual love that can take place only in a marriage between a man and a woman. If a person engages in pre-marital, extramarital, or homosexual acts with knowledge and freedom, then he or she is guilty of serious sin.

However, it is very important to note that the Church draws a distinction between homosexual *activity*, which is always wrong, and *homosexual orientation*. A true homosexual orientation is an enduring sexual attraction to persons of the same sex. This typically results in a desire to engage in genital, sexual activity with members of the same sex.

A true homosexual orientation is *not* sinful because a person does not choose to have these desires. (Similarly, a person is not "guilty" of being tall or short.) To date, science has not discovered the precise cause of a homosexual orientation. Is it genetic, hormonal, learned or induced through sexual experience, family rearing, or a combination of one or more factors? No one knows for sure. Regardless, homosexual orientation is not sinful if a person does not deliberately choose it.

Our culture, tragically, often fails to distinguish between a homosexual orientation and homosexual acts. As a result, society often stigmatizes persons with same-sex attraction as sex-fiends who cannot or refuse to control their sexual behavior. These prejudgments are cruel and unjust. People are not morally blameworthy for having a homosexual orientation. It is prejudice of the worst kind to lump everyone together, claiming that all persons with a homosexual orientation are evil and condemnable.

Jesus expects us to treat every human person with dignity and respect. Those who have a homosexual orientation "must be accepted with respect, compassion, and sensitivity. Every sign of unjust discrimination in their regard should be avoided" (*CCC*, 2358). To hate, display violence toward, or reject anyone is *un-Christian*, and sinful. We can disapprove of sinful activity (either heterosexual or homosexual), but we must *always* love others as our brothers and sisters.

# fifty-nine ➤ ➤ ➤ ➤ ➤ ➤ ➤

*I think I may be gay, and I am scared to death. What should I do?*

The first thing to remember is that you are a child of God. Period.

The second thing to remember is that persons with same-sex attractions often falsely conclude that they are exclusively homosexual in orientation. However, psychologists tell us that one's identity is always developing. It may take many years for people to discover their true sexual orientation. It rarely happens in the teen years.

This leads to a third point: Please examine exactly why you think you might be gay. Because of inexperience, some teens mistakenly conclude that they have a homosexual orientation because of one of the following characteristics or experiences. But *none* of these mean you are homosexual.

- *Previous engagement in sexual activity with someone of the same sex or strong feelings of attraction to particular people of the same sex.* A one-time experience, whether experimental or a form of sexual abuse, does not determine your sexual orientation. Generally, sexual identity is considered more complex than just gay or straight. So, just because there are feelings of same-sex attraction or an experiment with someone of the same sex does not mean that you aren't also attracted to people of the opposite sex.

- *Awkwardness around members of the opposite sex.* Even if it seems that all your peers have it more together than you do, know that most people feel uneasy in the presence of members of the opposite sex. It takes some people years to get over their shyness. Be patient with yourself. Many people don't start dating until the college years and even later.

- *Strong, same-sex friendships with powerful feelings of affection.* This is normal and healthy for human growth and development. And it is natural to admire physically attractive persons of your own sex. This doesn't mean you are gay. It simply means that you have a good eye for natural beauty. Again, it may take years to figure out if this attraction is an orientation, or just a temporary phase accompanied by a growing sexual maturity.

- *A certain personality type.* It is perfectly normal if a guy is quiet, shy, gentle, and sensitive. It is OK if some girls are aggressive, rough-and-tumble, and athletic. Having these types of personalities does not mean a person is homosexual.
- *Someone of the same sex hits on you.* This simply means you are an attractive person.

What should you do? Your best bet at this point is to talk your fears over with someone you trust—a parent, a priest, a counselor. It is perfectly normal for teens—as they mature—to experience confusion about their sexuality. What you need is someone to tell you that *you* are lovable for who you are as a human being. Sexuality is only a part of who you are; it is not the total picture. This is why it is wrong for a person to identify so strongly with his or her sexual orientation. A person should never forget that he or she is first a lovable child of God, endowed with dignity, intelligence, and free will, and a brother or sister to Christ and all others.

Confusion over sexual identity can engender fear, shame, self-hatred, and panic over the thought of someone finding out. Since many people in our society brand those with a same-sex attraction as sick, evil, and disgusting, you also might be angry at God for "making me this way." So, please discuss your feelings with someone. Realize that the orientation is not sinful. Our Lord through the Church will offer you help to live a chaste life. And a Catholic group like Courage can be a great source of support. (Their website: http://couragerc.net.)

Finally, please remember to be compassionate toward all those who are struggling with questions about sexual identity. We should recall Jesus' warning to the bystanders who wanted to kill the woman caught in adultery: "Let the one among you who is without sin be the first to throw a stone at her" (Jn 8:7). We *all* need Christ's love, forgiveness, and compassion to live upright, pure lives—no matter our sexual orientation.

# ?sixty ➤ ➤ ➤ ➤ ➤ ➤ ➤ ➤ ➤ ➤ ➤

*Why is the Church so against a guy and a girl living together? Living together before marriage may help to lower the divorce rate.*

Some people live together as a type of "trial marriage." They often claim they are doing this to see if they are sexually and emotionally "compatible" for the serious relationship of marriage.

Cohabitation ("living together") involves a relationship in which a man and woman are sexually active while sharing a household. But they are unmarried and thus involved in *premarital sex*, that is, they are engaged in the total intimacy of love (sex) without having made the unconditional commitment of marriage. The quality and degree of the commitment falls far short of the public, no-strings-attached promise of marriage. Not surprisingly, then, the couples who cohabit before marriage have a fifty percent *greater* chance of divorce than those who don't. Furthermore, sixty percent of couples who live together before marriage break off their relationship without marrying. Finally, one researcher discovered that women who cohabit are more than twice as likely to be the victims of domestic violence than married women.[6] Thus, the common misperception that cohabitation is good preparation for marriage is patently false.

To understand more of the Church's reasoning, think of sexual intercourse as the communication of profound realities. As body-language, sex says: "I am giving you my entire self, completely and exclusively. This act is a declaration of our total commitment to each other." For this action to be moral, that is, in harmony with God's plan, then it should take place only when the reality of the relationship is one of total self-giving. This reality takes place only in marriage, where a couple has openly promised to love each other "for better or for worse, in sickness and in health" as long as they both shall live.

To engage in sexual intercourse outside of marriage—even out of motives of "love"—is to misuse this profound and beautiful symbol of communication. In reality, people are being dishonest when they engage in premarital sex. They are not being true to themselves. Sexual love-making should speak the language of full commitment. But actually the man and woman who are not married can always bail out. They are not ready for total commitment. People always get hurt when they misuse God's gifts. And this can happen even with couples who say that they love one other.

True love speaks the language of forever. The Church promotes saving sex until marriage because sexual intercourse is both the symbol and expression of the permanent commitment of true love. Premarital *love* is the best preparation for marriage. Note how St. Paul lists *patience* as the first quality of love in 1 Corinthians 13. If you really love someone, you will wait for marriage before having sex. The advantages of self-discipline and patience before marriage are many, including:

- a stronger marriage with a greater chance for success,
- a closer friendship,
- deeper intimacy and communion,
- and the learning of problem-solving and communications skills.

# sixty-one > > > > > > > >

### How do I resist someone who is pressuring me for sex?

The old saying goes, "An ounce of prevention is worth a pound of cure." The best way to thwart any pressure for sex from a date is to prepare yourself ahead of time. Consider the following game plan:

1. *Know your standards beforehand.* Even before you go out, in your mind and heart say no to any activity beyond hand-holding, hugs, and light kisses. (See Question 56.) Draw the line ahead of time and never cross it. Remember, you are a child of God, not a commodity. You don't owe someone sex just because he paid for a nice dinner or bought you expensive clothing.

2. *Dress modestly.* Some girls love to tease guys to distraction, but in their minds they never intend for the guys to get to "first base." Many guys think with their groins, not their brains. If one person is sending out nonverbal, "seduce-me" messages, the partner will often interpret them as "anything goes." So girls, stay away from tight, low-cut, clothes that are known to turn guys on. And guys, dress and speak modestly yourselves, and only date girls who respect themselves as persons, not objects for lust.

3. *Avoid sexually suggestive movies and conversation.* Stay away from sexually explicit films that are likely to enflame your passions and heighten your lust. Do not talk about sexually suggestive topics, especially concerning your own relationship. Improper talk does lead to improper actions.

4. *Stay away from alcohol and drugs.* Nothing lowers the resolve to be chaste more than alcohol and other drugs. They lessen the ability to think clearly, to know right from wrong. Alcohol and drug abuse are the slippery slope to promiscuity. Make a contract with yourself and your date *not* to drink or do drugs when you are out together (or any other time, either).

5. *Plan the specifics of your date ahead of time.* When you have "nothing to do," you may end up getting sexually involved. Always have back-up plans in case your main plans fall through, for example, find other friends to hang around with.

6. *Avoid parking in "make-out" locales.* Besides the obvious temptations, you are also likely prey to criminals and scrutiny by the police in such places.

7. *Just say no if your date begins to pressure you.* Many guys have learned to push the right buttons to get what they want. Remember, you do not have to explain your no to your partner. And you don't owe your date a consolation prize of oral sex if you refuse intercourse. (You can contract some serious STDs through oral sex.) If your date persists, ask him to take you home. If he refuses, leave him and call a parent or a friend to come to pick you up. You might be a bit embarrassed. But that's a small price to pay to maintain your integrity.

One last point: While this is focused on women, there has been a sea change in our culture in regard to young women's attitudes toward sex. For many reasons, girls have become far more aggressive sexually. Many of these same rules-of-thumb apply to guys. In the end, decide your own limits. Don't let the other person decide your limits for you.

## Saying NO with Feeling

Here are three lines people use to pressure another into having sex and some possible responses. Devise clever ways to say no to the lines that follow.

"I love you. Don't you love me?"

R: "Yes, I do. And that's why I am saying no. And if you *really* loved me, you'll respect my wishes."

"Everyone is doing it."

R: "That's not so because *I'm* not!"

(Reality check: "The percentage of high school males who have ever had sex declined from 57% in 1991 to 48% in 2003. The proportion of high school girls who reported having sex decreased from 51% in 1991 to 43% in 2001.[7])

"It's not that big a deal."

R: "It is to me. I'm saving sex for my future spouse. That's how God wants it. That's how I want it." (In one survey, eight in ten girls and six in ten boys who had sexual intercourse said they wish they had waited.[8])

"I heard you're a big prude about sex. Prove it isn't so."

R:

"Who are you saving it for?"

R:

"Is there something the matter with me?"

R:

"We don't have to go all the way."

R:

# sixty-two ➤ ➤ ➤ ➤ ➤ ➤ ➤

*An actual letter from a college freshman:*
*Can you help me?*

Dear Doc,

As a former student, I recall that you once said if anyone ever needed to talk about anything, you would listen. Well, I have a problem that most probably would not bother most guys. Before I start, I need to say that I have taken to heart most of the values and morals taught by the Catholic Church, including those that deal with intercourse. Anyway, I've been going out with a girl for a while now and we are getting very close. The problem is not whether we should have sex; it is how I should deal with the knowledge that has she done it with boyfriends before. (She told me that she was with three guys before.)

She never seemed the type that would have done this before marriage, but I was wrong. Waiting until marriage is something that I hold dear. This is getting to me because I am getting along better with her than any other girl I've dated before. The possibility that this relationship might work out seems good, but it's hard for me to think about marrying a girl who has been with other guys while I was still a virgin. It just feels like we're on different levels, but I don't want to change the level I am on. I'm sure you can understand how I feel, that's why I thought about you.

Of course, she says she regrets doing it, but what I don't understand is why it took three separate guys, probably multiple times with each, for her to come to the conclusion that she didn't want to do it. I've thought about breaking up . . . but this would be hard since we like each other so much. . . . If things go so far that we would ever get married, I don't know how I could deal with being with her on our wedding night. It would be my first time. . . . I would definitely feel unequal, at a time when a couple is supposed to be sharing its' love and equality.

I don't know what to do and I know that you can give me some words of wisdom.

Thank you.
Your former student

Dear Friend,

God bless you for being such a great guy—so moral, so desirous of living an upright, wholesome life. I am honored that you ask for my advice.

I put myself in your shoes and think of what I would be feeling. I think my thoughts and feelings would be very much like yours. You truly are looking at this issue very realistically. What caused her to have sex with three different guys? Is she a reliable and trustworthy person now? Will these experiences taint your relationship down the road, especially if you marry? Will her memories of her other boyfriends—and their intimacy— color her relationship with you? What does she see in you that she did not see in the other guys? These are great questions.

My first concern, from a practical point of view, is whether she is disease-free. I hate to be so crass as to raise this issue, but you are certainly entitled to an answer to this question before you proceed with the relationship. You are worthy of a life, and it would be a shame for her past mistakes and misjudgments to imperil you in any way.

More positively, she must have some tremendous qualities to "come clean" and reveal to you her past relationships. This can display honesty, trust, and real evidence that she has left her past ways behind her. Without a doubt, I tremendously believe in the power of forgiveness and its ability to heal. If she is a Catholic, I would counsel her to seek God's forgiveness in the sacrament of Reconciliation if she has not already done so.

This can give her a tremendous new start and begin the process of healing.

Not knowing your girlfriend, I don't really know what to tell you about the future or your relationship. I can assure you that a person of your character would be mighty attractive to a host of young ladies. With patience on your part, I am sure the Lord would send you somebody else. On the other hand, maybe she has been sent to you for you to rescue her and transform into a vision of purity and loveliness.

I think, my friend, that I would counsel patience on your part, time, and prayer. Patience (coupled with self-control on both of your parts) will be a great test if this is the real thing. Time will prove whether what appears great now has the staying power to last. Prayer will help you see what the Lord wants for you. As corny as it sounds, you might ask her to pray with you sometime, too. And prayer will strengthen you to keep your virtue.

I feel I haven't helped you a whole lot. But I can promise you my prayers. Trust your heart on this one. Your feelings of discomfort could be genuine instincts that this is not meant to be and should be broken off before things get too involved. Yet, your feelings of affection for her also indicate that it is worth spending a bit more time in the relationship. It is not inevitable that you will get married one day if you stay with her now. It may give you the time to figure out why she had to have sex with three different guys. Was she immature? Was she reacting to a bad home life, pursuing love in the wrong places? Was she trying to fit in to be accepted?

The point now is: Is she a new person? Is she a good person? Is she a reformed person?

And remember a ton of girls would love to have you as a boyfriend if they knew what I know about you. Trust your own goodness.

Good luck, my friend. God bless you.

With fondest wishes,
Mike "Doc" Pennock

## Chapter FIVE

# CATHOLIC HEADLINES ON THE FRONT PAGE

Issues of Controversy, Confusion, and Concern

T he Catholic Church has been making headlines a lot in recent years. Not all the news, of course, is good or welcome. Take the scandal of pedophilia, the sexual abuse of children by clerics. Because of the misdeeds of a small minority of priests and the mishandling of them by some bishops, the Church has been subject to severe criticism and even outright ridicule. Another example occurs whenever the Holy Father or the bishops come out with a statement that promotes life against the culture of death, immediately you can be sure the talk-show pundits and editorial writers make their opinions known that the Church is just too old-fashioned to be relevant today.

The Church stands for Jesus. And Jesus came both to comfort people who were upset and to upset people who were too comfortable. Some of the teachings of the Church upset people in today's society because the Church takes the viewpoint of eternity, not the short-term goal of what is popular today.

This chapter will take up some of the topics in today's Church that provoke controversy—issues like why women can't be priests, a celibate clergy, papal infallibility, and Catholic devotion to Mary. It will also address some issues that grab the headlines, for example, what should be our attitude toward terrorists whose goal in life is to kill. What is a Christian response in the face of such evil?

# sixty-three ➤ ➤ ➤ ➤ ➤ ➤

*It seems every time I turn on the TV or read the newspaper, someone is criticizing the Catholic Church. Why does it seem that so many people today dislike Catholics and the Catholic Church?*

The Constitution of the United States prides itself on protecting all citizens from discrimination. However, today's media often take shots at the Catholic Church that they wouldn't take against other groups in our society. Fr. Mark S. Massa, S.J., in his recent study entitled *Anti-Catholicism in America*,[1] traces the historical roots of anti-Catholic prejudice. Some of these roots are cultural, going back to the founding of this country by Protestant Reform groups that wanted nothing to do with the Church of Rome. Still other roots are economic as newly arrived Catholic immigrants competed for jobs with the non-Catholic majority. Still other anti-Catholic sentiments grew out of an intellectual tradition that profoundly emphasizes the individual and downplays communal responsibility that the Church teaches as part of its Christian message. This tradition, held by many academic leaders, holds for a very strict separation of Church and state. According to this view, religion should be a private affair and religious leaders should not try to teach society as a whole how it should act.

On this last issue, however, the Church that Jesus founded has the duty to get involved in public life. On issues like abortion, war, capital punishment, social justice, sex education in the schools, school vouchers, and a host of other issues, the Church has the responsibility to teach its members and our fellow citizens the truth about how we should deal with these in a way that respects human life. Because the Catholic Church has not been quiet about these social issues, it has been on the receiving end of sometimes harsh and unfair attacks.

A wise person once observed that, "You can avoid criticism by saying nothing, doing nothing, and being nothing." Much of the criticism against the Catholic Church in America today results from it saying, doing, and being something, namely, countercultural. As the "big kid on the block," it is the target of bigotry because it preaches the gospel, stands for absolute values, and represents Christ.

Preaching the gospel truth in the public arena will eventually result in negative comments, even hatred. But this should not surprise us. Jesus himself said that if we want to follow him, we should pick up a cross. Getting this kind of reaction means the Church is probably doing something right. As it is said, "It is human to stand with the crowd; it is divine to stand alone."

Fr. Massa's book gives a good overview of the discrimination experienced by Catholics since the founding of America, discrimination that resulted in the burning of convents, attacks by the Ku Klux Klan, the publication of popular books that ridiculed Catholic faith, the mockery of Catholic beliefs by television evangelists, fiercely anti-Catholic Internet websites, and so forth. But he also observes that today violence against Catholics is virtually nonexistent.

Typically, the problem today is that frequently the secular media are championing an agenda completely at odds with the Church's teaching. The coverage of such issues as gay marriage, sex education, cloning, stem cell research, and abortion "rights" all show a media that are promoting actions and world views directly opposed to the Church. The Catholic journalist Russell Shaw says one way the media inflames anti-Catholic sentiment is by giving preferential treatment to dissenters in the Catholic Church. Furthermore, an impartial study—*Media Coverage of the Catholic Church*—documents the media's unfair treatment of official Church teaching. If the media are distorting Catholic teaching, we can certainly understand why some people dislike Catholics. Prejudice, after all, is a prejudgment made on insufficient information.

Unfortunately, there has also been legitimate criticism of the Church in recent years that resulted from the pedophilia crisis in the Church. The sexual molestation of children and adolescents is a terrible crime and sin, even more so when committed by trusted representatives of God. Some bishops greatly mishandled offenders who came to their attention, some genuinely believing that the priests had repented of their sin and were cured and others who were tragically too weak to act decisively in their roles as shepherds. In reassigning priests with deep psycho-sexual problems to new parishes, the problem was both avoided and compounded simultaneously. In hindsight, attempts to cover up the scandal to preserve the image of the Church were scandalously wrong. Media coverage brought this tragic story to public attention and forced bishops to find a better way to handle offending priests.

In this case, freedom of the press has helped the Church reform its procedures. Many of the media reports were fair and balanced, but others exploited the issue to attack the Church, especially on issues like celibacy and the hierarchical governing structure of the Church. The crisis did great harm to the reputation of the Catholic Church in the United States. It lessened the moral authority of our Church leaders to speak out on some of the great moral issues confronting our world today. We can only pray that God will help the American Church regain its footing as a moral leader in a society that so greatly needs both morality and leadership.

A closing thought: Sailors in the North Sea marvel at how icebergs float in the opposite direction of powerful winds. The reason for this is that eight-ninths of the mass of the typical iceberg is underwater and reacts to the hidden currents. It is like that with the Church. The Holy Spirit is guiding the Church and helping it to resist—even in the face of criticism—the contrary winds of the modern age.

**What Do You Say?** ➤ ➤ ➤ ➤ ➤ ➤ ➤ ➤ ➤ ➤ ➤ ➤ ➤ ➤

1. Is your own Catholic faith visible enough that it would upset radical anti-Catholics?
2. If it were a crime to be a Catholic, would there be enough evidence to convict you?

◄ ◄ ◄ ◄ ◄ ◄ ◄ ◄ ◄ ◄ ◄ ◄ ◄ ◄ ◄ ◄ ◄ ◄ ◄ ◄ ◄ ◄ ◄ ◄ ◄ ◄ ▼

# sixty-four ➤ ➤ ➤ ➤ ➤ ➤

*Why is the Church so rich? Why doesn't it sell everything and give it to the poor?*

A long-standing charge, often spread by the enemies of the Church, is the supposed wealth of the Catholic Church. As a matter of fact, in some recent years, the Vatican as well as many dioceses around the world operate at a deficit or barely break even. In America, the Church in some dioceses is struggling because of an economic downturn and the fall-off in contributions following the sex-abuse scandal in the Church. Vital services to the poor have been cut back, schools have closed, and parishes have been forced to drop programs.

An interesting statistic from the United States Catholic Bishops: In 2002, there were 15.9 million registered active Catholic households in the United States; their average contribution to the Sunday collection was $455 each.[2] This kind of contribution does not make a filthy rich Church. Outside this country, many parishes in Third World countries are closer to being dirt poor.

True, the Church does own many buildings and the property on which they stand. But these are at the service of the people. Consider the network of Catholic schools the Church runs. This is the largest network of private schools in the country with over 2.54 million students enrolled in 6,736 elementary schools and 1,378 high schools[3] at an enormous savings to taxpayers. Countless hospitals, orphanages, nursing homes, churches to worship in, and similar agencies serve millions of people, many of them poor and non-Catholic. One example is the Catholic Charities network, the nation's fourth largest non-profit and one of its most efficient. It serves 1,400 local agencies and institutions nationwide and provides vital services to more than seven million people a year, regardless of religious, social, or economic backgrounds.[4]

For historical reasons, the Church does own many valuable works of art. Vatican City itself is a museum. People of all faiths can go there to enjoy and appreciate the stunning achievements of some of humanity's greatest artists. Beautiful cathedrals, priceless paintings, sculptures, and similar works give testimony to the human spirit. They are tangible signs of the faith of people whose creative efforts reflect the glory of a brilliant Creator. Humanity would be less if the Church divested itself of these treasures that are meant for the ages. To see this, imagine if the Church did sell all the art. Assuming that this sale brought in several billion dollars which were then distributed directly to the most impoverished people, each poor person would only get a few dollars, not enough to materially improve their lives. They would remain poor and humanity would witness a priceless collection of art would be broken up and scattered across the globe.

Your question is a good one, though. Through the ages, some in the Church have misused resources. We cannot excuse these abuses. Jesus identified very strongly with the poor and calls all people to be generous to poor people (Mt 25). When we respond to their needs, we are responding to Jesus himself. St. Ignatius of Loyola stated well the challenge before all Christians: "What have you done for Christ? What are you doing for Christ? What will you do for Christ?"

**Challenge** ➤ ➤ ➤ ➤ ➤ ➤ ➤ ➤ ➤ ➤ ➤ ➤ ➤ ➤ ➤ ➤

- How do you personally respond to the needs of poor people?
- Do you contribute to the support of your parish? the missions? special collections?

◄ ◄ ◄ ◄ ◄ ◄ ◄ ◄ ◄ ◄ ◄ ◄ ◄ ◄ ◄ ◄ ◄ ◄ ◄ ◄ ◄ ◄ ◄ ◄

# sixty-five ➤ ➤ ➤ ➤ ➤ ➤

### Why can't women be priests?

This continues to be a thorny issue, despite a definitive statement by Pope John Paul II in 1994—*Ordinatio Sacerdotalis*—that "the Church has no authority whatsoever to confer priestly ordination on women and that this judgment is to be definitely held by all the Church's faithful."

The question persists, however, because of several factors. Other Christian denominations like the Anglican community, which is similar to our Church in many ways, have authorized the ordination of women. The debate has also frequently been framed as a rights issue. Because women have been discriminated against in the past both in society and in the Church, some have concluded that a male-only priesthood is just one more example of injustice against women.

Those who support the ordination of women believe that this Church tradition—like optional celibacy—should change to accommodate today's women who feel called to serve as priests. They also hold that baptized women—like men—can signify Christ to the community. According to their view, any cultural reasons for forbidding women priests do not apply today. Therefore, they reason, the Church should allow them to serve as priests.

Despite these arguments, the Church teaches that it *cannot* ordain women to the priesthood. First, let us state firmly that a male-only priesthood is not a women's rights issue. The Church strongly affirms that men and women are equal in their humanity, both made in God's image and likeness. But equality does not mean sameness; women can give birth, men can't.

The Church cannot ordain women because Jesus is the one who set up the priesthood and the one who called men to be priests. In his earthly ministry, Jesus chose only male apostles— there was not a single woman among the twelve. However, he had a high regard for women and repeatedly stressed their dignity against many repressive laws of his own day. He had women as his close followers, defended their equality before the law in marriage, and broke with the customs of his day by associating with women freely in public. In many ways, his attitude and practice toward women was revolutionary for his time. Had he desired women to be priests, surely he would have given some indication of this desire.

Furthermore, Jesus did not include his mother, Mary, among the apostles, the forerunners of the bishops. She, the greatest of all saints, was not called to serve as a priest or bishop. Surely, this shows that the non-admission of women to the priesthood is not a matter of discrimination against them or that women have less dignity. There is simply no greater human being than the Blessed Mother. The apostles, those closest to Jesus during his earthly ministry, simply imitated Jesus' example and his clear intention when they chose only male collaborators to succeed them in their ministry (*CCC*, 1577).

Church teaching also stresses that sacramental signs—both persons and objects—should represent what they signify by natural resemblance. The priest is a perceptible sign, "another Christ." He represents Jesus when he presents to God the prayer of the Church, especially the Eucharistic sacrifice (*CCC*, 1552). Because Christ was a male, the priest must be a male.

Priesthood is a gift that Jesus Christ gives to his Church. It is not a right which anyone deserves, but a call by God to serve the Church in a particular way (*CCC*, 1578). Many other ministries are open to women and men. Simply put, the Church does not have the authority to change what Jesus Christ established. This is not discrimination against women, which is clearly contrary to Christ's teaching.

**What Do You Think?**

- What is a ministry in the Church that you feel called to?
- What special gifts do have that you think could contribute to the building up of the Church?
- How do you see yourself serving the Church ten years from now?

## sixty-six

*Wouldn't the pedophilia crisis be solved if priests could marry? Wouldn't the vocation crisis be solved, too? In other words, why can't priests marry?*

Pedophilia is a sickness that affects a certain number of people in our society. No one fully understands its cause. Is it genetic or learned behavior or caused by being abused as a child? No one knows for sure, although theologically it is yet another tragic result of the Fall. What is certainly true is that the vast majority of child molesters in our society are *married* heterosexual males. Simply put, priestly celibacy is *not* the cause of pedophilia.

Second, a married clergy may or may not solve the shortage of priests. Arguably, God calls sufficient men to the priesthood but because of the culture we live in and all its enticements (an obsession with materialism, individualism, and hedonism), enough men are not responding to the call. Furthermore, parents don't encourage vocations to the religious life like they did in the past. In the end, it would be false to conclude that a married clergy would be an automatic solution. Look at the vocation of marriage today. Unfortunately, it too is under serious threat. There is such a high incidence of divorce, including, sadly, Catholics.

Third, we realize that the requirement for a non-married priesthood—clerical celibacy—in the Roman Catholic Church is not a divine law. Nothing in Jesus' teaching reveals that he *required* priests to remain unmarried. Peter himself had a wife (see Mk 1:30). And tradition holds that all the apostles, except for John, had wives and families.

Though our Lord did not require celibacy, it can be said that he did strongly *encourage* it (Mt 19:10f, Mk 10:29, and Lk 14:26) for those who commit themselves totally to the spread of God's kingdom. God's love and work in our world is the most important reality. Celibate priests do, in fact, follow the example of Jesus himself who remained unmarried for the sake of God's kingdom. And St. Paul himself also counseled celibacy (1 Cor 7:32f) so persons could completely devote themselves to serving God's people.

What is the further history of the celibacy rule for priests? The Western Church (or Latin rite), from the earliest centuries, highly valued priestly celibacy. Thus, in 306, the council of Elvira in Spain issued a law requiring a celibate clergy. Gradually, other local councils enforced priestly celibacy. Finally, the Second Lateran Council in 1139 adopted a celibate priesthood for the entire Western, Latin-rite Church.

The Eastern Church, made up of various rites (e.g., the Byzantine rite) in communion with the pope, permits a married man to be ordained a deacon or priest. But the Eastern rites forbid a priest to marry *after* ordination. They also require that bishops remain unmarried.

John Paul II did accept some married Anglican and Episcopalian clergy to receive holy orders in the Catholic Church. The pope extended this special dispensation to certain converts so they could continue serving as official ministers after becoming Catholics. Since the celibacy rule is not a divine law, the Holy Father can make exceptions when circumstances warrant.

According to the Holy Father, priestly celibacy is a gift to the Church. By means of it, priests can serve us wholeheartedly without the distractions that family responsibilities require. Finally, priestly celibacy is a "sign of contradiction" to the world. It reminds us that in eternity there will be no marriage. We will all be one in a loving union with God. The celibate priest is a living symbol in the present of the future that awaits all God's people.

With the shortage of priests, and in wake of the sex abuse scandal, you will see more and more people calling for optional celibacy for today's priesthood. There are many good arguments pro and con on this issue. Current Church leadership, however, has decided that celibacy is still the better of the two options. For example, the Twenty-First Synod of Bishops, which met in October of 2005 with around 250 bishops in attendance, reaffirmed the Church's stance on priestly celibacy in the recommendations they submitted to Pope Benedict XVI. Regardless, we should always pray for generous hearts and courage to accept any call God might be making to our young people to serve as priests or in the religious life.

**To Think About** ＞ ＞ ＞ ＞ ＞ ＞ ＞ ＞ ＞ ＞ ＞ ＞ ＞ ＞ ＞ ＞

- What qualities do you like to see in priest?
- What are you doing to support and give friend-ship to priests and others in religious life?

# sixty-seven ➤ ➤ ➤ ➤ ➤ ➤

*If the pope is only a man, why do
Catholics believe he is infallible? Does
this mean he can't make mistakes?*

A uthor John Deedy recounts the story of Cardinal James
Gibbons of Baltimore, who had just returned from Rome.
A reporter asked Cardinal Gibbons if he thought the pope
was infallible. Gibbons replied, "All I know is that he kept
referring to me as 'Jibbons.'"[5]

The pope at the time was the Italian Leo XIII who, as Italians
do, pronounced "g" as "j." The story may not be true. But it
does tell us that papal infallibility does not mean the pope is
perfect. He can make mistakes in his private opinions. And, as
a man, he can sin.

*Papal infallibility* refers to the spirit of truth, a *charism* or gift
which Jesus gives to the Church. It results from Jesus' promise
to Peter that he would never permit "the gates of the nether-
world" to overpower the Church (see Mt 16:16–19). In this gift,
Jesus through the Holy Spirit will not allow the Church, in its
*official* teaching on faith and morals, to betray the vision he has
entrusted to it.

The Christian community originally gave great respect to
the teachings of the apostles and later to the local churches
founded by the apostles. From the earliest centuries special
respect was given the Church of Rome and its bishop, since this
was the place of St. Peter's death and his community. By the
fifth century, the great St. Augustine captured perfectly the attitude of Catholics toward papal teaching, "Rome has spoken;
the case is concluded."[6]

In 1870, the First Vatican Council declared the infallibility of
the pope an official Church dogma. The Second Vatican
Council reaffirmed this teaching and also defined how the

bishops also teach infallibly when united to the pope. Quoting the *Dogmatic Constitution on the Church*, the *Catechism of the Catholic Church* puts it this way:

> "The Roman Pontiff, head of the college of bishops, enjoys this infallibility in virtue of his office, when, as supreme pastor and teacher of all the faithful—who confirms his brethren in the faith he proclaims by a definitive act a doctrine pertaining to faith or morals. . . . The infallibility promised to the Church is also present in the body of bishops when, together with Peter's successor, they exercise the supreme Magisterium," above all in an Ecumenical Council (*CCC*, 891).

Note how this gift of freedom from error holds only when the pope invokes the highest authority of his office, that is, when he teaches *ex cathedra* (from the chair of Peter). Furthermore, the pope and bishops speak infallibly only on *traditional* teachings, doctrines that the Church has always taught and believed. They cannot invent new doctrines. They can only solemnly define teachings that have been part of the Church's heritage. There have only been two papal infallible statements declared in the last 150 years or so: the Immaculate Conception of Mary (1854) and the Assumption of Mary into Heaven (1950).

# sixty-eight ➤ ➤ ➤ ➤ ➤ ➤

*Why is Mary so important to Catholics?
Do we really worship her as some
people say Catholics do?*

C atholics, like all Christians, worship and adore God alone.
To worship anyone or anything else is to commit *idolatry*,
forbidden by the first commandment. But Catholics do
*venerate* (that is, "honor" and "respect") Mary and the saints
because of their wholehearted love and service of God and
their holiness of life. We give Mary *greater* reverence than the
other saints because she is the queen of the saints, the Mother of
God. She is also our mother because Jesus gave her to the
Church when he told the beloved disciple John "Behold, your
mother" (Jn 19:27) as he hung dying on the cross.

When we admire Mary, God's great masterpiece, we are
honoring the Divine Artist. Mary herself proclaimed, "The
Mighty One has done great things for me, and holy is his
name" (Lk 1:49).

When we venerate Mary and the saints, we are not praying
to them. Rather, we are praying in solidarity with them.
Because they are our ancestors in the faith, they pray alongside
us, interceding for us before God. Mary is a powerful interces-
sor. The incident at Cana—where Jesus changed water into
wine because Mary requested him do so—shows how valuable
a loving mother's intercession can be. For centuries, Catholics
have recognized the power of Mary's help whenever they recite
the Hail Mary. In this prayer, we petition Mary, "pray for us sinners now and at the hour of our death."

We also honor Mary and the saints when we try to imitate
their holy lives, especially their virtues. Mary deserves special
honor because she is a tremendous exemplar of the Christian
virtues.

- *Mary brought God to humanity, the task of all Christians.* She showed the way by being a perfect example of faith. Not knowing how or even why, she said yes to God's invitation to be the mother of Jesus. In the Lord's Prayer, we pray, "Thy will be done." Mary perfectly shows how to achieve this.

- *Mary remained faithful her entire life.* Her commitment to the Lord was not a flash in the pan. She stayed the course, even in the extremely difficult days of her son's passion and death. Mary embodies the meaning of discipleship.

- *Mary was humble.* The most blessed of all women and men, she gave God credit for what he accomplished through her. She *praised* God unceasingly. All we are and all we have are pure gifts from a loving God. Mary teaches us how to say "thank you" to our incredibly generous Father.

- *Mary lived only to know, love, and serve God.* Our faith teaches that our primary goal in life is to know, love, and serve God in this life and to join him in an eternity of perfect happiness. Mary lived her life in a sinless, exemplary way doing what God calls us all to do. She deserves our respect, honor, veneration, and imitation.

# sixty-nine ➤ ➤ ➤ ➤ ➤ ➤ ➤

## How does the Church decide who becomes a saint and who doesn't?

T he Church sets aside All Saints' Day (November 1) to honor the countless anonymous saints who are with the Lord in heaven. These are the uncanonized saints. Undoubtedly, among these millions of saints are many of your own relatives from past generations. If their faith and love were heroic while here on earth, you can be sure they are in heaven. This is the day of the liturgical year when the Church remembers their lives.

*Canonization* is the official process the Church uses to declare that a person is in heaven and may be honored as a saint. The word *canonization* comes from a Greek word that means "measuring rod" or "standard" and has come to mean "to be on the list officially." In the early Church, the title of saint was bestowed on a person locally when the people who knew the saint acclaimed him or her to be one. Over time, abuses set in and Pope John XV in 993 took steps to formulize the process of declaring a person a saint. Pope John Paul II revised the saint-making process in 1983 and 1997 and renamed the Vatican congregation in charge as the Congregation for the Causes of Saints. There are three major steps involved in being put on the official list of saints:

1. Supporters in a local diocese nominate a candidate's name after his or her death by petitioning the bishop to investigate the person's qualifications for sainthood, that is, whether he or she lived a holy life of faith and morals and exemplified the theological and cardinal virtues to an extraordinary degree. The bishop appoints a postulator to examine the person's life. If the bishop believes a

good case has been made, he gives the results of the cause to Rome where the Congregation for Causes of Saints determines if the person lived a heroic life of virtue. If the answer is yes, then the person is given the title "servant of God" or "Venerable" and the cause moves to the next stage.

2. Stage two is known as "beatification" where the person's life and writings are carefully examined to make sure they conform to Catholic teaching. This step involves interviewing known living acquaintances of the saint. For the process to proceed, it must show that praying to the candidate resulted in one miracle because of his or her intercession. (However, a martyr—someone who died for the faith—is not required to have a miracle.) If the candidate passes this stage, the Church declares the person "Blessed." This means Catholics can venerate this person within a certain geographical area or in the religious community to which he or she belonged.

3. Step three (canonization) involves an exhaustive examination of the candidate's life by the Congregation for the Causes of the Saints. A second miracle is necessary, "attributed to the intercession of the Blessed and having occurred after his beatification"[7] before the commission of bishops and cardinals present the cause to the pope. If the pope approves, he will issue a Bull of Canonization, which proclaims the person a saint of the Catholic Church. Catholics may now honor this saint publicly throughout the world. Bishops can name churches after the saint. And the Church may assign a liturgical feast day to the newly canonized saint.

As you can see, the process of canonization is complex. You may have noticed that many canonized saints belong to religious orders. Does this mean that lay people, like married couples, are not holy? No! The practical reason is that religious orders have the financial means and staying power to promote the cause of a particular candidate over a long time period.

Most saints are anonymous. It is the hope of the Church that one day Christians will also pray to and honor you. Christ calls each person to be a saint. He wants us to live our ordinary lives in an extraordinary way by loving and serving him through others. As the song goes, may you be "in their number when the saints go marching in."

## Of Interest:

You might enjoy checking on the progress of the canonization process of the following individuals.

- **Blessed Mother Teresa:**
  www.motherteresacause.info
- **Bishop Sheen:**
  www.archbishopsheencause.com

Also, you might want to examine the biographies and pictures of some recently beatified and canonized persons at the Vatican website: www.vatican.va

(Type in "canonization" under the Search engine.)

## seventy

*My Protestant friend says it is wrong to pray to the saints. Why do we Catholics do so?*

First of all, then, I ask that supplications, prayers, petitions, and thanksgivings be offered for everyone. . . . This is good and pleasing to God our savior, who wills everyone to be saved and to come to knowledge of the truth (1 Tm 2:1, 3–4).

T he author of the First Letter to Timothy instructs Christians to pray for one another. Haven't you done that when you asked someone to pray for you before a test, a big game, or a visit to the dentist's office? Hasn't a friend or family member asked you to pray for him or her? Praying for others is, in fact, a great way to demonstrate our love and unity with others.

As Christians, we are truly members of one big family. This family, the communion of saints, includes those of us still alive on earth, as well as those in heaven or in purgatory. As Christians, we believe that death does not destroy our spiritual relationship with each other. In fact, it can intensify it because our friends and relatives in heaven are vitally alive and care for us very much. They show their continuing love and concern by praying for us before God.

When we pray "to" the saints, we are really asking them to pray *with* us and *for* us to our Lord Jesus, our unique mediator and Savior. All graces and salvation come through him alone.

The saints led heroic lives of holiness on earth. They gave God great honor when they lived among us. They continue to inspire us to imitate their example. When we pray to them for intercession, we are rejoicing with them. We unite our own prayers with theirs, praying to Jesus who takes all of our petitions to our Heavenly Father.

Jesus told us of the special power of joining our prayer to those of others (Mt 18:19–20). The New Testament frequently instructs us to pray for each other (for example, Jas 5:16). Surely you have experienced in your own life the spiritual power of several voices joined in prayer on your behalf. Even medical science has produced a number of studies that seem to show that praying for others actually helps the healing process. When you pray to the saints you show that you firmly believe that our union with the members of Christ's family goes beyond death. Why not pray to God with the saints—our friends in high places—who sit before God's heavenly throne? It is good to do so.

# seventy-one ➤ ➤ ➤ ➤ ➤

*Our parish still uses bingo to raise money for the school. Isn't gambling immoral?*

M any Bible-based Christian denominations claim that gambling is immoral. However, the Catholic Church teaches that gambling is morally neutral. Games of chance can even be positive when they are a form of entertainment, help raise funds for good causes, or boost the economy of local communities.

However, the Church holds that gambling is immoral if

- the money that is wagered comes from funds needed to support one's family,
- a person is forced to participate in it,
- gambling supports an immoral cause,
- or the games of chance are rigged.

In addition, the *Catechism of the Catholic Church* warns, "The passion for gambling risks becoming an enslavement" (*CCC*, 2413). Compulsive gambling is a form of enslavement because a person cannot resist the impulse to gamble. It is a serious and growing problem in our society (from 1–3% of the population is affected). It damages countless families both economically and legally.

Bingo is a form of gambling that charitable organizations, including the Catholic Church, has used for years to raise funds for worthy causes like parish schools. Based on the principles outlined above, bingo can be a moral and even fun way to raise money.

In recent years, more and more bishops are asking pastors in their dioceses to phase out bingo. An important reason is that many senior citizens, who live on fixed incomes, often play bingo with funds that they cannot afford to lose. For some bingo has become an addiction. Also, bingo as a fund-raising activity often depends on outsiders coming to the bingo nights. This encourages parishioners to shirk their duty of supporting the parish out of their own funds. In fact, the majority of Catholic parishes do not have bingo nights.

# seventy-two ➤ ➤ ➤ ➤ ➤

### How can the Church consider certain wars just but teach capital punishment is unjust? Isn't this inconsistent?

The Catholic Church stands for a consistent ethic of life, what the late Cardinal Joseph Bernardin referred to as "a seamless garment" of respect for life from "womb to tomb."

Human life is a precious gift from God. It is sacred because humans are made in his image and likeness and possess dignity. Humans are also sacred because we are in a special relationship to our Creator. Our goal in life is to be united to God forever in eternity. God alone is the Lord of life. Therefore, no one anywhere at any time by any means has the right to destroy an *innocent* human life. This is why the Church strongly condemns murder, abortion, direct euthanasia, acts of terrorism, torture, forced sterilization, and other violent assaults on human life.

The Church is also *against* war because of all the evils and injustices entailed by the waging of war. Every citizen and every government must work unceasingly for peace by removing the anger, hatred, greed, and envy that lead to war. However, the Church recognizes that we live in a sinful world and that as a *last* resort, legitimate governmental authorities have the right to engage their citizens in what is known as a just war. For a war to be just, all of these conditions must be present:

- "the damage inflicted by the aggressor on the nation or community of nations must be lasting, grave, and certain;
- "all other means of putting an end to it must have been shown to be impractical or ineffective;
- "there must be serious prospects of success;
- "the use of arms must not produce evils and disorders graver than the evil to be eliminated. The power of modem means of destruction weighs very heavily in evaluating this condition" (CCC, 2309).

Even if the proper authorities decide a nation must regrettably go to war, the war must be conducted morally. Therefore, "Non-combatants, wounded soldiers, and prisoners must be respected and treated humanely" (CCC, 2313). And military actions that aim to destroy whole cities or vast territories are horrible crimes that can never be justified.

The just war teaching of the Church recognizes that nations, just like individuals, have the right to self-defense against unjust aggressors. Minimum force must always be used to stop an unjust aggressor. But if the minimum force regrettably results in the death of the attacker, then it would be permitted. It is allowed because when individuals or nations defend themselves, two outcomes result: the saving of one's own life (or that of the nation) and the killing of the aggressor. The good effect (self-preservation) is intended; the killing is not—it is a sad outcome of an innocent person or nation preserving its own life.

In a similar way, the Church has taught that societies have the right to protect themselves against the unjust and evil attacks of criminals. Traditionally, the Church has taught that a *society does have the right to inflict the death penalty* (capital punishment) if the guilty party has been justly identified and if the person's death is the only possible way of defending human lives against this criminal.

However, the Church teaches that if non-deadly ways can protect citizens against criminals, then they must be used because they more effectively promote the common good and human dignity. Today, in fact, the criminal justice system has effective ways to prevent criminals from causing further harm. Therefore, the Church teaches that "the cases in which the execution of the offender is an absolute necessity 'are very rare, if not practically non-existent'" (CCC, 2267).

In a recent statement entitled, *A Culture of Life and the Penalty of Death*, the American Bishops call for the abolishment of the death penalty in the United States. Their reasons are compelling:

Our nation should forgo the use of the death penalty because

- The sanction of death, when it is not necessary to protect society, violates respect for human life and dignity.
- State-sanctioned killing in our names diminishes all of us.
- Its application is deeply flawed and can be irreversibly wrong, is prone to errors, and is biased by factors such as race, the quality of legal representation, and where the crime was committed.

We have other ways to punish criminals and protect society.[8]

## What Do You Think? » » » » » » » » » » » »

- According to just-war teaching, was the United States justified in going to war in Iraq in 2003?
- Can you think of any case today where the execution of an offender would be "absolutely necessary?"

« « « « « « « « « « « « « « « « « « « « « «

# seventy-three ➤ ➤ ➤ ➤

*How is a Catholic supposed to love terrorists? They are so evil.*

The FBI defines terrorism this way:

> the unlawful use of force against persons or property to intimidate or coerce a government, the civilian population or any segment thereof, in the furtherance of political or social objectives.[9]

According to this definition, (1) Terrorists engage in illegal actions involving force. (2) The purpose of their acts is to intimidate or coerce. (3) They engage in this activity to promote a political or social objective.

The Catholic Church condemns terrorism. "Terrorism threatens, wounds, and kills indiscriminately; it is gravely against justice and charity" (*CCC*, 2297).

Pope John Paul II in his annual message for peace in 2002 observed the ever-growing scourge of terrorist networks that have appeared in recent decades. He noted how terrorism springs from hate and is built on contempt for human life, especially when terrorist organizations encourage their followers to use themselves as weapons in suicide bombings. The Holy Father brands terrorism as a "true crime against humanity."[10]

The pope wisely noted how terrorism often is rooted in a fanatic fundamentalism that holds that one's own view of truth must be forced on everyone else. This is a gross violation of human dignity. And to do so in God's name, as some terrorists do, is to exploit God, making him an idol to be used for one's own purpose.

On both the international and personal levels, the last pope, John Paul II, taught an essentially Christian way to deal with the aftermath of terrorism: *"No peace without justice, no justice without forgiveness."*[11] In his Message for the World Day of Peace in 2004, John Paul II reminded governmental authorities that the use of force is not enough to stop and contain terrorism. He taught that leaders must discover and then eradicate the underlying causes of unjust situations that drive people to terrorist acts. Then they must insist on education that teaches the respect for human life in every situation.[12]

Terrorism is grossly evil. It is part of the great mystery of evil that haunts the human heart as a result of original sin. John Paul II vigorously condemned it in the strongest terms and outlined a way for nations to deal with it. But what can *you* do?

- *You can pray for the evildoers.* Jesus is our model. He taught us to love our enemies. He showed the way as he hung dying on the cross, "Father, forgive them, they know not what they do" (Lk 23:34). When we pray for terrorists, we are not denying the terrible evil of their acts; nor are we saying that they should not be brought to justice. We can never justify their crimes against humanity. What we are praying for is the conversion of the terrorists. We are praying that Christ's redemptive acts will touch their hearts and they will turn away from their hatred of humanity.
- A second thing you can do is *to pray that you might learn to forgive your enemies*, those who dislike you personally or harm you. Pray that you learn forgiveness in your own heart because forgiveness begins there, in your family, in your school. If you can learn to forgive in the little things that affect you directly, then the Holy Spirit will give you the courage to forgive in big things. "There can be no peace without justice, *no justice without forgiveness.*"

- Third, *commit yourself to living a just life* in your dealings with all people. Be honest. Defend others who are unfairly attacked. Write letters to newspapers and governmental officials in the support of prolife causes. Remember, *"There can be no peace without justice,* no justice without forgiveness."

- Finally, *avoid at all costs any sweeping generalizations,* for example, assigning blame to a whole nation or religion for the terrorist acts of a small minority of misguided fanatics. Not all Muslims, Arabs, Palestinians, or whatever, are terrorists. It is unjust to be prejudiced against any group of people.

# seventy-four ➤ ➤ ➤ ➤ ➤

### I have a friend who claims Catholics are not Christian. Is she right?

**Q-1:** Do you believe in the divinity of Jesus Christ as the only Son of God, our Lord and Savior?

**Q-2:** Have you been baptized in the name of the Father, and of the Son, and of the Holy Spirit?

If you answer yes to these two questions, then you are a Christian. Obviously, Catholics believe in Jesus Christ as the second person of the Blessed Trinity and receive the sacrament of Baptism. So without a doubt, Catholics are Christians.

But are all Christians "Catholic"? No. A Catholic is a Christian who believes that Jesus himself established the Catholic Church and that this Church, as the one Christ intended, possesses the fullness of truth and all the means necessary for salvation. Practically, this means that Catholics:

- Believe in the "one, holy, catholic, and apostolic Church" and all that it teaches through the pope and bishops who are the successors to Peter and the apostles.
- Accept all seven sacraments of the Catholic Church.
- Submit to the teaching authority of the Magisterium (the pope and bishops who are in union with him) in matters of faith and morals.

A little history about the terms *Christian* and *Catholic*. Recall that Jesus was a Jew and so were the apostles and most of their early converts. This group of Jewish believers proclaimed that Jesus was the Messiah (*Christos* in Greek, from which the name *Christian* is derived). In the early years after the resurrection, they did their best to convince their co-religionists that Jesus was the promised one. But many Jews did not accept this teaching; some even persecuted the Christians who, to their way of thinking, were teaching blasphemy by proclaiming that Jesus of Nazareth was the Son of God.

Because Jesus was truly "good news," early Christian preachers like St. Paul also began to proclaim Jesus to non-Jews, that is, to the Gentiles. Their preaching took them to every corner of the Roman Empire and met with considerable success. Many Gentiles converted to Christianity. The new faith became truly *universal* because it could be found everywhere. Furthermore, this new religion was open to accepting all kinds of people—slaves, merchants, soldiers, and even some royal figures.

When Christianity finally separated from Judaism after the Jewish Revolt (AD 66–70), it clearly became a distinct religion. In his *Letter to the Smyrnians*, written in AD 110, St. Ignatius of Antioch wrote his famous line, "Wherever the bishop appears, let the people be there; just as wherever Jesus Christ is, there is the Catholic Church." The Church was Catholic (universal) because of Jesus' presence to it.

Following St. Ignatius, and clearly by the end of the second century, *Catholic* and *Christian* were very often used to describe the very same religion, especially to distinguish it from some of the heretical groups of the day. The terms were interchangeable. To be a Christian was to be a Catholic. To be a Catholic was to be a Christian. If you weren't Catholic, you weren't Christian. If you weren't Christian, you weren't Catholic.

A major change in terminology took place in 1054 when the Eastern Schism took place. Schism means "division" or "split," that is, a rupture in unity. Many theological, philosophical, and political reasons caused this unfortunate break in Christian unity between Western Christians and Eastern Christians. The bottom line was that the Eastern Christians would not accept the authority of the pope. They became known as *Orthodox* Christians. Orthodox Christians hold many beliefs in common with Catholics, including recognizing seven sacraments. However, the Orthodox Christians do not submit to the authority of the Holy Father.

In the Western Church, you will recall that a German monk by the name of Martin Luther protested against some Church abuses that were taking place in the sixteenth century. Among these abuses was the unfortunate practice of selling indulgences to raise money for the building of St. Peter's. Instead of working to reform the Church from within, Luther taught some things that were heretical. He refused to change his views and thus began the Protestant Reformation. Since the sixteenth century, unfortunately, other Christian groups have also protested against various beliefs and practices. A common estimate holds that today there are in excess of 20,000 Protestant denominations.[13]

Sadly, this directly contradicts the stated desire of Jesus to his disciples that believers "may all be one."

> I pray not only for them, but also for those who
> will believe in me through their word, so that
> they may all be one, as you, Father, are in me
> and I in you, that they also may be in us, that

the world may believe that you sent me
(Jn 17:20–21).

There is plenty of blame to go around for the fractured unity in the Body of Christ. Although we believe that the unity Christ desires for his Church exists in the Catholic Church, the Church and individual Catholics must pray for unity among Christians and do all in our power to understand, explain, and live our faith.

St. Francis of Assisi said, "Preach the Gospel at all times. When necessary, use words." His point was that if others could see Christian love in action, they would be attracted to it. In a world of terrorists and extreme, lethal poverty, Christians must unite in an effort to show that the way of love, and not the way of hate, is the path to true peace and harmony. May it once again be said, "You can tell they are Christians by their love."

# seventy-five ➤ ➤ ➤ ➤ ➤

### Why doesn't the Church stay out of politics?

B ecause the Church lacks political power, it cannot force people or governments to act one way rather than another. But the Church does have the duty to teach in Christ's name. It can persuade Catholics and other open-minded people to consider seriously the requirements of the gospel calls to love, to promote justice, and to care for the weakest people in our midst. The Church can encourage Catholics to be faithful citizens, that is, to be informed, responsible, and active in the political process so that the culture of life can be promoted.

Consider some of the problems facing us today: terrorism security; equal rights for women and racial and religious minorities; fairness for workers in a global economy; abortion, assisted suicide, and euthanasia; the ever-present scourge of poverty that results in 30,000 children dying of hunger each day; global warming; war; and unethical biomedical engineering. These and many other local, state, national, and international issues beg for an intelligent and Christian response.

The Church is the Body of Christ, his presence in the world. As the Lord taught his generation to love and care for the "least of these" in our midst, so must the Church follow his example. As the American bishops argue in *Faithful Citizenship: A Catholic Call to Political Responsibility*, the Catholic community can bring three strong assets to the political arena:

- a consistent moral framework based on the word of God that teaches the dignity of human life and effective principles of justice and peace;
- a wide experience of serving those in need that gives practical expertise on how justice works in the real world;
- and a large and diverse faith community that is committed to the promotion of human life.[14]

Jesus revealed that all of us have tremendous worth and dignity because we are all children of a loving Father. Thus, the Church must continually call people to respect everyone's basic dignity. It *must* judge social, political, and economic matters, especially when persons' rights and their salvation require it.

Church social justice teaching of the past one hundred and ten plus years proceeds from the principle that certain economic and political rights flow from our basic dignity as persons. This teaching includes certain principles of reflection, criteria for judging, and guidelines for action. For example, Church social teaching condemns any theory that makes the disordered desire for money the basis of an economy. It also condemns any system that would reduce a human being to a mere means of profit. The first evil leads to materialism and consumerism. The second evil destroys the individual dignity of persons.

Issues of economy and politics entwine. They result from real people making real decisions. Hence, the Magisterium of the Church asks people to reflect on basic questions. For example, in the area of economics, we should ask: "What does the economy do *for* people? What does it do *to* people? And how do people *participate*?" By asking these questions, the Church challenges people to participate responsibly in the social order to make laws and set up policies that protect human rights.

As Christ's representative, the Church must especially speak out for the poor, the powerless, and the defenseless. This includes watching out for the rights of the unborn and needy people at home and abroad. It also means speaking out for minorities who are receiving unjust treatment in a political or economic system controlled by the wealthy.

Though it would not be advisable for the Church to form political parties, the Church must teach in Christ's name. It must promote justice, the virtue of fairness that gives persons their due as children of a loving God. Like a good mother looking out for her children, the Church also encourages her sons and daughters to participate actively in the political and economic arenas. Lay people especially have a key role to play in promoting justice in the political order.

## What Do You Say? ➤ ➤ ➤ ➤ ➤ ➤ ➤ ➤ ➤ ➤ ➤ ➤ ➤ ➤

"If anyone is well off in worldly possessions and sees his brother in need but closes his heart to him, how can the love of God be remaining in him?"

Is it moral for us to keep for our own exclusive use what we don't need when others lack the basic requirements for a decent life?

Should groups that have been discriminated against in the past be given special treatment in affirmative action programs to level the playing field so they can catch up economically? Explain.

Would a career in politics on the local, state, or national level appeal to you? Why or why not?

# ? seventy-six ➤ ➤ ➤ ➤ ➤ ➤

## Can I support a politician who is not pro-life?

T his is an important question and shows that you are serious about applying your faith to make the world around you a better place. One good place to start is the document the American bishops issue every four years before presidential elections entitled *Faithful Citizenship: A Catholic Call to Political Responsibility.* In this document, the bishops remind Catholics that they must look at issues through the eyes of faith. They admit that people of good will and sound faith may disagree on how to apply Catholic moral principles, but Catholics in public life have a special responsibility to apply their faith and moral principles to their public offices.

The Church cannot and will not tell citizens to vote or not to vote for a *specific* candidate. What it can do is to judge how particular candidates and the policies they endorse protect or "undermine the life, dignity, and rights of the human person, whether they protect the poor and vulnerable and advance the common good."[15]

Our obligation as Catholics is to look beyond a politician's political party. We must support candidates according to principle and not our own self-interest. The bishops write,

> We hope that voters will examine the position of candidates on the full range of issues, as well as on their personal integrity, philosophy, and performance. We are convinced that a consistent ethic of life should be the moral framework from which to address issues in the political arena.[16]

This consistent ethic of life flows out of seven principles of Catholic social teaching, namely:

- **Life and Dignity of the Human Person:** Because we are made in God's image, every human life, womb to tomb, must be regarded as sacred.
- **Call to Family, Community, and Participation:** We are social beings. Marriage between a man and woman and the family are the foundation of society and must be supported and strengthened, not attacked. Every person has a right to participate in social, economic, and political life and work for the common good.
- **Rights and Responsibilities:** Every human being has a fundamental right to life, the basis of all other rights that make it possible to live decently, rights like faith and family life, food and shelter, education and employment, health care and housing. We must help others achieve these rights, and we must exercise our rights responsibly toward each other as well.
- **Option for the Poor and Vulnerable:** God has special concern and love for poor and vulnerable people. We as individuals must also reach out in a special way to the poor and work to have our public policies serve the needs of the weakest in our midst.
- **Dignity of Work and the Rights of Workers:** We must see that economic policies serve the people, not the other way around. Work helps us participate in God's creative activity; therefore, the rights of workers must be protected and exercised to promote the common good.
- **Solidarity:** We belong to one human family. Therefore, we must be responsible for the welfare of people around the world. We must promote peace by working for justice for all people everywhere.

- **Caring for God's Creation:** God created the world and its goods for all people throughout the ages. We must care for it with respect.

To return to your exact question, the bishops affirm that the right to life is "the right that makes all other rights possible." Thus the pro-life issues—stem cell research, euthanasia, and most crucially, abortion—are the most fundamental in elections when such rights are at stake. The scandal of Catholic politicians supporting abortion rights while hiding behind the rhetoric of being "personally opposed" to abortion came to national prominence when the pro-abortion Catholic Senator John Kerry ran for the presidency in 2004. A furor broke out among American bishops over the possibility of denying communion to such candidates. In order to clarify the Church's position, Cardinal Ratzinger, who would the next year become Pope Benedict XVI, wrote a memo to the archbishop of Washington, D.C. The memo explicitly highlighted the centrality of the pro-life position: "There may be a legitimate diversity of opinion even among Catholics about waging war and applying the death penalty, but not however with regard to abortion and euthanasia."[17]

Cardinal Ratzinger went on to clarify the duties of voting Catholics with regard to these fundamental issues:

> A Catholic would be guilty of formal cooperation in evil, and so unworthy to present himself for Holy Communion, if he were to deliberately vote for a candidate precisely because of the candidate's permissive stand on abortion and/or euthanasia. When a Catholic does not share a candidate's stand in favor of abortion and/or euthanasia, but votes for that candidate for other reasons, it is considered remote material cooperation, which can be permitted in the presence of proportionate reasons.[18]

It is the clear duty, then, of every Catholic to support the fundamental right to life. However, supporting such a right in the ballot box involves a variety of prudential choices. For example, certain political positions have very limited or no impact on such fundamental issues, and therefore the stance of such politicians on the right to life can be reasonably disregarded. In elections to such positions, you can safely move quickly to see how they promote or oppose the other principles listed above. In presidential elections, however, the position of the candidates on their favored Supreme Court Justices and who they would appoint becomes particularly crucial. In the end, like the problems that face America, your question has no crystal clear answer. But certainly incumbent upon every Catholic is the building of the culture of life, whether by voting, by conversations with friends, or by speaking out to wider audiences through letters to the editor and other forms public engagement.

# seventy-seven ➤ ➤ ➤ ➤

*I have doubts about several of the Church's teachings. I also know people who do what the Church calls sinful (for example, premarital sex). Yet we all consider ourselves Catholics. Is there anything wrong with that?*

One important aspect of faith is trust. And trust involves risk. If this were not so, faith would not be faith but knowledge. Believing in Church teachings requires trust in the reliable testimony of prior generations of Catholics. It also means trusting that Jesus remains with his Church, guiding and directing it in truth.

A certain amount of questioning, confusion, and uncertainty, and even difficulty with this or that aspect of Catholic teaching is normal, and this is certainly true of teens who are trying to make the Catholic faith their own. In fact, questioning can be a sign of maturity, a desire to understand Church teaching, some of which directly opposes today's secular values and "truisms."

What should you do? First, believe that our Lord will strengthen you as you seek the truth about him and his Church. Pray for his help. Be confident that he will help you preserve the gift of faith that he has given to you. Second, be humble enough to admit that you don't know everything. Consult the wisdom of teachers in the Church, those trained to help you understand the truths of the faith. This would include parish priests and religious educators. Third, be patient with yourself. Try to live as a faithful disciple of Jesus. With Christian living comes Christian understanding.

Concerning the second part of your statement, don't forget that *all* Catholics are sinners. Remember, Jesus came to minister to sinners, to be the Divine Physician to those who need healing. The Church is not an exclusive club for saints, but a hospital for sinners.

A further question remains: Are the people you spoke of willing to seek repentance if they come to understand that their behavior is sinful? People who persist in a life of sin, without being sorry and making a firm purpose to amend their lives with God's help, are insincere. Their hypocrisy at not making an effort to live as Christians or Catholics reveals that they are not "good" Catholics. "Good" means that they are making an honest effort to live as Christ wants us to live. Jesus himself said,

> "Not everyone who says to me, 'Lord, Lord,'
> will enter the kingdom of heaven, but only the
> one who does the will of my Father in heaven"
> (Mt 7:21).

The issue you raise is actually more serious for adult Catholics who are often referred to as "cafeteria Catholics." They choose only those teachings of Christ and his Church they wish to believe and follow—something also more recently termed "Catholic Lite." Jesus did not found a smorgasbord or cafeteria Church where a person can pick and choose what to believe and what not to believe. Dining at his table means digesting all his Church's teachings. It means making an honest, even heroic, effort at putting them into practice. And, if we fall short, it means asking for the Lord's forgiveness and striving, with his help, to be faithful to him in the future.

> *"Ten thousand difficulties do not make one doubt."*
>
> ~CARDINAL JOHN HENRY NEWMAN

## What Do You Say? ⪢ ⪢ ⪢ ⪢ ⪢ ⪢ ⪢ ⪢ ⪢ ⪢ ⪢ ⪢ ⪢ ⪢

**Agree or disagree?** People don't leave the Church because they have an *intellectual* difficulty with a particular Church teaching. They often leave because they are behaving immorally and don't want to hear the truth about their sinful lives.

⪡ ⪡ ⪡ ⪡ ⪡ ⪡ ⪡ ⪡ ⪡ ⪡ ⪡ ⪡ ⪡ ⪡ ⪡ ⪡ ⪡ ⪡ ⪡ ⪡ ⪡

## Chapter SIX

# Do the Right Thing

### God's Plan for My Life

More than ninety years ago, a father, mother, and nine children from Scotland had scrimped and saved for years to immigrate to America. However, they were destined to be disappointed. Before departing on the much-anticipated trip, the youngest son was bitten by a dog. Because of the danger of rabies, the family was quarantined for two weeks and missed the ship that was to take them to America.

You can imagine the bitter letdown of the father of the family who stood on the dock and sadly saw the ship depart. In his anger, he shouted to God his sense of betrayal as the ship disappeared from view.

By the way, the name of the ship was the *Titanic*, touted to be unsinkable. Five days later, it struck an iceberg and slipped into the sea. Of the more than 2,220 people on board, it is estimated that 1,513 of them perished in the disaster, including the American millionaire John Jacob Astor. Had the Scottish family been on the ship, it is highly likely that several or all of its members would have drowned in the tragedy.

When the father of the family heard the news, he praised God and thanked him for turning what he initially saw as a major disappointment into a saving blessing.

Once again, remember the expression we have referred to before: "God writes straight with crooked lines." What we sometimes think is misfortune is really God guiding our lives in a different direction. It takes faith, prayer, and openness to see that life is an adventure with God guiding our lives, if we let him.

This final chapter takes up questions about how to discern how God can work in your life and what he wants of you. It discusses questions on how to grow in the Christian life—questions about Jesus' teaching, prayer, vocation, decision making, and college. As you read them, consider other questions you may have about your faith. Be sure to seek out answers from other Catholics whom you respect and trust.

# seventy-eight ➤ ➤ ➤ ➤

### How should I pray?

Your question shows that you consider prayer to be very important. And it is. It is to the spiritual life and friendship with the Lord what water and food are to physical life. The sign outside the church has it just about right: "Seven days without prayer makes one weak." Or, as one perceptive person remarked, "Prayer is a way of life, not just a case of emergency."

The first step in prayer is to find a regular time for it. (You always make time for what is important, and prayer is important.) Next, find a special place for prayer. Distractions are the plague of regular pray-ers. Finding a good place to pray—your bedroom, a chapel or church, a peaceful place outside in God's beautiful creation—can help cut down (but never eliminate) distractions that will inevitably come along.

The next step is to calm yourself down for the purpose of freeing yourself for prayer. You may wish to relax by doing deep breathing exercises. Let the cares of the day drain away. An agitated body leads to an agitated spirit at prayer.

When you are ready to begin your prayer time, try the following:

- Become aware of God's presence all around you. God holds you in the palm of his hand. You are always in his mind. You are like a fish swimming in an ocean of God's love.

- Approach God as you would a friend. The Lord Jesus *is* your friend, and prayer is essentially a conversation with the greatest friend you'll ever have. It involves talking and listening.

- In the *talking* part of your prayer, praise and thank God for all the good gifts he's given you that make life worth living: life, friends, health, talents. Also express to God your sorrow for your sins, your mistakes, your lack of attention to other people and to him. Believe that God, like any good friend, forgives and accepts you. He won't dwell on your past failings, and neither should you. Just ask the Lord for the strength to continue to be and do better.

- Now you are ready to take your concerns to the Lord. Jesus told us to petition God often and to be persistent in doing so. Speak to God simply as a child would to a loving parent. Share your concerns, your joys, your thoughts, your fears with him. Ask the Lord for "daily bread"—what you need physically, psychologically, and spiritually. Remember to pray for your family, your friends and relatives, the poor and the needy, as well as for your enemies.

- Prayer also involves *listening* to God. Ask the Lord to speak to you. Look over your past day—the people, the events, the successes and the failures, the joys and the sadness. Ask God to reveal to you more of their meaning in the overall context of your life. Stop and listen to your life. Is

God telling you through others to slow down, to stop worrying, to be more generous? Some people find it helpful to read from one of the gospels or epistles, stopping periodically to let God's word speak to their hearts. You might also want to try reading from other scriptures or some other spiritual book in the listening part of prayer.

- Enjoy God's presence around you, "basking in the sunshine of God's love"—without thinking in words at all. St. Jean Vianney tells of a saintly old peasant who reported on his prayer life: "I don't say anything to God. I just sit and look at him and let him look at me."

You might like to conclude your prayer with a promise or pledge to God. For example, you might tell him you are going to enjoy the beautiful world around you by taking a walk and noticing all the bright colors. Or you might make a point to be more considerate of those you meet during the day. Or you might pledge to thank someone or express to a parent or friend what they mean to you. You might also promise to say quiet prayers of love to the Lord at different times during the day, for example as you begin each class at school.

## Words of Wisdom about Prayer

"In praying, do not babble like the pagans, who think that they will be heard because of their many words. Do not be like them. Your Father knows what you need before you ask him."
~Mt 6:7–8

"Prayer is the raising of one's mind and heart to God or the requesting of good things from God."
~St. John Damascene quoted in *CCC*, 2559

# seventy-nine ➤ ➤ ➤ ➤

*Do my prayers affect God? For
example, can they get God to change
his mind?*

Prayer brings together two great mysteries. The first is of
an eternally loving God who knows all that was, all that
is, and all that ever will be. The second involves the mystery of our own free will, which enables us to accept or reject
God's invitation to love.

When we pray, we are praying to a loving God who has
known our prayers from all eternity. Thus, when we pray, we
are not telling God anything "new." Nor do we exercise any
power over him, for example, the power to persuade him to
change his mind about something. In fact, it is the Holy Spirit
who first inspired us to pray. As a result of knowing and inspiring our prayers from all eternity, God has included them in his
plan for the world. Furthermore, the very prayers that God
knew we would ask have been answered!

Therefore, prayer does not change God. Prayer changes us.
Prayer is essential for the Christian life because it makes us
reflect on our needs and turn to the One who can fulfill those
needs. Conversation and time spent with a good friend builds
trust, demonstrates love, and deepens the friendship. Prayer
does the same in our relationship with God. It also helps us
appreciate his great love for us, and it helps us become more
grateful for all he has done for us. It also helps us realize that
we must accept God's will and strengthens us to do it. In short,
when we pray, we allow the mystery of a loving God to touch
and change us.

Jesus knew the power that prayer has of conforming us to
God. This is why he himself prayed often throughout his life,
showing both how and why to pray. Jesus revealed that some

of God's activity in the world relies on our free and open response to it. For example, God's love is not forced on you. God offers it to you as a wonderful gift, which you can accept or reject. Prayer helps you recognize the invitation. It opens you up to God's activity. It heightens your awareness of God's hidden but powerful presence in everything around you. It helps you see that God will give you many gifts if you pray. As Jesus said, if you don't ask, you won't get.

We learn how to pray from the teacher of prayer *par excellence*: Jesus. He told us to pray often, both alone and with others. He instructed us to be open to God and to pray with childlike faith. He taught us to trust that our God—like a loving parent—will give us what is good for us.

Jesus also encouraged us to be persistent in our prayers and to pray with forgiveness in our hearts. If we harbor grudges, our hearts will be hard and the warmth of God's love will not touch us. If we follow Jesus' example and his advice on how to pray, God will indeed change us and answer our prayers.

## Read and Reflect

Read Luke 11:1–13. Reflect on what this passage tells you about prayer.

> "Prayer is the place of refuge for every worry, a
> foundation for cheerfulness, a source of constant
> happiness, a protection against sadness."
>
> ~ St. John Chrysostom

# eighty ➤ ➤ ➤ ➤ ➤ ➤ ➤ ➤ ➤ ➤

*God never answers my prayers, so why should I bother praying?*

Jesus told the parable of the Persistent Widow (Lk 18:1-8) to remind us of the importance of the virtue of patience in prayer. We can't be like the person who said, "Dear Lord, help me be patient—*right now*!" God answers our prayers, but in God's time, not ours.

Scripture offers several reasons why our prayers might not be answered according to our wishes. For example, God may want to answer our prayers, but our own actions and attitudes close us to him. A sinful heart on my part may bar me from a good hearing, for example, if my motive for asking for something comes from a lustful heart. The Letter to James says, "You ask but do not receive, because you ask wrongly, to spend it on your passions" (Jas 4:3). A second reason might be because we fail to pray with forgiveness in our hearts as instructed by Jesus, "When you stand to pray, forgive anyone against whom you have a grievance, so that your heavenly Father may in turn forgive you your transgressions" (Mk 11:25). But perhaps the most common reason we don't receive the desired answer is because we lack faith.

> But he should ask in faith, not doubting, for the one who doubts is like a wave of the sea that is driven and tossed about by the wind. For that person must not suppose that he will receive anything from the Lord, since he is a man of two minds, unstable in all his ways (Jas 1:6–8).

The antidote to doubtful prayer is the example of the father who begged Jesus to cure his child: "I do believe, help my unbelief!" (Mk 9:24).

At other times, we think God doesn't hear our prayers. Yet we really fail to understand his plans for us. God does answer our prayers, but we don't always recognize his answer. An unknown Confederate soldier put it well:

> I asked God for strength that I might achieve.
> I was made weak that I might learn humbly to obey.
> I asked God for health that I might do greater things.
> I was given infirmity that I might do better things.
> I asked for riches that I might be happy.
> I was given poverty that I might be wise.
> I asked for power that I might have the praise of men.
> I was given weakness that I might feel the need of God.
> I asked for all things that I might enjoy life.
> I was given life that I might enjoy all things.
> I got nothing that I asked for—
> but everything I had hoped for.
> Almost despite myself, my unspoken prayers were answered.
> I am among all men most richly blessed.

Remember that God always answers *sincere* prayer. But again his answer might be something we don't expect. Sometimes he answers no to our desires because they would harm us. At other times, God helps us see that what we are praying for is something that we can accomplish on our own with gifts he has already given us. Consider, for example, the student who begs God for an "A" on a test. But the student fails to study. In this case, it's unlikely that God will give the student the desired grade. Remember the adage, "God helps those who help themselves."

But God will always give his superabundant love to those who pray. Recall Jesus' own promise:

What father among you would hand his son a snake when he asks for a fish? Or hand him a scorpion when he asks for an egg? If you then, who are wicked, know how to give good gifts to your children, how much more will the Father in heaven give the holy Spirit to those who ask him (Lk 11:11-13)?

In conclusion, please note the wise observation of Trappist Basil Pennington on prayer:

God will give us whatever we want, asking in prayer—what we truly want, not what we say we want or even think we want. God listens to the heart, not to the lips. He knows, too, how limited our understanding and knowledge are. He sees our truest desires and knows how they can best be fulfilled. And this is what he grants. We may not see it at the moment, but we will in time. . . . If God seems to be saying "No" to some prayers, it is because he is saying "Yes" to the deepest prayer of our hearts.[1]

There are three answers to prayer: Yes, No, and Wait Awhile.

## Modern Parable on Prayer

A man left his Rolex in a hotel in another town. When he got home, he called the hotel. He told the manager his problem and she went to look for the watch. She found it, placed it in the hotel safe, and returned to the phone to tell the absent-minded caller the good news. But the caller had hung up the phone without leaving his name.

# eighty-one ➤ ➤ ➤ ➤ ➤ ➤ ➤

### What are Jesus' most important teachings? How should I respond to them?

"This is the time of fulfillment. The kingdom of God is at hand. Repent, and believe in the gospel."

~Mark 1:15

Jesus never wrote a book, yet the libraries of the world contain more works about him and his teaching than any other historical figure. Jesus never founded a college, yet countless millions have joyfully studied and discovered life in his lessons. Jesus was a brilliant teacher. Even his contemporaries recognized as much. The telling of parables was a favorite method he used to convey his unique, memorable, and life-changing teachings. His remarkable message centered on his Father's kingdom, God's reign. Jesus taught the following lessons, each with a built-in call for a personal response:

1. *God's kingdom is here right now.* The kingdom or reign of God refers to God's liberating activity in human history. Jesus preached that God is reconciling and renewing all things through the Son. Right now! God's reign is taking place on earth as it is in heaven. Although this process of renewal appears small like a mustard seed, God guarantees its inevitable growth. On the one hand, salvation is taking place through Jesus. On the other hand, the kingdom will reap a bounteous harvest at the end of time when the process begun in Jesus will perfectly reach its completion. We should live our lives in the realization that we are in the presence of God and God's reign.

2. *God's kingdom is a gift, open to everyone.* God loves everyone, especially sinners and outcasts. Like a good shepherd, God searches for the lost sheep. Like the merciful father of the prodigal son, God joyfully and unconditionally welcomes back wayward children. He only requires that we accept his freely given love and forgive others as he has forgiven us.

3. *The gospel requires a whole-hearted response.* Always prepared for Jesus's return, we should be like the man who sold every possession to buy the treasure that was hidden in a field. In short, we must be willing to sacrifice everything for God's reign.

4. *Because a new age has dawned, change your ways!* Reality is different now than it was before. Thus, we should uproot sin in our lives and ask for God's gift of forgiveness. We should develop a relationship with our loving God in prayer, addressing him on intimate terms as *Abba*, Father. We should always be confident that the Lord will answer our prayers. And we must be like God, sharing our gifts with the poor and not hoarding the many good things he has given us.

5. *Love everyone.* Jesus taught us to love everyone, even our enemies. "Love God above everything and our neighbors as ourselves," Jesus tells us. We prove that we love God when we love our neighbors, especially the least of our brothers and sisters. Love is not empty words but concrete acts: feeding the hungry, giving drink to the thirsty, welcoming the stranger, clothing the naked, visiting the sick and the imprisoned.

6. *Accept the challenge of the kingdom.* To follow Jesus' teaching requires sacrifice. We must pick up a cross in imitation of him. We do this when we accept the pain and suffering that comes our way for living a Christian life of service. In doing so, we, like Jesus, are promised fulfillment in this life and incredible happiness in the next.

**See for Yourself** ➤ ➤ ➤ ➤ ➤ ➤ ➤ ➤ ➤ ➤ ➤ ➤ ➤ ➤ ➤

Read these three beloved parables of Jesus, all found in Luke's gospel. They contain key points of Jesus' teaching.
- The Good Samaritan (Lk 10:25–37)
- The Prodigal Son (Lk 15:11–32)
- The Rich Man and Lazarus (Lk 16:19–31)

◄ ◄ ◄ ◄ ◄ ◄ ◄ ◄ ◄ ◄ ◄ ◄ ◄ ◄ ◄ ◄ ◄ ◄ ◄ ◄ ◄ ◄ ◄ ◄

# eighty-two ➤ ➤ ➤ ➤ ➤ ➤ ➤

### How should I read and interpret the Bible?

**M**uch of the Bible deals with a time, people, and culture that are foreign to us. Therefore, it takes effort to profitably read the Bible. Thanks to the efforts of countless scholars, the scriptures have been opened up so that all can *interpret* the Bible correctly.

The basic aim of *biblical interpretation* is to bring together the world of the reader and the world of the biblical text so the meaning of the text makes sense to the reader. Biblical interpretation has two essential tasks: (1) **gathering information** about the text, and (2) **explaining** the meaning of the text.

One approach to avoid in interpreting the Bible is *biblical fundamentalism*, which interprets scripture in an absolutely *literal* way. Fundamentalists believe God dictated the exact words in the Bible and the meaning of these words is obvious and clear. This overly literal approach ignores the human role in the composition of the Bible. Fundamentalism fails to account for changes in language over the centuries and overlooks the cultural differences between our age and that of biblical times. It even ignores the obvious inconsistencies that sometimes appear in the biblical accounts. For example, fundamentalists have a tough time explaining that the first chapter of Genesis says humans were the first creatures God made, while the second chapter states we were the last beings created.

Catholics do not approach the Bible from a fundamentalist perspective. Rather, Catholics endorse the *historical-critical method* of biblical interpretation. This method tries to understand biblical texts in their original setting, discovering the intention of the original author. For example, the historical-critical method will try to identify what the story of the snake talking to Adam and Eve meant to the original audience. It attempts to figure out if the teller of the story meant us to take it literally or not. In addition, it studies similar stories from other cultures in the ancient world in an effort to try to identify their literary form.

This method of reading the Bible relies on many important historical and literary methods like textual, literary, form, and redaction criticism, transmission history, archaeology, and sociology.

Biblical scholarship is beyond the present learning of most of us. We need the help of the experts to discover the text's original meaning. But personal Bible reading can help us discover what the scriptures mean for our personal lives. You can use the following six-step Bible-reading plan to help you apply the Bible to your own life:

**Step 1:** Choose a readable study Bible. It is readable if you can write, mark, underline, and highlight it. It is a study Bible if it contains an introduction to each book of the Bible and has good explanatory notes in the margins or at the bottom of the page.

**Step 2:** Begin with a short prayer by putting yourself in God's presence. Ask the Holy Spirit to open your mind to understand the biblical word. Ask the Holy Spirit to deepen your love for God and others as you spend your time studying and praying with the holy word.

**Step 3:** First Reading. Read the text. Try to get the overall picture without getting bogged down. What is taking place?

What strikes you? What confuses you? What new ideas did you get?

**Step 4:** Study the text. Go back and reread the text slowly. Be a detective. Engage your imagination, pretending that you are part of the story. Identify the following:

- *Who* is speaking? Who are the other people in the story?
- *What* is happening? *Why?*
- *Where* and *when* are the action, speech, and event taking place?

Fit this passage into the larger context. For example, what happened before?

Note any questions you might have. For example, pick out words you don't understand.

**Step 5:** Rely on helps. There are many ways to deepen your knowledge:

- Look at the introductions to the particular biblical book you are reading. Fix the passage in its historical context.
- Check the explanatory notes given in your Bible for the meaning of specific words and confusing passages.
- Look for cross-references. Reading other related scripture passage will sometimes clarify the text.
- Consult a biblical atlas, dictionary, or commentary for more in-depth information.

**Step 6:** Put it all together. Ask yourself these questions:

- What did this passage mean to its original audience?
- What does this passage mean to me? For example, what does it tell me about God, myself, other people, or life in general?
- Apply an insight you gained from your study to your life. For example, say you read about Jesus' compassion toward sinners. Perhaps you can resolve to be more forgiving to a classmate who

has recently done some harm to you. Or you studied one of the Psalms that praised God for his beautiful creation. Perhaps you could take a walk outside and notice God's marvelous handiwork and thank him for the gift of life and all its beauty.

**Try It Yourself** ➤ ➤ ➤ ➤ ➤ ➤ ➤ ➤ ➤ ➤ ➤ ➤ ➤ ➤ ➤ ➤

- Read the **Sermon on the Mount** (Matthew 5–7) using the format outlined above.

◄ ◄ ◄ ◄ ◄ ◄ ◄ ◄ ◄ ◄ ◄ ◄ ◄ ◄ ◄ ◄ ◄ ◄ ◄ ◄ ◄ ◄ ◄

# eighty-three ➤ ➤ ➤ ➤ ➤

*Where is Jesus today?*
*How can I meet him?*

A famous story tells of a group of salesmen rushing to catch a plane at a Chicago airport. One of the salesmen kicked over a table that held baskets of apples. Apples flew everywhere while the men dashed down the concourse.

However, knowing full well that he was guaranteeing that he would miss his flight, one man stopped and went back to help the sixteen-year-old girl whose apple stand was upset.

The girl was blind. The salesman helped her gather the apples and reset her display. Finally, he gave her $30 for the bruised fruit and asked her if she would be OK.

Crying gently, she said yes. After he apologized once more, the girl asked the compassionate salesman, "Sir, are you Jesus?"

Imagine the wonderment in the man's heart as he went to the ticket agent to reschedule his missed flight. He kept asking himself, "Am I Jesus?"

C ertainly, for those of us who wish to follow the Lord, we should act like him, just like this salesman did. So a good place to start when asking where to meet Jesus today is for you to look in the mirror! Then, turn to your neighbors and picture Jesus in them also. With the eyes of faith, the Holy Spirit enables us to see that we are God's adopted children. Through our baptisms, we are brothers and sisters of Jesus and, in him, brothers and sisters of one another. Here are some more clues and information about where you can meet Jesus today:

*Find Jesus in yourself.* Jesus lives in you! This earth-shaking truth sums up a key aspect of the gospel. So precious are you in God's eyes that his Son Jesus, our risen Lord, has chosen to be present in the world through his disciples. Jesus says,

"I am the true vine,
and my Father is the vine grower. . . .
I am the vine,
you are the branches" (Jn 15:1, 5).

*Find Jesus in the Church.* Whenever two or three gather in his name, Jesus is present (Mt 18:20). The Church is the body of Christ. Jesus is the head; you are one of the members. Baptism incorporates you into the body. You must use your individual talents to build up the body and continue Jesus' work of salvation and sanctification in the world.

*Find Jesus in the sacraments.* Jesus is present to us through sacred signs called the sacraments, visible signs of his care and love for us.

Jesus instituted the sacraments so he can remain close to his Church. The sacraments use materials symbols like words, actions, and concrete signs to express the love, concern, forgiveness, and real presence of the Lord.

The Eucharist is the central sacrament. It celebrates and creates Christian community. It reenacts the Paschal Mystery of God's unlimited love for you in Jesus. It challenges you to be Christ for others, to be "bread for the world."

Catholics believe that Jesus is wholly present in the consecrated bread and wine in the Eucharist, that is, "the body and blood, together with the soul and divinity, of our Lord Jesus Christ and, therefore, *the whole Christ is truly, really, and substantially contained*" (CCC, 1374).[2]

Jesus is also present in the priest who leads the worship. He is present in the community which comes to celebrate Jesus' loving actions. Furthermore, he is present in the scripture readings proclaimed at Mass. Finally, when we receive Holy Communion, we receive the Lord himself, not to keep him to ourselves but to let him shine through us as we become "light of the world" and "salt of the earth." We receive Christ to be Christ for others.

*Find Jesus in the Bible.* Think of the Bible as the words of the Word. The gospels, for example, contain the teachings of Jesus, teachings that can touch us and change our lives. The sacred scriptures are love letters sent to us from the one who loves us the most. God's word is a powerful sign of his presence and love. Reading the Bible often will help you meet the living Lord.

*Discover Jesus in prayer.* To experience Jesus as a living, concerned friend means spending time communicating with him. Prayer is simply conversation with the Lord. It helps you notice his presence and allows him to influence your mind, will, imagination, feelings, and memory. Conversing with the Lord as your closest, most understanding friend reassures you of his abiding love.

*Meet Jesus in the weak and humble.* Jesus especially identified himself with people society considered to be lowly and outcast. You can meet Jesus, just like the man in the story did, whenever you welcome the stranger, feed the hungry, give drink to the thirsty, or visit the sick and the imprisoned. You will *not* find

Jesus if you ignore those who are lonely, the poor, the physically and mentally challenged, the victims of prejudice, or old people who need your care. As Jesus says,

> "Amen, I say to you, what you did not do for
> one of these least ones, you did not do for me"
> (Mt 25:45).

*Find Jesus in love.* Scripture tells us that God is love. When we love, we will find Christ Jesus, God's great gift of love to us all:

> Beloved, let us love one another, because love is
> of God; everyone who loves is begotten by God
> and knows God. Whoever is without love does
> not know God, for God is love (1 Jn 4:7–8).

# ? eighty-four ➤ ➤ ➤ ➤ ➤ ➤

*I hear a lot about justice today. What does it mean for a Catholic teen to be just?*

An old Arab proverb says, "One hour of justice is worth a hundred of prayer." Philosophers have defined justice as "truth in action." The Bible tells us to do justice and love mercy. Pope Paul VI once wrote that we cannot have peace without justice.

St. Thomas Aquinas described justice as the virtue where we consistently give to each person what is his or her due by right. In other words, all people have certain inalienable rights because they are created in the divine image. Justice involves respecting the rights of others in the religious, social, political, and economic areas of life.

Here are twenty practices that can help you become a just person:

1.   Develop your God-given talents and then use them for the good of others.

2. Always be honest.
3. Always tell the truth.
4. Obey all just laws, including legislation on alcohol consumption and speed limits.
5. Treat with respect your classmates, coworkers, and those in authority.
6. Don't participate in gossip, especially about another's reputation.
7. Respect the property of others.
8. Give an honest day's work for an honest day's pay.
9. Be a peacemaker.
10. Identify and then try to overcome any prejudices you might have toward members of any racial or cultural group.
11. Show concern for the poor by limiting your spending habits and by sharing your good fortune with the needy.
12. Don't waste food.
13. Participate in food drives conducted at school or in your parish.
14. Fast on occasion to identify with the hungry.
15. Volunteer at a food bank.
16. Volunteer at senior citizens' home.
17. Dispose of waste materials responsibly. For example, don't litter. Participate in community recycling efforts.
18. Pray for peace.
19. Research possible careers that directly deal with social justice (for example, local politics, social work, inner-city teaching). Read about inspiring leaders who worked for justice (for example, Dorothy Day, St. Vincent de Paul).
20. Stay informed about one of the great social issues of our day. Examples abound—war, abortion, hunger, environmental issues, racism, sexism. Write letters to newspapers and politicians expressing your views on the topic.

Anglican Archbishop Desmond Tutu won a 1984 Nobel Peace Prize. His moral authority helped abolish the unjust separation of the races and its resulting discrimination in South Africa known as apartheid. He reminds us why we are here.

> God places us in the world as God's fellow workers—agents of transfiguration. We work with God so that injustice is transfigured into justice, so that there will be more compassion and caring, that there will be more laughter and joy, that there will be more togetherness in God's world.[3]

May we take our vocation as God's co-workers seriously and become agents of justice and compassion.

## What Would You Do?

Develop a plan to put justice into practice that you can act on in the next week. Develop another long-term plan that you can enact in the next six months.

# eighty-five

### How can I spread my Catholic faith?

Before ascending to heaven, Jesus gave this great commission to his apostles:

> Go, therefore, and make disciples of all nations, baptizing them in the name of the Father, and of the Son, and of the holy Spirit, teaching them to observe all that I have commanded you. And behold, I am with you always, until the end of the age (Mt 28:19–20).

The Church has always understood this passage to apply to all Christians. Technically, we are called to *evangelize*, that is, to spread the good news of Jesus Christ, to help him in his task of making the kingdom of God more visible on earth.

What does this mean for a teen? Does it mean going door-to-door for a year after graduation from high school (like Mormon youths do) to tell the world about Catholicism? Does it mean engaging in arguments with non-believers to try to win them over to Christianity with clever tactics? Does it mean signing on as a missionary to a foreign land?

The *Catechism of the Catholic Church* tells us simply that evangelization is "the proclamation of Christ by word and the testimony of life" (CCC, 905).

So the first way you can evangelize is by word, by sharing your faith with those who are searching and questioning. Perhaps a classmate asks you why you don't join in the mocking of another classmate. You can simply share your faith that this is not something a brother or sister of Jesus would do. Perhaps a coworker teases you for getting up on a Sunday morning to go to Mass. With a dose of good-natured humor, you might respond that you need this spiritual recharging because you grow close to Jesus and your Christian family when you receive Holy Communion, being sure to invite the person to join you. Perhaps a non-Catholic friend asks you a pointed question like one posed in this book, for example and you are prepared with a good answer.

At your age, a very good way to evangelize by word is simply to keep learning your faith so you know why the good news is truly good and why your Catholic faith is so precious. Then, you will be prepared to share it when people ask you questions or defend it when it is attacked.

But perhaps the best way for you to evangelize as a teenager is through the testimony of your life, that is, by your good example and by striving to live a life of virtue, justice, and love toward everyone. Jesus told us in the Sermon on the Mount that his followers were to be salt of the earth and light of the world. Just like salt preserves meat or adds flavor to food, a Christian's acts of love help Jesus' saving deeds touch lives and change the flavor of the world for the better. Just as light illuminates the way in the dark, the Christian who lets Christ shine through him or her is like a beacon pointing to the heavenly home that is meant for all at the end of our earthly journey. Jesus is the Way, the Truth, and the Life. Non-believers learn about Jesus from those who live Christ-like lives and who can point to Jesus who is our Savior.

If you live a life of love, spreading goodness into our world, people will take notice. They will see that you are different. They will ask you about your motivation. And you can then tell them why you are the way you are.

The Christophers have a motto, "It is better to light one candle than to curse the darkness." When you try to live a good Christian life, you will throw off plenty of light and will lead others to Christ.

May God bless you for wanting to share your faith. Finally, remember the last part of the quote in the great commission from Matthew's gospel: "I am with you always." You will not be alone. The Lord and his Holy Spirit will be with you.

# eighty-six ➤ ➤ ➤ ➤ ➤ ➤ ➤

*I don't particularly like people of other races. What's so wrong about that?*

You've probably heard the adage, "I don't have to like you, but I do have to love you." Christians have no option in loving. We must love everyone, including those who are different, even our enemies.

Liking has to do with preferences, our attraction to one thing, activity, or person, rather than another. Liking the familiar is normal and natural. However, when it comes to *not liking* people, be careful.

An African-American minister once remarked, "If you don't like me because of my ignorance, that's fine. I can go to school. If you don't like me because I'm dirty, I guess that's OK. I can wash and get clean. But if you don't like me because of my skin color, then *you* have a problem. Your problem is with God who made me this way."

A wise priest once asked his class, "How many races are there?" The students gave various answers, but they were all wrong. The correct response is: "There is only one race—the human race." We are all children of a loving God who made us. He loves us all equally. Jesus is the brother to us all. To dislike a brother or sister of the Lord is to tell God that he was wrong when he made us a rainbow of colors.

You need to ask: "Why is it that I dislike people who are different? Is it because I suffer from prejudice? Am I racist?"

*Racism* is the erroneous belief that some humans are inherently superior and others are innately inferior simply because of race. Racism is a form of prejudice (a prejudgment made without enough evidence) that can result in negative and harmful practices like speaking and listening to slurs against members of the other race (for example, crude jokes and characterizations), avoiding members of different racial groups, or being involved in violence toward members of a certain group. *Discrimination*—denying people their due rights on the basis of race—is another terrible effect of racism. Genocide—the killing of a particular race or ethnic group—is the worst consequence of racism. The twentieth century produced many evil people who engaged in genocide, but this vicious crime is still occurring even in this new millennium.

Racism is a serious sin because it insults God's children by violating essential human dignity. It is both unloving and unjust. The Church has vigorously condemned all forms of discrimination against people "on the basis of their race, color, condition of life, or religion" (*Declaration on the Relationship of the Church to Non-Christian Religions*, #5).

Ambrose Bierce, the American short-story writer, defined prejudice as "a vagrant opinion without visible means of support." Examine why you don't like certain people. If it is a matter of being close-minded, you can change. Make a serious effort to get to know and even befriend a classmate or co-worker who is different. Always remember there's only one race—the human race.

# eighty-seven ➤ ➤ ➤ ➤ ➤

*How can I decide the best course for my life? Right now, I have no idea.*

had a student who was out drinking with some friends. Inebriated, they drove their car across some railroad tracks thinking they could beat an oncoming train. They didn't. But miraculously, my student escaped serious injury. When I talked to him about this incident, he told me his life was spared because God had a plan for his life. I agreed with him. God does have a plan for each of us. A mature Christian will try to discover it, just as you are doing.

God's will for all of us is that we should be happy. And he has revealed the secret to happiness: Do something loving with your life using the gifts God has given you. The starting point for discovering and then doing God's will is to ask yourself honestly, "Do I want to be a good person? Do I want to be a person who loves?" Answer these questions with an enthusiastic yes and you will be on your way to discerning God's specific will for you.

Jesus said, "Seek and you will find" (Mt 7:7–8). You can't go wrong trying to find out God's will. However, two preliminaries are necessary for your search. First, *make God a part of your life.* You can do this by following the commandments of Christ and his Church. You will be in a better position to recognize

God's activity in your life. Second, *learn from Jesus.* Frequently read and reflect on the gospels. Pray to Jesus as your best friend and as one who perfectly discovered his Father's will. He will guide you on your quest.

To these two general practices, cultivate a spirit of prayerful reflection. Here are a few more helpful suggestions:

1. *Get to know yourself.* Jesus wants you to develop those gifts he has given you. What are your deepest inclinations and attractions? What brings you a feeling of peace and harmony? What jobs and careers appeal to you?

   Ask yourself, "What is holding me back? Am I too 'attached' to something that keeps me from being my true self? For example, do I always need to be in control? Do I always need others to approve of what I am doing?" Discovering what you need to work on can help free you to do God's will.

   Frequently ask yourself the question that St. Ignatius Loyola put to himself: "Where am I going and what for?" Are you on the right track to heaven, or are you going down the wrong road? If you keep your end goal in sight, the Lord will show you the means to get there.

2. *Ask for help.* Seek a wise counselor, an adult who knows you well. Openly discuss your dreams with this trusted friend. Also take to heart the advice that St. Paul gave his recent converts: "Test everything; retain what is good. Refrain from every kind of evil" (1 Thess 5:19).

3. *Be patient with yourself.* Thank God often for your many gifts. Ask for forgiveness when you sin. Relax. Reflect on these words of Blessed Francis Libermann:

In order to go to God with your heart, your mind must be undisturbed, indifferent. Keep it quiet. Do things simply, without too much analysis. If you really want to please God and intend to be in full agreement with His Will, you can't go wrong.[4]

# eighty-eight ➤ ➤ ➤ ➤ ➤

*How do I know if I have a religious vocation?*

Jesus Christ has a vocation, that is, a "calling" for all of his followers. He calls us to love, to be holy people who serve him through other people. Simply, your vocation is to be another Christ. But the way you will live out this general call will take place in one of four specific ways: as a single person, as a married person, as one who has entered religious life by professing vows like poverty, chastity, and obedience, or as an ordained deacon, priest, or bishop. (Some ordained men may also be a member of a religious community.)

Perhaps God is calling you to serve him as a priest, sister, or brother. This call may be subtle but also persistent. It often begins with an interior attraction, a yearning or desire to be as close as possible to God. Your interest may also be piqued by friendship with a priest, brother, or sister who is happy and fulfilled in his or her life of service. Don't stifle this attraction because of what you think others might say or because you find it a bit scary.

Here are several things to do to help you determine if the priesthood or professed religious life is for you:

- First, look at the type of person you are. Do you have the qualities needed to serve God as a priest or vowed religious? For example, are you basically a kind, genuine, moral person concerned about the welfare of others? Do you have a strong desire to serve Christ and his gospel? Are you unselfish, able to take direction, flexible, cooperative, loving? Are you emotionally well-balanced, of good intelligence, and physically healthy?

These are the basic qualities that the Church is looking for in candidates for the priesthood or religious life. The people who interview candidates are also looking to see if candidates can live the vow of celibacy. At this stage, though, don't be too worried about this. If the Lord is really calling you, he'll give you the graces to live out this vow for the sake of God's people.

Church or community officials also want to discover a person's *motives* for wanting to be a priest, sister, or brother. Service is an excellent motive. Seeking security or prestige, or escaping from loneliness or failed relationships are not good motives.

- Second, pray! Prayer is essential to friendship with Jesus and to discovering your vocation. He wants you to discover your calling, so honestly discuss your heart's deepest longings with him. Ask him for insight and courage about a possible vocation.

- Third, try out different ways to serve God. For example, help out with school or parish liturgies; volunteer to help in the grade-school religious education program; get involved in social justice and other service projects at school or as part of your parish youth group. Using your talents to serve others will help you discover if indeed God wants you to minister to his Church.

- Finally, if after some time your desire and yearning continue to persist, speak about your feelings with someone you admire who is already living out a similar calling. Once, this person had the same feelings as you do now. Without exerting pressure, he or she can gently direct you to which step to take next.

## Prayer for Vocations[5]

*Merciful and holy Lord,*
continue to send new laborers
into the harvest of your Kingdom!
Assist those whom you call
to follow you in our day;
contemplating your face,
may they respond with joy
to the wondrous mission
that you entrust to them
for the good of your People
and of all men and women.
~ Pope John Paul II

> > > > > > > > > > > > > > > > > > > > > >

## Might God Be Calling You to Serve His Church?

To see if you have some of the necessary qualities to serve God and his people as a priest, brother, or sister, mark the following questions using this scale:

>    0 — never/no
>    1 — sometimes/somewhat, but not strongly
>    2 — often/pretty strong/yes
>    3 — always/very strong/yes

_____ 1. Do you like helping others?

_____ 2. Is prayer important to you?

_____ 3. Do you like sharing your faith with others?

_____ 4. Are you a people person?

_____ 5. Would you like to make your life a miracle, that is, do something really worthwhile that makes a difference in people's lives?

_____ 6. Are you more interested in what God thinks of you than what the world thinks of you?

_____ 7. Do you love God above everything and your neighbor as yourself?

_____ 8. Are you proud of your Catholic faith?

_____ 9. Do you admire priests and religious sisters and brothers?

_____ 10. Are you a happy person who loves life?

_____ 11. Do you like talking to people, and do people like talking to you?

_____ 12. Do you like some quiet time to be alone and reflect on what's going on in your life?

_____ 13. Is receiving the Lord in Holy Communion important to you?

_____ 14. Do any of the ministries that priests and professed religious do attract you?

_____ 15. Do you think the Lord might be calling you to the religious life or priesthood?

Did you score a lot of *2's* and *3's*? If so, why not discuss with a priest or religious what God might be asking of you?

# eighty-nine ➤ ➤ ➤ ➤ ➤ ➤

### How do I keep in touch with my Catholic faith when I go to college?

Going away to college is both an exciting and frightening prospect. It is exciting because of the new-found freedom and novel experiences: a new roommate, deciding on an academic major, choosing class schedules, handling a budget, and the like. Furthermore, Mom and Dad are not on your back, telling you what to do and when to do it. But this new experience can be a little scary; you may get homesick. And you may not be sure that you can handle all the freedom. You might know someone who got into the party-scene or couldn't handle the academics at college and lasted only a semester. You wonder: "Can this happen to me?"

Well over 95 percent of the twelve thousand students I have taught in my thirty-six years of teaching went on to college, survived, and are now pursuing careers. Most of them are raising families. Over the years, more than thirty have even returned to my high school as teachers. All four of my own children have made it through college. As far as I can tell, most of these have kept the faith through the challenges college life presents to believers. Here are four main challenges to your faith that you will likely face when you go away to college, with suggestions for handling them in a positive way.

1. Expect to meet classmates who will disagree with you about everything from your prolife stand to your politics to your attitude to religion to your taste in music. The list is endless. In general, there is a "live-and-let-live" attitude toward all these issues.

   Many of your classmates will have absorbed the morality of our popular culture that holds that all values are merely a matter of taste. This conventional morality denies any absolutes in right or wrong. Thus, it contradicts Christ and the Church's teachings that some behaviors are wrong despite the circumstances or a person's intention. Most likely, you will hold a minority position on issues like abortion and the value of chastity.

2. You will likely have professors who will ridicule religion, belittle and vilify the Catholic Church, and deny the divinity of Jesus. Don't let this surprise or shock you. Many of them have also rejected absolute truth. Religion, especially the Catholic faith, which is the largest denomination in the United States, threatens many people.

3. You might encounter some fundamentalist religious groups on campus who will try to win you over to their religion. Their evangelistic outreach can be at times overwhelming. Tell them that you are a Catholic. Let them

know that you have professed faith in Christ since the time of your baptism. Make sure to connect with a Catholic community on or near campus (see below).

4. The biggest threat to your faith is likely to be yourself! You will be tempted to cave into the various freedoms of college life. These temptations are especially strong in the areas of sex, drinking, and drugs. But remember, the inappropriateness of these actions does not change because of your new environment or because others are doing them.

One excellent way to keep the faith at college is to find like-minded friends, including a roommate, who share your faith and values. They can help you keep your standards and find good, healthy ways to have fun without going along with what everyone else is doing. These friends can also go to Mass with you, a practice that goes by the wayside with too many college students.

Another help is Catholic campus ministry, a service present on both Catholic and non-Catholic campuses. The purposes of campus ministry include forming faith communities, helping students live the faith by forming Christian consciences, educating for justice, and aiding religious development.

Campus ministry may sponsor organizations like the Newman Club, a longtime Catholic organization on college campuses. Clubs like these promote the spiritual, intellectual, and social growth of their members. Former students of mine have joined such organizations, often emerging as leaders. They have told me what a lifeline these organizations were in helping their Catholic identity actually grow and develop while in college.

Many campus ministry programs sponsor Christian life communities, which sometimes share living quarters in a house off campus. You might want to join such a community.

Make sure that when you visit a prospective college, you set up an appointment with the director of Catholic campus ministry. This person will be most happy to tell you about life as a Catholic on that campus.

## Check These Out ➤ ➤ ➤ ➤ ➤ ➤ ➤ ➤ ➤ ➤ ➤ ➤ ➤ ➤ ➤ ➤

*The National Catholic College Admission Association*
www.catholiccollegesonline.org
- Great search engine to match your interests with a Catholic college

*Catholic Campus Ministry Association*
Links to Catholic Campus Ministry websites:
www.ccmanet.org/ccma.nsf/campussites?OpenPage

*Catholiclinks.org: Campus Ministries*
*—Newman Club Links*
www.catholiclinks.org/newmanunitedstates.htm

# ninety ➤ ➤ ➤ ➤ ➤ ➤ ➤ ➤ ➤ ➤ ➤

*In the last analysis, how will God decide whether or not I get into heaven?*

In a word, you must *love*. You must love God above all else, with all your heart, with all your soul, with all your mind, and with all your strength. And you must love your neighbor as yourself (cf. Mk 12:28–34).

- Loving God with all your heart means loving him with all your desires and inclinations. Do you desire God to be first in your life? Or does something else take his place: pleasure, popularity, possessions, power? If you make something else your god, you are on the wrong path to heaven.

- Loving God with all your soul means loving him with your very life. Have you chosen God as the goal of your life? Are you willing to commit your life to God—by serving him and following his will? Would you be willing to give up your life for him?

- Loving God with all of your mind means you keep God in your thoughts. It means you have an active prayer life, talking and listening to the Lord as your best friend. If God would forget you for an instant, you would cease to exist. But how often do you think of God? Do silly, trivial thoughts distract you from what is really important? Do you pray to God often?

- Loving God with all your strength means your energy goes into doing his will, not to accumulating worldly riches and honors. Only what God thinks of you is important. All else is secondary.

How do you love the invisible God you do not see? By loving his beautiful creations—especially the people around you. First, thank God for creating you and giving you marvelous gifts. Second, love yourself by respecting yourself. Third, develop the gifts God has given you. Fourth, use those gifts for other people.

Vince Lombardi, the legendary football coach, once said that a secret to his teams' success was that each player cared for one another, thinking about the next guy so he wouldn't get hurt, doing his job well so the other guys could do theirs as well. For Lombardi, the difference between mediocrity and greatness was the care and love the guys had for each other.

This describes wonderfully our life as Christians. We are members of the same team, the same family really. We must care for each other. Remember Jesus' parable of the Last Judgment (Mt 25: 31–46). Jesus tells us in this famous story that the sheep will inherit God's kingdom; the goats, on the other hand, will merit eternal punishment. The basis of judgment is simple: Did you feed the hungry, give drink to the thirsty, and welcome the stranger? Did you clothe the naked and visit the sick and imprisoned? In other words, whatever you do—or fail to do—to and for others will come back to you. And this is especially true if you respond to or neglect the least of God's children.

Once again, Jesus will ask you one simple question at judgment time: "Did you love—God, neighbor, self." If you can answer yes, then God will reward you in heaven beyond what you can possibly imagine. Isn't this the greatest news of our Catholic faith?

## A Concluding Word from the Author

Thank you for reading this book. Remember it is OK to ask questions. Never hesitate to approach a parish priest, a catechist, or a knowledgeable Catholic adult to help you answer them. Or research some answers for yourself at some of the Catholic websites listed in the next chapter. May God continue to bless you as you grow in knowledge of your Catholic faith. Please pray for me, as I will for you. May these words sustain you all the days of your life:

> May the road rise to meet you.
>
> May the wind be always at your back.
>
> May the sun shine warm upon your face.
>
> And rains fall soft upon your fields.
>
> And until we meet again,
>
> May God hold you in the hollow of His hand.
>
> — Traditional Irish Blessing

## Chapter SEVEN

# HELP ALONG THE WAY

Some Resources to Help You Live a Christian Life

## CATHOLIC AND CHRISTIAN LIVING
## SEVEN STEPS ON THE ROAD TO HEAVEN

### ONE. Avoid Sin and What Leads Us to Sin

#### Types of Sin:

- **Original sin:** sin of disobedience of Adam and Eve whereby they lost the grace of original holiness and became subject to death. Every person is born into the state of original sin with a fallen nature. Christ redeemed us from it.

- **Actual sin:** sins we commit through our actions or failure to act. The two kinds of actual sin are:

1. **Mortal sin:** "deadly sin" that involves (1) grave matter, (2) sufficient reflection, and (3) full consent of the will. It destroys our union with God and the Church and requires sacramental confession to be forgiven.
2. **Venial sin:** does not destroy divine life in the soul, but it lessens God's love in our hearts and weakens us to resist temptation. It usually involves lesser matters of

the moral law, or in serious matters a person acts without full knowledge or complete consent.

- **The Seven Capital Sins** (these are the root of other sins and vices)

  1. Pride
  2. Covetousness
  3. Lust
  4. Anger
  5. Gluttony
  6. Envy
  7. Sloth

## Express Sorrow for Your Sins by Celebrating the Sacrament of Reconciliation and by Reciting an Act of Contrition

My God, I am sorry for my sins with all my heart. In choosing to do wrong and failing to do good, I have sinned against you whom I should love above all things. I firmly intend, with your help, to do penance, to sin no more, and to avoid whatever leads me to sin. Our Savior Jesus Christ suffered and died for us. In his name, my God, have mercy.

## T W O. Follow the Pathway to Heaven

A. Live your life as Jesus instructed—the **Two Great Commandments**: "You shall love the Lord, your God, with all your heart, with all your soul, and with all your mind. You shall love your neighbor as yourself" (Mt 22: 37, 39; CCC 2055, 2083).

B. **Follow the Ten Commandments** (CCC, 2084–2557).
   1. I am the LORD your God; you shall not have strange Gods before me.
   2. You shall not take the name of the LORD your God in vain.

3. Remember to keep holy the LORD'S day.
4. Honor your father and your mother.
5. You shall not kill.
6. You shall not commit adultery.
7. You shall not steal.
8. You shall not bear false witness against your neighbor.
9. You shall not covet your neighbor's wife.
10. You shall not covet your neighbor's goods.

## THREE. Make Friends of the Angels

*In Greek, angel means "messenger," an important task God gave to them in communication with humans. The Old and New Testaments mention three angels by name: Michael, Gabriel, and Raphael.*

*Angels are pure spirits God created out of his love before the beginning of the world. They are friends of the Lord to whom we can pray for their intercession before the Lord. According to the tradition of theologians of the Middle Ages, there are nine choirs of angels, traditionally listed in groups of three.*

**Messengers (angels who minister to humans)**
1. Angels
2. Archangels
3. Principalities

**Governors (angels who have power over nature)**
4. Dominations
5. Virtues
6. Powers

**Counselors (angels who are constantly worshipping God)**
7. Thrones
8. Cherubim
9. Seraphim

- Read more about angels at this website: www.catholic.org/saints

- Pray this traditional prayer to your Guardian
  Angel:

Angel of God,
my Guardian dear,
to whom His love
commits me here,
ever this day (or night)
be at my side,
to light and guard,
to rule and guide.
Amen.

## FOUR. Observe the Holy Days of Obligation

On holy days, the Church celebrates special feasts. Catholics over the age of reason have a serious obligation to attend Mass on these days and avoid unnecessary work. There are six holy days in the United States:

1. Mary, Mother of God (January 1)
2. Ascension Thursday (40 days after Easter which is the Thursday of the Sixth Week of Easter; bishops in certain provinces can vote to have this feast celebrated on the Seventh Sunday of Easter )
3. Assumption of Mary into Heaven (August 15)
4. All Saints' Day (November 1)
5. Mary's Immaculate Conception (December 8)
6. Christmas (December 25)

## FIVE. Practice the Fruits of the Holy Spirit

The fruits of the Holy Spirit are perfections that the Holy Spirit forms in us as the first fruits of eternal glory (CCC, 1831).

1. Charity
2. Joy
3. Peace
4. Patience

5. Kindness
6. Goodness
7. Generosity
8. Gentleness
9. Faithfulness
10. Modesty
11. Self-Control
12. Chastity

## SIX. Put Your Faith into Action (CCC 2447)

*Corporal Works of Mercy (Mt 25:31–46)*

1. Feed the hungry.
2. Give drink to the thirsty.
3. Clothe the naked.
4. Shelter the homeless.
5. Visit the sick.
6. Visit the imprisoned.
7. Bury the dead.

*Spiritual Works of Mercy*

1. Counsel the doubtful. (Give advice to those who need it.)
2. Instruct the ignorant.
3. Admonish the sinner. (Correct wrongdoers.)
4. Comfort the sorrowful.
5. Forgive injuries.
6. Bear wrongs patiently.
7. Pray for the living and the dead.

## SEVEN. Receive the Holy Eucharist

The *Catechism of the Catholic Church* has the following names for the Eucharist, a word that means "thanksgiving" (see *CCC*, 1328-1329).

1. The Lord's Supper
2. Breaking of the Bread
3. Eucharistic assembly
4. Memorial of the Lord's passion and resurrection

5. Holy sacrifice of the Mass (also, Sacrifice of Praise, Spiritual Sacrifice, and Pure and Holy Sacrifice)
6. Holy and Divine Liturgy
7. Celebration of the sacred mysteries
8. Most Blessed Sacrament
9. Holy Communion
10. Holy Mass

## IT'S ALL ABOUT JESUS

### His Name and Important Titles (CCC, 430–455)

*Jesus*

Jesus' proper name. Means "Yahweh is salvation." Describes Jesus' role for humanity. To distinguish him from others, he might have been called Jesus the Nazarene; Jesus the Carpenter; or Jesus, Son of Joseph.

*Christ*

From the Greek word *Christos*, which translates the Hebrew word for *Messiah*. Means "anointed one." Jesus fulfilled Old Testament prophecies and became the savior of all people.

*Lord*

From the Greek word *Kyrios* which renders the Hebrew name for God, YAHWEH. To call Jesus Lord is to express faith in his divinity.

*Prophet, Priest, King*

"Prophet" refers to Jesus' mission of speaking for God the Father, "Priest" refers for his being the unique go-between God and humans, and "King" marks him as ruler of the world who came to serve, not be served.

*Son of David*

In the line of Israel's first king, this title acknowledges that Jesus has the authority to establish the Kingdom of God on earth. He is the promised Messiah, the anointed one.

*Son of God*

Reveals Jesus' identity as God's unique Son and his role as savior of the world.

### Son of Man

The most common title Jesus used of himself (found over eighty times in the New Testament). Stresses his humanity and identification with us. But following the book of Daniel, it highlights Jesus' saving role as God's unique agent who will usher in God's kingdom.

## The Seven Last Words of Jesus from the Cross

1. "Father, forgive them, they know not what they do" (Lk 23:34).
2. "Woman, behold, your son." . . . "Behold, your mother" (Jn 19:26–27).
3. "I thirst" (Jn 19:28).
4. "Amen, I say to you, today you will be with me in Paradise" (Lk 23:43).
5. *"Eli, Eli, lema sabachthani?"* "My God, my God, why have you forsaken me?" (Mt 27:46; also, Mk 15:34).
6. "It is finished" (Jn 19:30).
7. "Father, into your hands I commend my spirit" (Lk 23:46).

## SEVEN SACRED SYMBOLS FOR JESUS

**Alpha and Omega.** In the book of Revelation, the Risen Lord says, "I am the Alpha and the Omega, the one who is and who was and who is to come, the almighty." The Alpha and Omega are the first and last letters of the Greek alphabet. The symbolism points us to Christ's eternal nature.

**Chi-Rho.** Early Christians took the first two letters for the word Christ in Greek to develop this sacred monogram to profess their faith in Jesus Christ.

**Fish.** A secret sign used by early persecuted Christians to designate themselves as followers of Jesus. The Greek word for fish is *ichthus*. The early Christians thought of this as a Greek acronym for *Iesous* (Jesus) *CHristos* (Christ) *THeou* (God) *Uiou* (Son) *Soter* (Savior). Thus the fish is short hand for "Jesus Christ, Son of God, Savior."

The first three letters of the Greek word for "Jesus." The horizontal line that forms a cross is the sign for an abbreviation. Another common interpretation is that these are Latin letters to represent the words *In hoc signo* (*vinces*)—"In this sign, you will conquer." A historical reference here is to the Emperor Constantine who saw a vision of the cross before marching to victory. (Some mistakenly think these are English letters meant to represent the words "I have suffered.)

INRI On top of the cross, posted in Hebrew, Latin, and Greek, was the crime of the crucified (Jn 19:19-20). INRI is an abbreviation of Jesus' crime in the Latin language: I=Jesus N=of Nazareth R=King I=of the Jews

**Cross.** The most common cruciform is the Latin cross, which reminds us of Christ's supreme sacrifice. The cross is empty to symbolize the resurrection and our hope for eternal life.

**The Shepherd.** The Good Shepherd is found in the Catacombs. It symbolizes the Lord's loving care for each of us and his willingness to give up his life for his flock.

## 15 GREAT SAYINGS OF JESUS

### 5 Sayings to Comfort You

1. Therefore I tell you, do not worry about your life, what you will eat [or drink], or about your body, what you will wear. Is not life more than food and the body more than clothing? . . . Do not worry about tomorrow; tomorrow will take care of itself. Sufficient for a day is its own evil.
~Matthew 6:25, 34

2. Come to me, all you who labor and are burdened, and I will give you rest. Take my yoke upon you and learn from me, for I am meek and humble of heart; and you will find rest for yourselves. For my yoke is easy, and my burden is light.
~Matthew 11:28–30

3. Ask and you will receive; seek and you will find; knock and the door will be opened to you. For everyone who asks, receives; and the one who seeks, finds; and to the one who knocks, the door will be opened.
~Luke 11:9–10

4. I am the resurrection and the life; whoever believes in me, even if he dies, will live, and everyone who lives and believes in me will never die. Do you believe this?
~John 11:25–26

5. For God so loved the world that he gave his only Son, so that everyone who believes in him might not perish but have eternal life.
~John 3:16

### 5 Sayings to Call You to Greatness

1. But I say to you, love your enemies, and pray for those who persecute you, that you may be children of your heavenly

Father, for he makes his sun rise on the bad and the good, and causes rain to fall on the just and the unjust.

~Matthew 5:44–45

2. Whoever wishes to come after me must deny himself, take up his cross, and follow me. For whoever wishes to save his life will lose it, but whoever loses his life for my sake and that of the gospel will save it.

~Mark 8:34–35

3. Take care to guard against all greed, for though one may be rich, one's life does not consist of possessions.

~Luke 12:15

4. Much will be required of the person entrusted with much, and still more will be demanded of the person entrusted with more.

~Luke 12:48

5. I give you a new commandment: love one another. As I have loved you, so you also should love one another. This is how all will know that you are my disciples, if you have love for one another.

~John 13:34–35

## 5 Sayings to Take to Heart

1. But I say to you, whoever is angry with his brother will be liable to judgment.

~Matthew 5:22

2. But many that are first will be last, and [the] last will be first.

~Mark 10:31

3. But I tell you, if you do not repent, you will all perish.

~Luke 13:5

4. You also must be prepared, for at an hour you do not expect, the Son of Man will come.

~Luke 12:40

5. He [the Son of Man] will answer them,
"Amen, I say to you, what you did not do for
one of these least ones, you did not do for me."

And those will go off to eternal punishment, but the righteous to eternal life.

~Matthew 25:45–46

## Some Interesting Catholic Facts to Know

### By the Number

Did you know that . . .

- Catholics numbered 1.085 billion in 2003, 17.2% of the world's population
- 50% of the world's Catholics live in the Americas
- Worldwide, there are about 4,700 bishops and 405,500 priests
- 23% of the population of the United States (around 68 million people) are Catholic
- Approximately 40%—or 29 million—of U.S. Catholics are Hispanic
- There are more than 19,200 parishes in the 195 dioceses and eparchies (dioceses of the Eastern Catholic Church) in the United States
- The average age for priests in the United States is 61
- The Catholic Church runs the largest network of private schools in the United States. Over 2.53 million students are enrolled in its 6,736 elementary schools and 1,378 high schools
- 772,000 students attend 234 Catholic colleges and universities in the United States
- Between 900 and 1,000 people live in Vatican City; about 3,000 lay workers live outside the city

(When asked how many people work in the Vatican, with a twinkle in his eye, Pope John XXIII said, "About half of them.")

**Sources:** *2004 Pontifical Yearbook; 2006 Catholic Almanac*; the United States Conference of Catholic Bishops, *Catholic Information Project* "The Catholic Church in America—Meeting Real Needs in Your Neighborhood" found at: http://usccb.org/comm/cipfinal.pdf; *The World Factbook; Catholic Review Online*; and Center for Applied Research in the Apostolate (CARA)

## About the Popes

Did you know that . . .

- John Paul II was the only Polish pope and the first non-Italian to be elected pope in 450 years and had the third-longest papal reign in history.
- Benedict XVI is the 265th pope, the first German pope in close to 500 years, and a brilliant scholar who was the right-hand man of John Paul II.
- The longest reigning pope was Pius IX (1846-1878)—thirty-two years.
- John is the most commonly used name (twenty-five times, including two anti-popes but not including John Paul I and John Paul II); next, Gregory (sixteen times) which is tied with Benedict (sixteen times).
- According to the Catholic Encyclopedia, there have been thirty anti-popes (men whose elections were declared uncanonical, contrary to Church law).
- The Pope wears white because Pope St. Pius V (1566–1572) was a Dominican who wore his white habit during his papacy. This began the tradition of the pope wearing white.

- There has been only one English pope—Adrian IV (1154–1159).
- Pope Celestine V (Peter di Morone) resigned from being pope in 1294 after only five months in office. He was a holy hermit, eighty-four years of age, when elected to follow Nicholas IV (1288–1292) and soon realized he was not able to deal with worldly leaders. He died two years later and was canonized in 1313.
- Pope Paul VI (1963–1978) was the first to address the United Nations.
- That besides having the title *pope*, the Holy Father is also known as the Bishop of Rome, the Supreme Pontiff of the Universal Church, the Vicar of Christ, the Primate of Italy, and the Patriarch of the West.
- Jesus changed the name of Simon to Peter who was to became the first pope (AD 42–64?/67?). But John II (533–535) was the first pope to change his name after election. His baptismal name was Mercury.
- Pope Leo XIII (1878–1903) appeared in a short film in 1896, only a year after the invention of the motion picture. The film has the pope getting out of a carriage and walking to a bench in the Vatican gardens where he sat down and began to read.

### About the Church Through the Centuries

Did you know that . . .
- The Roman Emperor Constantine finally legalized Christianity in 313 in the Edict of Milan. Thus ended three centuries of on-and-off again persecution against Christians.
- The first ecumenical (worldwide) council took place in a small town in Turkey—Nicaea—in 325 to define clearly that Jesus was divine and not

merely God's greatest teacher, as held by the Arian heretics.
- The Great Schism (split) took place between the Eastern Orthodox churches and Roman Catholicism in 1054.
- The Church established the first European universities.
- The "Babylonian Captivity of the Church" began in 1309. For seventy years the papacy was in Avignon, France, and under the thumb of the French king.
- Martin Luther, a major player in the Protestant Revolt, was an Augustinian priest who at first tried to reform the Church from within.
- The first Catholics in the United States were from Spain and settled in Florida.
- John Carroll (1735–1815) was the first bishop appointed to serve American Catholics; his cousin Charles was a signer of the Declaration of Independence.
- Pope John XXIII convened the twentieth ecumenical council, namely, the Second Vatican Council (1962–1965).

## About Catholic Practices

Did you know that . . .
- You can pray simply by sitting in God's presence and saying no words.
- Fasting is a form of prayer.
- Christians at one time turned toward Jerusalem to pray.
- When we kneel in prayer, we are showing our humility before God.
- When you bless yourself with holy water, you are renewing your baptism and showing your faith

in the Blessed Trinity in whose name you were baptized.

- Easter is a movable feast that occurs on the first Sunday after the vernal equinox (when the sun is directly above the equator); thus, it can occur any time between March 22 and April 25.
- A monstrance holds the host when the Blessed Sacrament is exposed for worship.
- When we say Amen to end our prayers, we are stating our agreement with what we just spoke. It means "So be it" or "It is true."
- Alleluia (or hallelujah) is from the word Hallel, the greatest expression of praise in the Hebrew language. Joined to Jah, a shortened form of the Hebrew name of God, JHVH (meaning "I AM"), it becomes Hallelujah. (Alleluia is the spelling in Latin.)
- The sacrament of Penance also has the names of the sacrament of Reconciliation, forgiveness, confession, or conversion (CCC, 1422f).
- The ministers of the sacrament of Matrimony are the couple themselves.
- The three degrees of ministerial priesthood are bishops, priests, and deacons.
- "Monsignor" is a title of honor, meaning "my lord."
- The month of May is dedicated to Mary.
- The Blessed Mother is the patron saint of the United States under the title the Immaculate Conception.

**To learn more about the saints, check these websites:**

**Catholic Online**

www.catholic.org/saints

**Catholic Community Forum**

www.catholic-forum.com/saints/indexsnt.htm

**Catholic Doors Ministry**

www.catholicdoors.com/misc/patron.htm

## CATHOLIC SYMBOLISM

### Catholic Mottoes, Phrases, and Abbreviations

**AMDG** (*Ad Majorem Dei Gloriam*)
"For the Greater Glory of God"
Motto of St. Ignatius of Loyola and the Society of Jesus (Jesuits)

**Benedicere, Laudare, Praedicare**
"To bless, To praise, To preach"
Motto of the Dominican Order

**BVM**
Blessed Virgin Mary

**DV** (*Deo Volente*)
"God willing"

**Deo gratias**
"Thanks be to God."
Response at the end of liturgy.

**Deus Meus et Omnia**
"My God and My All."
Motto of the Franciscan Order

**Deus vult!**
"God wills it!"
Motto of the Crusades

**DOM** (*Deo optimo maximo*)
"To God who is the best and greatest"
Motto of the Benedictine Order

**Habemus Papam!**
"We have a Pope!"
Said after a new Pope is elected.

**JMJ** *"Jesus, Mary, and Joseph"*
Written on the top of papers by many Catholic students to dedicate their work to the Holy Family

**In hoc signo vinces**
"In this sign you will conquer."
Sign of the Cross seen in the sky by Constantine

"It is better to light one candle than to curse the darkness."
Motto of the Christophers

**Laus Deo semper**
"Praise God always."
Motto of saints, especially monks

**Mea culpa, mea culpa, mea maxima culpa**
"Through my fault, through my fault, through my most grievous fault."
Said while striking one's breast three times as a sign of repentance during the Confiteor at Mass

**Ora et Labora**
"Pray and Work."
Motto of the Benedictine and Trappist Orders

**Pax Christi**
"Peace of Christ"

**R.I.P.** (*Requiescat In Pace*)
"May he or she rest in peace."

**Totus Tuus**
"Totally yours"
Motto of Pope John Paul II

**¡Viva Cristo Rey!**
"Long live Christ the King!" (Spanish)

Battle cry of defenders of Catholicism against Communism in the Spanish Civil War, and of the Mexican "Cristeros" who fought against the Masonic-Bolshevik takeover of their country during the Mexican Revolution

## Liturgical Colors

**Black:** sign of death and mourning. Good Friday; along with violet and white, may be used for Masses of Christian burial.

**Gold:** royalty and purity; can be used in place of green, red, or white.

**Green:** hope, life, fidelity. Used on the Sundays in Ordinary Time.

**Red:** the color of blood, thus sacrifice; the Holy Spirit; charity. Used to commemorate the Lord's passion (Palm Sunday, Good Friday); feasts of the apostles and evangelists; martyrs—those who shed their blood for the faith; and the Holy Spirit (Pentecost Sunday).

**Rose:** joy in the midst of penance; may be used on the Third Sunday of Advent (Gaudete Sunday) and the Fourth Sunday of Lent (Laetare Sunday)

**Violet/purple:** penance, sorrow, preparation. Used during Advent and Lent.

**White:** purity, triumph, joy, virginity, innocence. Used on feasts of the joyful and glorious mysteries of our Lord's life (for example, Christmas and Easter), and on feasts of Mary, the angels, and saints who were not martyrs.

## Numbers

**1** = Unity
- There is only *one* God
- Jesus prayed that we all be one (Jn 17)

**2** = Duality
- There are two natures (divine and human) in Jesus Christ
- Good and Evil
- Night and Day

**3** = Perfection (all there is)
- Three Persons in the Blessed Trinity—Father, Son, and Holy Spirit
- Three theological virtues—faith, hope, and charity
- Three dimensions of a person—body, soul, spirit

**4** = Completion
- Four gospels and four evangelists
- Four weeks in Advent

- Four cardinal virtues—prudence, justice, fortitude, temperance
- Number sign of nature: four seasons

5 = Bad number
  - Five wounds of Christ
  - Five senses that lead us into temptation

6 = Sense #1: perfection 3X2=6
  - God creates in six days; his work brought to perfection
  - Sense #2: imperfection, since it falls one short of Seven, the perfect number

7 = Perfection (3+4=7); completion of a series; rest; totality
  - God rests on the seventh day (Sabbath)
  - Seven gifts of the Holy Spirit
  - Seven sacraments
  - Seven days of the week
  - Seven tongues of fire
  - Jesus spoke seven words from the cross
  - Seven petitions in the Lord's Prayer
  - Seven seals on the book of life
  - Seven churches listed in the Book of Revelation

8 = Regeneration, new beginning, resurrection (beginning of a new series 7+1)
  - Many baptismal fonts are eight-sided
  - Eight Beatitudes

9 = Mystery, perfection multiplied by perfection (3x3); perfect unity
  - Nine fruits of the Holy Spirit
  - Nine choirs of angels

10 = Complete, order and worldly power
  - Ten Commandments
  - Plagues of Egypt
  - Ten lepers

**12** = Complete cycle (2x6); universal completion (3x4); totality

- Twelve tribes of Israel
- Twelve apostles
- Twelve months of the year

**13** = Betrayal

- Thirteen people at the Last Supper, one of whom (Judas Iscariot) betrayed Jesus

**40** = Trial; one generation of people

- The Flood lasted forty days and forty nights
- The Chosen People wandered for forty years in the desert
- Jesus is tempted in the desert forty days
- Jesus ministers for forty days after his resurrection

**100** = Completeness, fullness (10 x 10)

**666** = Perfect imperfection

- The Beast of the Book of Revelation (most likely, the Emperor Nero who persecuted Christians)

**1000** = Very large number; eternity

**144,000** = Untold number

- 12 equals the total; 12X12 is the total total—everything or everyone
- Multiplying anything by 10, 100, or 1000 highlights the totality even more
- Thus, 144,000 represents the complete total of the saints that God will save, which includes an innumerable, immense, unimaginably large number

## SOME FAMOUS CATHOLICS[1]

### Celebrities: Deceased

Bing Crosby (singer, actor)
Bela Lugosi (actor: Dracula)
John Candy (comedian, actor)

Carroll O'Connor (actor: Archie Bunker)
Grace Kelly (actress)
Perry Como (singer)
Gene Roddenberry (Creator of Star Trek)

## Living Celebrities

Anthony Hopkins (actor)
Farrah Fawcett (actress)
Nicole Kidman (actress)
Conan O'Brian (TV host, comedian)
Regis Philbin (TV personality)
Moira Kelly (actress)
Pierce Brosnan (actor)
Brigitte Bardot (actress)
Sylvester Stallone (actor)
Faye Dunaway (actress)
Mel Gibson (actor)
Martin Sheen (actor)
Brooke Shields (actress)
Bill O'Reilly (journalist)
Jim Caviziel (actor, played Jesus in *The Passion of the Christ*)

## Musicians

Antonio Vivaldi (Baroque composer and priest)
John Michael Talbot (contemporary Christian singer)
Dave Brubeck (Jazz composer and pianist)
Celine Dion (singer)

## Authors

James Joyce (Irish writer)
J.R.R. Tolkien (the author of *The Lord of Rings*)
Flannery O'Connor (American author)
G. K. Chesterson (English author, Catholic Apologist)

## Sports Figures

Mike Piazza (baseball player)
Tom Brady (football player)
Babe Ruth (the legendary star of the New York Yankees)
Vince Lombardi (coach, daily communicant)

## Politicians

John F. Kennedy (U.S. president)
Jerry Brown (former governor of California)
Mario Cuomo (former governor of New York)
Geraldine Ferraro (vice-presidential candidate)
Lech Walesa (Polish labor leader and former president of
  Poland)
Rudy Guiliani (former mayor of New York City)
Tom Ridge (former governor of Pennsylvania; first Secretary
  of Homeland Security)
Jeb Bush (governor of Florida)
Antonin Scalia (Supreme Court; his son is a priest)
Clarence Thomas (Supreme Court; convert to Catholicism)
John Roberts (Chief Justice of the Supreme Court)

## Scientists

Louis Pasteur (French chemist, biologist)
Gregor Mendel (Austrian monk, founder of genetics)
Nicholas Copernicus (Polish astronomer, the heliocentric
  theory)
Blaise Pascal (French mathematician and writer)

## ELEVEN GOOD WORDS FOR CATHOLICS TO KNOW

**Annulment**—An official church declaration that what
appeared to be a Christian marriage never existed in the first
place.

**Beatific Vision**—Seeing God "face-to-face" in heaven, the source of our eternal happiness; final union with the Triune God for all eternity.

**Catechesis**—Process of systematic education in the faith for young people and adults with the view of making them disciples of Jesus Christ.

**Concupiscence**—An inclination to commit sin that can be found in human desires and appetites as a result of original sin.

**Dogma**—A central truth of revelation that Catholics are obliged to believe.

**Encyclical**—A letter on some important topic written by the pope and sent to the whole Church or to the whole world. An encyclical contains the ordinary teaching of the Magisterium.

**Hierarchy**—The official, sacred leadership in the Church made up of the Church's ordained ministers—bishops, priests, and deacons. The symbol of unity and authority in the Church is the pope, the Bishop of Rome who is the successor of St. Peter.

**Magisterium**—The official teaching authority of the Church. The Lord bestowed the right and power to teach in his name on Peter and the apostles and their successors, that is, the bishops and the pope as their leader.

**Sanctifying grace**—The grace, or gift of God's friendship, that heals our fallen human nature and gives us a share in the divine life of the Blessed Trinity. A habitual, supernatural gift, it makes us perfect, holy, and Christ-like (*CCC*, 1999).

**Subsidiarity**—A principle of Catholic social justice that holds that a community of a higher order should not interfere in the internal life of a community of a lower order, depriving it of its functions. For the sake of the common good, higher order societies should support and help lower order societies as needed.

**Transubstantiation**—The term used to describe that at the consecration of the bread and wine at Mass their entire substance is turned into the entire substance of the Body and Blood of Christ, even though the appearances of bread and wine remain.

## INTERESTING INTERNET SITES

### Good Youth Sites

DisciplesNow.com
www.disciplesnow.com
Life Teen
www.lifeteen.org
OmegaRock.com
www.omegarock.com
OneRock Online
www.onerock.com

### Good Catholic Research Sites

Catholic Information Network (CIN)
www.cin.org
Theology Library
www.shc.edu/theolibrary
eCatholicism.org
www.ecatholicism.org
Resources for Catholic Educators
www.silk.net/RelEd
Don't be fooled. This is a great source of information for students, too.
New Advent
www.newadvent.org
Lists top Catholic Internet sites as well as having the old *Catholic Encyclopedia*.
Catholic Pages
www.catholic-pages.com

**Go to the source:**

The Holy See
www.vatican.va
United States Conference of Catholic Bishops
www.usccb.org

## PRAYERS AND INSPIRATIONAL SAYINGS

### Let Go and Let God

MY LORD GOD, I have no idea where I am going. I do not see the road ahead of me. I cannot know for certain where it will end. Nor do I really know myself, and the fact that I think that I am following your will does not mean that I am actually doing so. But I believe that the desire to please you does in fact please you. And I hope I have that desire in all that I am doing. I hope that I will never do anything apart from that desire. And I know that if I do this you will lead me by the right road though I may know nothing about it. Therefore will I trust you always though I may seem to be lost and in the shadow of death. I will not fear, for you are ever with me, and you will never leave me to face my perils alone.

—Thomas Merton, *Thoughts in Solitude*
© Abbey of Gethsemani

### Christ Needs You

Christ has no body now but yours,
No hands but yours,
No feet but yours.
Your eyes are the eyes through which
Christ's compassion must look out on the world.
Yours are the feet with which
He is to go about doing good.
Yours are the hands with which
He is to bless us now.
          —St. Teresa of Avila

## Prayer for Peace (attributed to Saint Francis of Assisi)

Lord, make me an instrument of your peace.
Where there is hatred, let me sow love;
where there is injury, pardon;
where there is doubt, faith;
where there is despair, hope;
where there is darkness, light;
where there is sadness, joy.
O Divine Master, grant that I may not seek so much to be
consoled as to console;
to be understood, as to understand,
to be loved, as to love.
For it is in giving that we receive,
it is in pardoning that we are pardoned,
and it is in dying that we are born to eternal life.

## Prayer for Trust in God

GOD has created me to do some definite service; God has committed some work to me which has not been committed to another. I have my mission—I may never know it in this life, but I shall be told of it in next.

I am a link in a chain, a bond of connection between persons. God has not created me for naught. I shall do good. I shall do God's work. I shall be an angel of peace, a preacher of truth in my own place.

Whatever, wherever I am, I can never be thrown away. If I am in sickness, my sickness may serve the Lord; in perplexity, my perplexity may serve the Lord; if I am in sorrow, my sorrow may serve the Lord. God does nothing in vain. Therefore I will trust in the Lord.

—Cardinal John Henry Newman

## Let Nothing Disturb Thee

Let nothing disturb thee.
Let nothing affright thee.
All things are passing.
Patience obtains all things.
He who has God has everything.
God alone suffices.
— Saint Teresa of Avila's Bookmark

## A Prayer for Courage

Give me whatever you ask of me,
then ask of me whatever you will, Lord.
Remember that we are only dust,
for of dust you have made us!
But I can do anything
in him who strengthens me;
Lord, strengthen me, and I can do everything.
Give me whatever you ask of me,
then ask of me what you will. Amen.
—St. Augustine

## St. Patrick's Breastplate

Christ with me,
Christ before me,
Christ behind me,
Christ in me,
Christ beneath me,
Christ above me,
Christ on my right,
Christ on my left,
Christ when I lie down,
Christ when I sit down,
Christ when I arise,
Christ in the heart of every man who thinks of me,
Christ in the mouth of everyone who speaks of me,

Christ in every eye that sees me,
Christ in every ear that hears me.
   —St. Patrick

## Resolute Faith

No, in all these things we conquer overwhelmingly through him who loved us. For I am convinced that neither death, nor life, nor angels, nor principalities, nor present things, nor future things, nor powers, nor height, nor depth, nor any other creature will be able to separate us from the love of God in Christ Jesus our Lord.
   —St. Paul (Romans 8:37–39)

## Jesus Prayer

(to be recited for several minutes while breathing rhythmically—breathing in while reciting the first phrase, out with the second, and so forth)
   **Lord Jesus Christ, Son of God, have mercy on me, a sinner.**

## Prayer for Generosity

Lord, teach me to be generous.
Teach me to serve you as you deserve;
to give and not count the cost;
to fight and not heed the wounds;
to toil and not seek for rest;
to labor and not ask for reward, except to know
that I am doing your will. Amen.
   —St. Ignatius of Loyola

## Wise Words

Do not look forward in fear to the changes of life;
Rather look to them with full hope that as they arise,
God, whose very own you are, will lead you safely
through all things;

And when you cannot stand it, God will carry you in His arms.

Do not fear what may happen tomorrow;
The same everlasting Father who cares for you today
will take care of you today and every day.
He will either shield you from suffering or will give you
unfailing strength to bear it.

Be at peace and put aside all anxious thoughts and imaginations.

—St. Francis de Sales[2]

## What the Bible says about . . .

**Anxiety/depression:** Psalm 25; Psalm 130; Matthew 6:25–34
**Feelings of inferiority:** Jeremiah 1:4–10; John 15
**The need for forgiveness:** Psalm 51; Psalm 130; Luke 15:11–24
**Peer pressure:** Proverbs 1:7–19; Ephesians 5:1–20
**Seeking God's will:** Micah 6:6-8; Matthew 5:14–16;
1 John 4:7–21
**Taking up responsibility:** Proverbs 2:1–11; Isaiah 11:1–9;
2 Timothy 2:14–26
**Temptation:** James 1:12–18
**Tough decisions:** Psalm 139; Colossians 3:12–17

# NOTES

&gt;&gt;&gt;&gt;&gt;&gt;&gt;&gt;&gt;&gt;&gt;&gt;&gt;&gt;&gt;&gt;&gt;&gt;&gt;&gt;&gt;&gt;&gt;&gt;&gt;&gt;&gt;&gt;&gt;&gt;&gt;&gt;&gt;&gt;&gt;

*All websites in notes verified as active on dates listed.*

## Chapter 1: Parents and Other Mysteries of Life

1. American Association of Suicidology, "Youth Suicide Fact Sheet," <http://www.suicidology.org/associations/1045/files/AAS%20Suicide%20 Fact%20Sheet%20-%20Youth%20Suicide%20Fact%20Sheet.pdf> (21 December 2005).
2. Ibid.
3. National Adolescent Health Information Center, "Fact Sheet on Suicide: Adolescent & Young Adults," <http://youth.ucsf.edu/nahic/img/Suicide.pdf> (27 May 2004).

## Chapter 2: Why Do I Have to Go to Confession?

1. Quoted on the *EWTN Online's* tribute to Mother Teresa. "Mother Teresa of Calcutta: Peacemaker, Pioneer, Legend: A Vocation of Service," <http://www.ewtn.com/motherteresa/vocation.htm> (21 December 2005).
2. Quoted by *Catholic Answers*, "Infant Baptism," <http://www.catholic.com/library/Infant_Baptism.asp> (21 December 2005).
3. Here the *Catechism of the Catholic Church* is quoting from the Council of Trent (1551): DS1651.
4. The three quotes on the Eucharist in this section were found on the excellent website, *The Real Presence Association*. Be sure to check it out for some outstanding teachings about this sacrament of love: <http://www.therealpresence.org/>.
5. United States Conference of Catholic Bishops, *USCCB Online*, Committee on the Liturgy, "Non-Catholics and Holy Communion," <http://www.usccb.org/liturgy/q&a/mass/communion.shtml> (4 January 2006).
6. Found at *BrainyQuote*, <http://www.brainyquote.com/quotes/quotes/a/ abrahamlin106142.html> (21 December 2005).
7. All these facts are reported and documented on *Alcohol Policies Project: Center for Science in the Public Interest Online*, "Young People and Alcohol," May 2001, <http://www.cspinet.org/booze/alcyouth.html> (21 December 2005).
8. *US. NO DRUGS.com*, "Alcohol Statistics," <http://www.usnodrugs.com/alcohol-statistics.htm> (21 December 2005.
9. *Priests for Life Online*, "Interview with Dr. George Isajiw, MD," 1998, <http://www.priestsforlife.org/media/interviewisajiw.htm> (21 December 2005).
10. Niemoller and Hyde quotes found at *Priests for Life Online*, <http://www.priestsforlife.org/resources/storiesanecdotes.htm> (27 May 27, 2004).

278

11. You can read some of these Church laws for yourself in the *Code of Canon Law* on the Vatican's website. Check out Canons 1323, and 1331, 1398, <http://www.vatican.va/archive/ENG1104/_INDEX.HTM> (4 January 2006).

12. Luigi Fraschini, "What's Your Honesty Quotient?" *Driving Today*, 22 November 2001. Reprinted on *Drivers.com Online*, <http://www.drivers.com/article/477/> (21 December 2005).

13. Kathy Slobogin, "Survey: Many Students Say Cheating Is OK," *CNN.com/Education Online*, 5 April 2004, < http://www.cnn.com/2002/fyi/teachers.ednews/04/05/highschool.cheating/> (21 December 2005).

14. Clayton Wheat wrote this prayer. You can read it in its entirety online at the *American Heritage Library Online*, <http://www.constitutional.net/026.html> (4 January 2006).

## Chapter 3: God Writes Straight with Crooked Lines

1. *Council of Toledo XI (675): DS 530:26 quoted in the Catechism of the Catholic Church, 253.*

2. Quoting the Constitution on Divine Revelation, #11.

3. Quoting the Constitution on Divine Revelation, #8.

4. Barna Research Online, "The Bible," <http://www.barna.org/cgi-bin/PageCategory.asp?CategoryID=7> (22 December 2005).

5. Quoting the Constitution on Divine Revelation, #11.

6. Found at **Inspirational Christian Stories and Poems Archive,** <http://216.71.2.132/texts/topics/bible/bibleinfiftywords.shtml> **(22 December 2005).**

7. International Theological Commission, "Communion and Stewardship: Human Persons Created in the Image of God," July 23, 2004. Can be read at <http://www.vatican.va/roman_curia/congregations/cfaith/cti_documents/rc_con_cfaith_doc_20040723_communion-stewardship_en.html> (4 January 2006).

8. Quoted by Bishop Alexander Mileant, "Understanding the Bible, Part 9: The Book of Revelation," OrthodoxPhotos.com, <http://www.orthodoxphotos.com/readings/revelation/> (22 December 2005).

9. Margaret Wertheim, "Looking for God," *Science & Spirit Magazine*, June-July 2003, p. 27. Found on the Vatican Observatory Online, <http://clavius.as.arizona.edu/vo/R1024/News/Looking_for_God.pdf> (22 December 2005).

10. Jennifer Harper, "Most Americans Take Bible Stories Literally," *Washington Times*, February 17, 2004, Washington Times Online, <http://www.washtimes.com/functions/print.php?StoryID=20040216-113955-2061r> (22 December 2005). The Fox study was cited on PollingReport.com Online, <http://www.pollingreport.com/religion.htm> (22 December 2005). A 1999 poll conducted by Time.com found that 84% of American adults believed in miracles. This was reported in "The Religious Beliefs of America," Religious Tolerance.org Online, <http://www.religioustolerance.org/chr_poll4.htm> (22 December 2005).

11. The Lourdes Miracles," *Lourdes Magazine Online*, No. 139, December 2005-January 2006 issue, <http://www.lourdes-magazine.com/index.php?lien=savoir.php&contexte=en&id_actu=447> (22 December 2005).

12. John P. Meier, *A Marginal Jew*, II (New York: Doubleday, 1994), p. 512.

13. New York: Simon and Schuster, 1990. This is an excellent book. You would really enjoy reading it. It discusses not only the process of how the church canonizes saints, but also reviews the lives of some extraordinary Christians like Dorothy Day.

14. National Center for Health Statistics, Donna L. Hoyert, Ph.D., Hsiang-Ching Kung, Ph.D., and Betty L. Smith, B.S. Ed., "Deaths: Preliminary Data for 2003," National Vital Statistics Report, Vol. 53, No. 15, February 28, 2005, Centers for Disease Control and Prevention Online <http://www.cdc.gov/nchs/data/nvsr/nvsr52/nvsr52_13.pdf> (22 December 2005).

15. *The Harris Poll*® #90, December 14, 2005, "The Religious and Other Beliefs of Americans 2005," *HarrisInteractive*® Online <http://www.harrisinteractive.com/harris_poll/index.asp?PID=618> (22 December 2005).

16. You can find these addresses online at the Eternal Word Television Network website, EWTN Online, <http://www.ewtn.com/library/PAPALDOC/JP2HEAVN.HTM> (4 January 2006).

## Chapter 4: Let's Talk about Sex

1. Jason Evert, *If You Really Loved Me*, cited *by Catholic Answers Online* in a Question and Answer article on premarital sex, <http://www.catholic.com/chastity/Q1.asp> (23 December 2005).

2. *American Social Health Association Online*, "Facts & Answers about STDs," <http://www.ashastd.org/learn/learn_statistics.cfm> (23 December 2005).

3. *The Alan Guttmacher Institute Online*, "Facts in Brief: Teen Sex & Pregnancy," September 1999, <http://www.agi-usa.org/pubs/fb_teen_sex.html#tp> (23 December 2005).

4. About.com's Women's Issues, "Abortion Statistics," <http://womensissues.about.com/cs/abortionstats/a/aaabortionstats.htm> (23 December 2005).

5. *United States Conference of Catholic Bishops Online*, "Between Man and Woman: Questions and Answers about Marriage and Same-Sex Unions," 12 November 2003, <http://www.usccb.org/laity/manandwoman.shtml> (23 December 2005).

6. As cited by Bishop Robert Banks, "Cohabitation: Why the Church Opposes Practice," *Catholic Herald Online*, 13 February 2003, <http://www.chnonline.org/weddings/2003-02-13/special_supp5.html> (23 December 2005).

7. *The National Campaign to Prevent Teen Pregnancy Online*, "Facts on Abstinence," citing N. Brener et. al., "Trends in Sexual Risk Behaviors among High School Students—United States, 1991-2001," *MMWR*, 51(38), pp. 856-859, <http://teenpregnancy.org/resources/teens/avoid/abstinence/absfacts.asp> (23 December 2005).

8. *The National Campaign to Prevent Teen Pregnancy Online*, "General Facts and Stats" citing a 2003 study entitled "With One Voice: America's Adults and Teens Sound Off about Teen Pregnancy," <http://www.teen pregnancy.org/resources/data/genlfact.asp> (23 December 2005).

## Chapter 5: Catholic Headlines on the Front Page

1. New York: The Crossroad Publishing Company, 2003.
2. *United States Conference of Catholic Bishops Online*, Catholic Information Project, "The Catholic Church in America—Meeting Real Needs in Your Neighborhood," December 2003, <http://www.usccb.org/comm/cipfinal.pdf> (23 December 2005).
3. "Summary of School Statistics as of Jan 1, 2005," reported by *The Official Catholic Directory*. Cited in Matthew E. Bunson, D. Min., *Our Sunday Visitor's 2006 Catholic Almanac* (Huntington, IN: Our Sunday Visitor, Inc., 2005), p. 534.
4. *United States Conference of Catholic Bishops Online*, Catholic Information Project, op. cit.
5. John Deedy, *Retrospect* (Chicago: Thomas More Press, 1990), p. 52.
6. *Sermons* 131, 10.
7. Vatican Information Service, "Canonization Process," September 12, 1997, *Catholic-pages.com Online*, <http://www.catholic-pages.com/saints/process.asp> (23 December 2005).
8. United States Conference of Catholic Bishops, *A Culture of Life and the Penalty of Death* (Washington, D. C.: USCCB, 2005), p. 4. This document was accessed online at <http://www.usccb.org/sdwp/national/penaltyofdeath.pdf> (23 December 2005).
9. *Terrorism Files.org Online*, "Definition of Terrorism," <http://www.terrorismfiles.org/encyclopaedia/terrorism.html> (23 December 2005).
10. Pope John Paul II, "No Peace Without Justice No Justice Without Forgiveness," Message for the World Day of Peace, 1 January 2002, *The Holy See Online*, <http://www.vatican.va/holy_father/john_paul_ii/messages/peace/documents/hf_jp-ii_mes_20011211_xxxv-world-day-for-peace_en.html> (23 December 2005).
11. Ibid.
12. Pope John Paul II, "An Ever Timely Commitment: Teaching Peace," Message for the World Day of Peace, 1 January 2004, *The Holy See Online*, <http://www.vatican.va/holy_father/john_paul_ii/messages/peace/documents/hf_jp-ii_mes_20031216_xxxvii-world-day-for-peace_en.html> (23 December 2005).
13. *Religious Tolerance.org Online* reports the projections of the editors of the *World Christian Encyclopedia: A Comparative Survey of Churches and Religions— AD 30 to 2200* in which they state that there are 34,000 Christian groups in the world! See "Conservative & Liberal 'Wings' in Protestant Christianity," <http://www.religioustolerance.org/chr_divi.htm> (23 December 2005).

14. *Faithful Citizenship: A Catholic Call to Political Responsibility* (USCCB: Washington, D.C., 2003). Posted online at the United State Conference of Catholic Bishops Online's website, 3 March 2004, http://www.usccb.org/faithfulcitizenship/ bishopStatement.html#4> (23 December 2005).
15. *Faithful Citizenship.*
16. Ibid.
17. *Worthiness to Receive Communion. General Principles* Joseph Cardinal Ratzinger to Theodore Cardinal McCarrick. <http://www.priest forlife.org/maigsterium/bishops/ 04-07ratsingerommunion.htm> (24 December 2005).
18. Ibid.

## Chapter 6: Do the Right Thing

1. Basil Pennington, O.C.S.O., Challenges in Prayer (Wilmington, Delaware: Michael Glazier, Inc., 1982), pp. 61-62.
2. Quoting the Council of Trent (1551): DS 1651.
3. Found on Fr. Brian Cavanaugh's Apple Seeds® Online, Volume 19, No. 2, October, 2003, <http://www.appleseeds.org/oct%5F03.htm> (24 December 2005).
4. In Jill Haak Adels, Wisdom of the Saints (New York: Oxford University Press, 1987), p. 54.
5. Excerpt from a larger prayer given in the "Message of his Holiness Pope John Paul II for the 41st World Day of Prayer for Vocations," delivered on the Fourth Sunday of Easter, 2 May 2004, The Holy See Online, <http://www.vatican.va/holy_father/john_paul_ii/messages/ vocations/documents/hf_jp-ii_mes_20031205_xli-voc-2004_en.html> (25 December 2005).

## Chapter 7: Help Along the Way

1. This list was modified from the list at Our Lady of Perpetual Help Parish Online (La Follette, TN), <http://www.campbellcounty.com/~our lady/Famous%20Catholics.htm> (30 May 2004). Some of those listed were either baptized into the Catholic faith or converted. There is no guarantee that they all practiced or are practicing as faithful Catholics.
2. Found on Fr. Brian Cavanaugh, TOR, Apple Seeds® Online, <http://www.appleseeds.org/peace%5Fdesales.htm> (25 December 2005).

# INDEX ➤➤➤➤➤➤➤➤➤➤➤➤➤➤➤➤➤➤➤➤➤➤➤➤➤➤

# Index

**M**ichael Francis Pennock was a theology teacher for thirty-six years, thirty-four spent at St. Ignatius High School in Cleveland. He received his bachelor's in History from Loyola University, Chicago, his master's in Religious Education from St. John College of Cleveland, and his Ph.D. in Secondary Education from the University of Akron. He wrote his dissertation on the Catholic religious education theorist, Gabriel Moran. While educating Catholic leaders he wrote 24 Catholic textbooks, many of them best-sellers like *Your Life in Christ*. He has also written a number of other books, including *Ready for College* and *Seeker's Catechism*. Pennock and his wife Carol live in Austin, Texas, where he is now writing full-time. They have four children, Scott, Jennifer, Amy and Christopher, and four grandchildren.